To Steve.

My very best

wishes,

Karin.

God

A brief philosophical introduction

III

K. H. A. Esmail
Course Director and Tutor (Philosophy & Religious Studies),
Institute of Continuing Education, University of Cambridge

Series in Philosophy

www.vernonpress.com

In the Americas:
Vernon Press
1000 N West Street, Suite 1200,
Wilmington, Delaware 19801
United States

In the rest of the world:
Vernon Press
C/Sancti Espiritu 17,
Malaga, 29006
Spain

Series in Philosophy

Library of Congress Control Number: 2021933250

ISBN: 978-1-64889-210-3

For

A & K

Table of Contents

Introduction 9

Chapter 1 **The Nature of God** 29

Introduction 29

An all-knowing or omniscient thing and God's knowledge 43

An all-powerful or omnipotent thing and God's power 83

Chapter 2 **Evil being overridden & God bringing about a particular kind of universe** 127

Evil states of affairs and an evil state of affairs being overridden 127

God bringing about a particular kind of universe 129

God bringing about this particular kind of universe and evil being overridden in it 146

An observation on God bringing about this particular kind of universe and a moral theory 148

Chapter 3 **The Existence of God**

Are there sufficient grounds for the claim that God does not exist?

God and Evil 155

The principal arguments for the claim that God does not exist 155

Alvin Plantinga's response in *The Nature of Necessity* 159

Another response 166

Chapter 4 **The Existence of God**

Are there sufficient grounds for the claim that God exists? 173

Some Ontological arguments Anselm 173

Some Design arguments 185

Some Cosmological arguments 201

An argument from the religious experience of God 226

Main Conclusions 269

Appendix 1

God's sovereignty 277

Appendix 2

Evil being overridden and some discussions of God and evil 295

Appendix 3

Some of the moral and other features of God bringing about a particular kind of universe and God being morally perfect 305

Appendix 4

Are there sufficient grounds for the claim that, very probably, God does not exist? 315

Appendix 5

Theodicy and some theodicies 333

Appendix 6

Some further remarks on God and time 357

Appendix 7

Some further remarks on a living thing which possesses the power to do this or that *freely* 369

Select Bibliography 443

Index 445

Introduction

Religion

The great religions of the world are Hinduism, Buddhism, Judaism, Christianity, and Islam. Each of these great religions identifies the ultimate goal of a human being's life and it identifies a means *or* means to realise it. Here is an example: in Buddhism, the ultimate goal of a human being's life is to realise a particular state of being, *viz.* nirvāṇa;[1] the Eightfold Path is the means to realise it.

This ultimate goal is related in each great religion to something which is good and which is greater in value than anything else and which is not in a human being's ordinary experience. Here is an example: in Buddhism, the ultimate goal of a human being's life is related to something, *viz.* nirvāṇa, which is good; it is greater in value than anything else; it is not in a human being's ordinary experience.

There is a report (or reports) of an experience of this thing and a number of beliefs about it and a number of practices in relation to it in each of these great religions. Here is an example: in Buddhism, there is a report of an experience of this state of being in the life of the Buddha[2] and in the life of others; there is a belief about it that a human being does not have the "basic impurities" of a human being in it; there is the practice of the Eightfold Path in relation to it.

This thing is God in some of these great religions.[3] Traditionally, God is a thing which is alive and which is non-physical and which is among other things all-knowing and all-powerful and morally perfect and eternal and which has to be so and which has brought about the physical universe and human beings and which sustains the physical universe and human beings and which cares about the physical universe and human beings. God is worthy of worship. Someone who believes that God exists is *a theist.* Judaism, Christianity and Islam are the prime examples of religions which are theistic.

Analytic philosophy, the philosophy of religion, and this work

The western tradition of philosophy begins with the ancient Greeks in the 6th century BCE.[4] This tradition includes a sub-tradition, *viz.* analytic philosophy. This sub-tradition begins in the late nineteenth century and the early twentieth century. It is pre-dominant in the English-speaking world today. The origins of it lie in the work of (among others) Gottlob Frege and George Edward Moore and Bertrand Russell and Ludwig Wittgenstein.

Analytic philosophy includes regularly the analysis of (some) fundamental concepts;[5] it includes regularly the identification of arguments for this or that claim; it includes regularly the critical assessment of arguments for this or that claim; and, it is regularly detailed and rigorous.

The philosophy of religion is a sub-discipline of analytic philosophy. This sub-discipline is concerned above all with the claim that God exists. Its concern above all is with the analysis of the concept or nature of God *and* with arguments for and against the existence of God.[6]

This is a work in analytic philosophy. It is concerned in the main with the analysis of the nature God and with arguments for and against the existence of God. So, it is concerned in the main with what the philosophy of religion is concerned with above all.

An explanation of some key words or expressions used in (the analytic tradition of) philosophy and how some words or expressions are re-stated in this work

Analysis

The analysis of this or that is the following: the identification of its (ultimate) constituents. The analysis of this or that is regularly the identification of the constituents which are required and which are enough for it. Here is an example: the tripartite analysis of *someone knows this or that.* (This analysis of *someone knows this or that* is as follows: (that) this or that *is* the case; he *believes* (that) this or that; he has *sufficient grounds* or *justification* for his belief.[7])

What is required for this or that is regularly stated after the words "only if": this or that *only if* _______ - _______ is a statement of what is required. Here are some such statements: someone knows this or that *only if* (that) this or that is the case; someone knows this or that *only if* he believes (that) this or that; someone knows this or that *only if* he has sufficient grounds or justification for his belief.

What is enough for this or that is regularly stated after the word "if": this or that *if* ________ - ________ is a statement of what is enough. Here is such a statement: someone knows this or that *if* (that) this or that is the case and he believes (that) this or that and he has sufficient grounds or justification for his belief.

What is required and what is enough for this or that is regularly stated after the words "if and only if" (or "*iff*"): this or that *if and only if* (or *iff*) ________ - ________ is a statement of what is required and what is enough. Here is such a statement: someone knows this or that *if and only if* (or *iff*) (that) this or that is the case and he believes (that) this or that and he has sufficient grounds or justification for his belief.

What is required for this or that is stated in another way in this work: *not* this or that *unless* ________ - ________ is a statement of what is required. Here are some such statements: someone does *not* know this or that *unless* (that) this or that is the case; someone does *not* know this or that *unless* he believes (that) this or that; someone does *not* know this or that *unless* he has sufficient grounds or justification for his belief.

What is enough for this or that is also stated in another way in this work: this or that *in case* ________ - ________ is a statement of what is enough. Here is such a statement: someone knows this or that *in case* (that) this or that is the case and he believes (that) this or that and he has sufficient grounds or justification for his belief.

Finally, what is required and what is enough for this or that is also stated in another way in this work: this or that *just in case* ________ - ________ is a statement of what is required and what is enough. Here is such a statement: someone knows this or that *just in case* (that) this or that is the case and he believes (that) this or that and he has sufficient grounds or justification for his belief.

Argument(s)

An argument includes statements *or* propositions. (Statements *or* propositions have values: either the value *true* or the value *false*.[8]) An argument includes one *or* more statements *or* propositions which purportedly support another statement *or* proposition. The initial propositions *or* statements are premises and the proposition *or* statement they purportedly support is the conclusion. (A conclusion is preceded in ordinary discourse in English by a word such as "so" or "therefore".)

In a *valid* argument, the premises are such that the conclusion *follows* from them. Here is an example of such an argument: the Tate is a gallery; a gallery exhibits works of art; so, the Tate exhibits works of art. (The statement *or* proposition that the Tate is a gallery and the statement *or* proposition that a gallery exhibits works of art are the premises. The statement *or* proposition that the Tate exhibits works of art is the conclusion. The premises are such that the conclusion follows from them. Hence, this is a valid argument.) A valid argument is *sound* just in case its premises are true.

Incidentally, there is a form of argument which is used regularly in this work. It is used in order to establish that this or that statement *or* proposition is untrue. It includes one *or* more initial premises which are true and it includes this statement *or* proposition as a further premise, *viz.* a supposition, and it includes a further statement *or* proposition which follows and which is absurd. It concludes that this statement *or* proposition, *viz.* the supposition, is untrue for it is included and a further and absurd statement *or* proposition as a result follows. (This form of argument is referred to as *reductio ad absurdum.*)

In an *inductively strong* argument, the premises are such that the conclusion is *probable.* Here is an example of such an argument: water has boiled whenever we have heated it to a certain temperature; so, all water boils when it is heated to that temperature. (The statement *or* proposition that water has boiled whenever we have heated it to a certain temperature is the premise. The statement *or* proposition that all water boils when it is heated to that temperature is the conclusion. The premise is such that the conclusion is probable. Hence, this is an inductively strong argument.)

In an argument which is *not valid* and which is *not inductively strong,* the premises are *not* such that the conclusion follows from them *or* that the conclusion is probable. Here is an example of such an argument: the River Thames is polluted; so, there are visitors to the Tate gallery. (The statement *or* proposition that the River Thames is polluted is the premise. The statement *or* proposition that there are visitors to the Tate gallery is the conclusion. The premise is *not* such that the conclusion follows from it *or* that the conclusion is probable. Hence, this is an argument which is not valid and which is not inductively strong.)

Modal expressions

Here is a modal expression: *it is possible that.* This expression operates on statements *or* propositions to form more complex statements *or* propositions. It is an *operator.* Here is an example of its use: it is possible that the Tate gallery is not in London.

Here is another modal expression: *it is necessary that.* This expression also operates on statements *or* propositions to form more complex statements *or* propositions. It is an operator. Here is an example of its use: it is necessary that *3* is greater than *2*.

Here is another modal expression: *it is impossible that.* This expression also operates on statements *or* propositions to form more complex statements *or* propositions. It is an operator. Here is an example of its use: it is impossible that a thing is not identical with itself.

These expressions are stated in another way in this work. The expression "it is possible that" is stated as follows: *it can be that.* (It also operates on statements *or* propositions to form more complex statements *or* propositions.) Here is example of its use: it can be that the Tate gallery is not in London.

The modal expression "it is necessary that" is stated as follows: *it cannot be that* ________ *is not so* or, in places, *it has to be that.* (They also operate on statements *or* propositions to form more complex statements *or* propositions.) Here is example of the use of "it cannot be that ________ is not so": it cannot be that *3* is greater than *2* is not so.

The modal expression "it is impossible that" is stated as follows: *it cannot be that.* (It also operates on statements *or* propositions to form more complex statements *or* propositions.) Here is an example of its use: it cannot be that a thing is not identical with itself.

A way to understand these expressions is in terms of *possible worlds.* A possible world is how things as a whole, *viz.* a world, can be.[9] Here is how these expressions are understood in terms of possible worlds using examples from the preceding paragraphs. The first example, *viz.* it is possible that the Tate gallery is not in London, is understood as follows: there is a possible world which is such that the Tate gallery is not in London in it. The second example, *viz.* it is necessary that *3* is greater than *2*, is understood as follows: every possible world is such that *3* is greater than *2* in it. The third example, *viz.* it is impossible that a thing is not identical with itself, is understood as follows: there is no possible world which is such that a thing is not identical with itself in it. (Here is another statement of how it is understood: there is no possible world which is such that it includes a thing and that thing is not identical with itself.)

Some of the (fundamental) kinds of there are and some of their features according to this work

One of the principal concerns of western philosophy (including analytic philosophy) has been the following question: what (fundamental) kinds of thing are there? (This particular question is a concern of another sub-discipline, *viz.* ontology.) Well, here are some of the kinds of there are and some of their features according to this work.

Abstract and concrete things, states of affairs, facts, and (intrinsic) value

Things are abstract *or* concrete. Abstract things among other things are not in space and they do not change intrinsically and they are such that someone is able only to (mentally) apprehend them. Here are some examples of abstract things: concepts; propositions; numbers; possible worlds; states of affairs; properties.

Here are some examples of concrete things: God; instants and seconds; areas of space; the planets; the island which includes England; the Tate gallery in London. (Some concrete things such as God are not in space. Some concrete things such as an instant of time do not change intrinsically.)

Abstract things include states of affairs.[10] Here are some examples of states of affairs: that *3* is greater than *2*; that a thing is identical with itself; that the Tate gallery is in London; that the Tate gallery is one of a number of galleries in London; that *3* is not greater than *2*; that a thing is not identical with itself.

States of affairs are not conjunctive *or* conjunctive. The states of affairs in the pen-ultimate sentence are not conjunctive. The states of affairs which follow are conjunctive: that *3* is greater than *2 and* a thing is identical with itself; that the Tate gallery is in London *and* the Tate gallery is one of a number of galleries in London; that *3* is not greater than *2 and* a thing is not identical with itself.

States of affairs obtain *or* they do not obtain. Some states of affairs obtain and they have to obtain. Here are some examples: that *3* is greater than *2*; that a thing is identical with itself; that *3* is greater than *2* and a thing is identical with itself. (Such states of affairs are such that things *are* as they are in them *and* in that case it can be that things are as they are in them *and* indeed it cannot be that things are not as they are in them.)

Some states of affairs obtain and they do *not* have to obtain. Here are some examples: that the Tate gallery is in London; that the Tate gallery is one of a number of galleries in London; that the Tate gallery is in London and the Tate gallery is one of a number of galleries in London. (Such states of affairs are such that things *are* as they are in them *and* in that case it can be that things are as they are in them *and* it can be that things are *not* as they are in them.) States of affairs which obtain *represent* how things *are*.

Some states of affairs do not obtain and they *cannot* obtain. Here are some examples: that *3* is *not* greater than *2*; that a thing is *not* identical with itself; that *3* is *not* greater than *2* and a thing is *not* identical with itself. (Such states of affairs are such that things are *not* as they are in them *and* indeed it cannot be that things are as they are in them.[11])

Some states of affairs do not obtain and they can obtain. Here are some examples: that the Tate gallery is *not* in London; that the Tate gallery is *not* one of a number of galleries in London; that the Tate gallery is not in London and the Tate gallery is not one of a number of galleries in London. (Such states of affairs are such that things are *not* as they are in them *and* it can be that things are as they are in them.) States of affairs which do *not* obtain do *not* represent how things *are*. (States of affairs which are such that it can be that things are as they are in them represent how it can be that things are whether they obtain *or* they do not obtain.)

A state of affairs is *a part of* some other state of affairs just in case it has to be that it obtains in case that other state of affairs obtains. Here is an example: the state of affairs that the Tate gallery is in London is a part of the state of affairs that the Tate gallery is in London and the Tate gallery is one of a number of galleries in London for it has to be that it obtains in case the latter state of affairs obtains.[12]

Some parts of other states of affairs are (temporally) immediate parts of them and others are (temporally) non-immediate parts of them. A part is a (temporally) immediate part of some other state of affairs just in case it is a part of that other state of affairs *and* that other state of affairs – in case it obtains - obtains at some time and it obtains at that time, too. Here is an example: the state of affairs that the Tate gallery is in London is a (temporally) immediate part of the state of affairs that the Tate gallery is in London and the Tate gallery is one of a number of galleries in London. (It has to be that it obtains in case the latter state of affairs obtains *and* the latter state of affairs – in case it obtains - obtains at some time and it obtains at that time, too.)

A part is a (temporally) non-immediate part of some other state of affairs just in case it is a part of that other state of affairs *and* that other state of affairs – in case it obtains - obtains at some time and it does *not* obtain at that time.

Here is an example: the state of affairs that God judges human beings at some time is a (temporally) non-immediate part of the state of affairs that God brings about (in the very first instance) human beings who possess the power to act freely and who possess the power to lead lives. (It has to be that it obtains in case the latter state of affairs obtains *and* the latter state of affairs – in case it obtains – obtains at some time and it does *not* obtain at that time.)

What is a *fact*? Well, *this or that* in case the state of affairs that (that) this or that obtains. The *this or that* is a fact. Here is an example: *the Tate gallery is in London* in case the state of affairs that the Tate gallery is in London obtains; *the Tate gallery is in London* is a *fact.*

It can be that this or that in case the state of affairs that (that) this or that can obtain. This, *viz.* it can be that there is (that) this or that, is a fact in case that is so. Here is an example: it can be that the Tate Gallery is in London in case the state of affairs that the Tate gallery is in London can obtain; this, *viz.* it can be that the Tate Gallery is in London, is a fact in case that is so.

There are facts and they have to be facts. Here is an example: *3* is greater than *2*. This is so and this has to be so. This is so and this has to be so for the state of affairs that *3* is greater than *2* obtains *and* it has to obtain.

There are facts and they do not have to be facts. Here is an example: the Tate gallery is in London. This is so and this does not have to be so. This is so and this does not have to be so for the state of affairs that the Tate gallery obtains *and* it does not have to obtain.

Finally, *this or that* has an (intrinsic) *value.* (The theistic traditions of the Middle East and other traditions also maintain that what is so has an intrinsic value.) Let us take it that states of affairs which can obtain - whether they obtain *or* they do not obtain - also have this value in order to facilitate this discussion. States of affairs which *can* obtain *alone* have a value.

The value of a state of affairs (which can obtain) is good *or* bad *or* neutral. Here are some examples of good states of affairs: that someone is undertaking an act with good intentions; that someone is happy; that something is functioning properly; that something is well-proportioned.

Here are some examples of bad states of affairs: that someone is undertaking an act with bad intentions; that someone is unhappy; that something is not functioning properly; that something is not well-proportioned.

Here are some examples of neutral states of affairs: that someone is not undertaking an act with good intentions; that someone is not happy; that there is a small hole in the earth; that there is a small stone in the earth.

Good states of affairs and bad states of affairs have *a degree* of value. So, they have *relations* to each other: *greater than*; *equal to*; *less than*. Here is an example: the degree of value of the good state of affairs that someone is happy and someone else is happy is greater than the degree of value of the good state of affairs that that someone alone is happy.

Good states of affairs and bad states of affairs and neutral states of affairs also have relations to each other: *better than*; *neither better than nor worse than*; *worse than*. Here are some examples of these relations: a good state of affairs is better than a neutral state of affairs; a neutral state of affairs is neither better than nor worse than some other neutral state of affairs; a bad state of affairs is worse than a neutral state of affairs.

Some states of affairs are such that their value *or* their degree of value is determined by their parts. Here is an example: the value of the state of affairs that someone is not unhappy and someone else is not unhappy is neutral *for* the value of each of the states of affairs which are parts of it is neutral. (The state of affairs that someone is not unhappy and the state of affairs that someone else is not unhappy are the parts of this state of affairs. The value of each part is neutral.)

Properties and change

Abstract things also include *properties*. Here are some examples of properties: being in London; being identical with itself; being cube-like. Further, there is an instance of a property just in case there is a thing with that property. Here is an example: the Tate gallery being in London. (There is an instance of a property, *viz.* being in London, for there is a thing, *viz.* the Tate gallery, with that property.)

A property of a thing is a relational property of it *or* a non-relational property of it. A relational property of a thing is its being in some relation to something(s). Here is an example of a relational property of a thing (*viz.* the Tate gallery): the Tate gallery *being in London.* (The Tate gallery has a relation, *viz.* being in, to something, *viz.* London. Hence, this is a relational property of it.)

Incidentally, relational properties are extrinsic *or* intrinsic. An extrinsic relational property of a thing is its being in some relation to some *other* thing(s). Here is an example of an extrinsic relational property of a thing (*viz.* the Tate gallery): the Tate gallery *being in London.* (The Tate gallery has a relation, *viz.* being in, to some *other* thing, *viz.* London. Hence, this is an extrinsic relational property of it.)

An intrinsic relational property of a thing is its being in some relation to *itself.* Here is an example of an intrinsic relational property of a thing (*viz.* the Tate gallery): the Tate gallery *being identical with itself.* (The Tate gallery has a relation, *viz.* being identical with, to *itself.* Hence, this is an intrinsic relational property of it.)

Any other property of a thing is a *non-relational* property of it. Here is an example of a non-relational property of a thing (*viz.* the Tate gallery): the Tate gallery *being cube-like.* (The Tate gallery being cube-like is *not* its being in some relation to something(s). Hence, this is a non-relational property of it.)[13]

What is a *change* in a thing? Well, a change in a thing is the following: it has a property at some time and it does *not* have it at a later *or* earlier time. Further, a change in a thing is an *extrinsic* change in it *or* an *intrinsic* change in it. An extrinsic change in a thing is the following: it has an extrinsic relational property at one time and it does not have it at a later *or* earlier time. Here is an example of an extrinsic change in a thing (*viz.* the Tate gallery): the Tate gallery being in London at some time and the Tate gallery *not* being in London at a later time. (The Tate gallery has an extrinsic relational property, *viz.* being in London, at some time and it does *not* have it at a later time. Hence, it is an extrinsic change in it.)

An intrinsic change in a thing is the following: it has an intrinsic relational property *or* non-relational property at one time and it does *not* have it a later *or* earlier time. Here is an example of an intrinsic change in a thing (*viz.* the Tate gallery): the Tate gallery being cube-like at some time and the Tate gallery *not* being cube-like at a later time. (The Tate gallery has a non-relational property, *viz.* being cube-like, at one time and it does not have it at a later time. Hence, it is an intrinsic change in it.)

Incidentally, a thing which exists at some time and which does not exist at an earlier *or* later time is *not* an intrinsic change in it. It is not an intrinsic change in it for a change in a thing is its being this or that at some time and it not being this or that at an earlier *or* later time and in that case that thing exists at both times.

Notes

1. In this state of being, a human being's "basic impurities" have been (gradually) eliminated and there is among other things no "attachment" to things and there is a state of peace. (A human being's basic impurities are a desire for the sensual and a desire for continued existence or "manifestation" and an ignorance of the nature reality.)

This is "nirvāṇa with the substrate of life remaining" for the particular physical and psychological constituents of someone who has attained it remain.

There is "nirvāṇa without the substrate of life remaining" in death.

2. The origins of Buddhism lie in the life and teachings of Sid dhārtha Gautama, the Buddha. He lived in the 5th century BCE.

Traditional biographies include *The Acts of the Buddha* (c. 2nd century CE). These biographies claim that he attained nirvāṇa.

The Pali Canon (c. 1st century BCE) – the Pali Canon is a set of authoritative texts and it is the earliest such set which survives intact – also claims that he attained nirvāṇa.

3. Traditionally, God is transcendent in at least this way: "God is beyond the universe".

Some have understood the claim "God is beyond the universe" in the following way: "God is beyond the universe" where "universe" is *everything*. It is added that this is absurd. (For example, Kai Nielson in *Naturalism and Religion*, New York 2001, p.473.)

This is absurd. But, this is an improper understanding of the claim. Here is the proper understanding of the claim: God is a thing *and* he is not a physical thing *or* things in the physical universe *and* he is not the physical universe itself.

4. The epics of Homer, *viz.* the *Iliad* and the *Odyssey*, in particular inform the minds of the ancient Greeks prior to the first philosophers. (Homer lived in the 7th century BCE according to Herodotus (484 - 420 BCE).)

In these epics, the actions of the gods and necessity – in particular, in relation to the time of the death of a human being – and chance explain how things are in the physical and ordered universe.

The first philosophers in Miletus in Ionia or Greek Asia – modern day Turkey – seek an independent and single and rational explanation of the physical and ordered universe.

5. Which concepts? Well, in particular a concept which (to begin with) is the following:

(i) fundamental in relation to the physical universe *or* to human beings *or* to both

and

(ii) applies to something(s) *or* it can apply to something(s) *or* it is not evident that it cannot apply to something(s).

Such a concept is not subject to analysis *unless* the following is so:

(iii) its (ultimate) constituents are not evident

and

(iv) it lends itself to philosophical analysis.

Here is an example: the concept of being a living thing which knows this or that.

6. It is also concerned with among other things religious language and with non-rational grounds for the claim that God exists.

It is concerned with the concept or nature of God for it is a concept which (to begin with) is fundamental in relation to the physical universe and human beings *and* it is not evident that it cannot apply to something(s).

Further, its ultimate constituents are not evident *and* it lends itself (somewhat) to philosophical analysis.

7. Incidentally, this analysis will be considered in the course of the consideration of God's knowledge in the first chapter.

8. These are the *standard* values which a statement *or* proposition has in a key sub-discipline of philosophy, *viz.* logic.

9. This statement is not altogether satisfactory for "how things as whole, *viz.* a world, can be" includes a modal term, *viz. can.*

10. It is taken that states of affairs and propositions – for example, the proposition *a thing is identical with itself* – are *equivalent* to each other.

11. States of affairs are such that it can be that things are as they are in them *or* they are such that it cannot be that things are as they are in them.

12. A state of affairs is an *independent part of* some other state of affairs just in case it is a part of that other state of affairs *and* it is *not* a part of any other part of that other state of affairs.

Here is an example: the state of affairs that a particular person is experiencing a certain amount of unhappiness about what he is thinking about is an independent part of the state of affairs that he is experiencing a certain amount of unhappiness about what he is thinking about, *viz.* his own wrongdoing.

The state of affairs that he is experiencing a certain amount of unhappiness about what he is thinking about, *viz.* his own wrongdoing, includes the following parts: that he is experiencing a certain amount of unhappiness about what he is thinking about and that he is thinking about his own wrongdoing.

But, the state of affairs that he is experiencing a certain amount of unhappiness about what he is thinking about is *not* a part of the state of affairs that he is thinking about his own wrongdoing.

Hence, it is an independent part of the state of affairs that he is experiencing a certain amount of unhappiness about what he is thinking about, *viz.* his own wrongdoing.

13. Here is another distinction.

An *essential property* of a thing is a property which it has and which it has to have in order to be that thing.

Here is an example: the property *being a place to exhibit works of art* is a property of the Tate and it is a property which it has to have in order to be it.

An *accidental property* of a thing is a property which that thing has and which it does not have to have in order to be that thing.

Here is an example: the property of *being one of several large galleries in London* is a property of the Tate and it is *not* a property which it has to have in order to be it.

Chapter 1

The Nature of God

Introduction

The great religions of the Middle East are theistic. They claim traditionally the following: there is a thing which is alive and which is non-physical and which is among other things all-knowing and all-powerful and morally perfect and eternal and which has to be so and which has brought about the physical universe and human beings and which sustains the physical universe and human beings and which cares about the physical universe and human beings, *viz.* God, and God is worthy of worship. There is a further claim: God is good and God is such that it cannot be that there is a thing which is better (or greater) than him *or* equal to him. (This further claim is a denial of among other things the claim that, for anything which is good, it can be that there is a thing which is better.)

Incidentally, here is a way to re-state this further claim in terms of states of affairs:

a state of affairs which includes God and which is such that God determines its value is good;

there is *no* state of affairs which includes a thing and which is such that that thing determines its value and which is better (or greater) than that state of affairs;

there is *no* state of affairs which includes a thing other than God and which is such that that thing determines its value and which is equal to that state of affairs.

How is this further claim established in these religions? Well, here is a way to begin with to establish this further claim in these religions. (These religions subscribe implicitly *or* explicitly to the claims in the next few paragraphs.)

A thing is alive *or* it is not alive. A thing which is alive is *better than* a thing which is not alive. (The first of these things, *viz.* a thing which is alive, is good. The second of these things, *viz.* a thing which is not alive, is neutral. So, the first of these things is better than the second of these things. This is a denial of the claim that any such relation of a thing to some other thing is *only* to some other thing in the *same* category.)

A thing which is alive can know this or that. A thing which is alive and which is all-knowing is greater than a thing which is alive (and which knows this or that) and which is *not* all-knowing. (The first of these things, *viz.* a thing which is alive and which is all-knowing, is good. The second of these things, *viz.* a thing which is alive and which knows this or that and which is not all-knowing, is good. Good things have a degree of value. The degree of value of the first of these things is greater than the degree of value of the second of these things. So, the first of these things is greater than the second of these things.)

A thing which is alive and which is all-knowing and which *has* to be all-knowing is greater than a thing which is alive and which is all-knowing and which does *not* have to be all-knowing. (The first of these things, *viz.* which is alive and which is all-knowing and which has to be all-knowing, is good. The second of these things, *viz.* a thing which is alive and which is all-knowing and which does *not* have to be all-knowing, is good. Good things have a degree of value. The degree of value of the first of these things is greater than the degree of value of the second of these things. So, the first of these things is greater than the second of these things.)

A thing which is alive can possess a power *or* powers. A thing which is alive and which is all-powerful is greater than a thing which is alive (and which possesses some power(s)) and which is *not* all-powerful. (The first of these things, *viz.* a thing which is alive and which is all-powerful, is good. The second of these things, *viz.* a thing which is alive and which possesses some power(s) and which is not all-powerful, is good. Good things have a degree of value. The degree of value of the first of these things is greater than the degree of value of the second of these things. So, the first of these things is greater than the second of these things.)

A thing which is alive and which is all-powerful and which has to be all-powerful is greater than a thing which is alive and which is all-powerful and which does *not* have to be all-powerful. (The first of these things, *viz.* a thing which is alive and which is all-powerful and which has to be all-powerful, is good. The second of these things, *viz.* a thing which is alive and which is all-powerful and which does not have to be all-powerful, is good. Good things have a degree of value. The degree of value of the first of these things is greater than the degree of value of the second of these things. So, the first of these things is greater than the second of these things.)

This is a way to begin to establish the claim that God is good and God is such that it cannot be that there is a thing which is better (or greater) than him *or* equal to him in these religions. The claims in the preceding few paragraphs are true. Here are some examples of these claims: a thing is alive *or* it is not alive; a thing which is alive can possess a power *or* powers; a thing which is alive can know this or that.

Here are some further examples of these claims: a thing which is alive is better than a thing which is not alive; a thing which is alive and which is all-powerful is greater than a thing which is alive (and which possesses some power(s)) and which is not all-powerful; a thing which is alive and which is all-knowing is greater than a thing which is alive (and which know this or that) and which is not all-knowing. (These claims are true in case there are no other matters to consider.)

Traditionally, God is all-knowing and all-powerful.[1] Is God all-powerful and all-knowing? Well, God is in time. (The claim that God is not in time is considered in the course of what follows.) God cannot be all-knowing at some time in case it can be that he exists *and* it can be that a living thing possesses the power to bring about (in the very first instance) other living things which possess the power to do this or that freely as we shall see. God cannot be all-powerful at some time in case it can be that that is so as we shall also see. (The pen-ultimate sentence refers to living things which possess the power to do this or that *freely*. What is the power at issue? Well, the power at issue to begin with is as follows: it is such that it cannot be that a living thing possesses it unless it is *not* brought to exercise it by something else; it is such that it cannot be that a living thing possesses it unless it possesses the power to *not* do that this or that.[2])

Theists maintain that it can be that God exists. Most theists maintain that it can be that a living thing, *viz.* God himself, possesses the power to bring about (in the very first instance) other living things which possess the power to do this or that freely.

Ought a theist who maintains that it can be that a living thing possesses this power to be concerned that God cannot be all-knowing at some time and he cannot be all-powerful at some time in case it can be that that is so? Well, he ought not to be concerned that this is so for this is as we shall see in accord with God being worthy of worship. (God is such that it cannot be that there is some other thing which is better or greater than him or equal to him in case it can be that that is so.[3]*)*

In the Judaeo-Christian tradition, there is a significant tradition which claims that God is simple and that he is immutable. God cannot be simple in case it can be that he exists and it can be that a living thing possesses the power to bring about (in the very first instance) other living things which possess the power to do this or that freely as we shall see. God cannot be immutable in case it can be that that is so as we shall also see.

Ought a theist who maintains that it can be that a living thing possesses this power to be concerned that God cannot be simple and that he cannot be immutable in case it can be that that is so? Well, a theist ought not to be concerned that this is so for once more this is as we shall see in accord with God being worthy of worship.

Prior to considering these and some related matters, let us consider another traditional claim of theists. The claim is that it can be that there are instances of the kind living and non-physical thing. This claim is untrue *or* implausible according to many analytic philosophers today. Here is an argument (A1) for the claim that it cannot be that there are instances of the kind living and non-physical thing. The argument is in two stages. Here is the first stage (A1.1) :

it cannot be that a thing is distinguishable from some other thing unless it is so by its non-relational properties and extrinsic relational properties – properties which do not name a specific thing - *or* by its spatial location *or* both ;

it cannot be that a thing which is living and non-physical has a spatial location ;

so, it cannot be that a thing which is living and non-physical is distinguishable from some other thing unless it is so by its non-relational properties and extrinsic relational properties.

The conclusion follows from the first premise and the second premise. The first premise, let us accept, is true. The second premise is true. So, the conclusion is true. It cannot be that a thing which is living and non-physical is distinguishable from some other thing unless it is so by its non-relational properties and extrinsic relational properties.

Here is the second stage (A1.2). Its initial premises are as follows :

it can be that there are two things which are living and non-physical and which have the same non-relational properties and extrinsic relational properties in case it can be that there are two (or more) things which are living and non-physical ;

it cannot be that a thing which is living and non-physical is distinguishable from some other thing unless it is so by its non-relational properties and extrinsic relational properties.

Let us suppose that it can be that there are two (or more) things which are living and non-physical.

It can be in that case that there are two things which are living and non-physical and which have the same non-relational properties and extrinsic relational properties. (This initial conclusion follows from the first premise and the supposition.)

It can be in that case that there are *two* things which are living and non-physical and which have the same non-relational properties and extrinsic relational properties *and* which are *not* distinguishable. (This further conclusion follows from the second premise and the initial conclusion.) That's absurd!

So, it cannot be that there are two (or more) things which are living and non-physical.

The first premise is true according to an advocate of this argument. The second premise is true. The supposition is such that an absurdity follows with its addition. So, the conclusion – the conclusion is the denial of the supposition – is true. It cannot be in other words that there are *instances* of the kind *living and non-physical thing.*

Is this so? Well, the first premise of this stage is *untrue* in case it can be that God exists and it can be that a living thing possesses the power to bring about (in the very first instance) other living things which possess the power to do this or that freely. Here is an argument (A2) for this claim. It is in three stages. Here is the first stage (A2.1) :

it can be that God possesses the power to bring about (in the very first instance) other living things which possess the power to do this or that freely in case it can be that he exists and it can be that a living thing possesses this power ;

it can be that God possesses the power to bring about (in the very first instance) other living things which possess the power to do this or that freely *and* which are *not* physical in case it can be that he possesses the power to bring about (in the very first instance) other living things which possess the power to do this or that freely ;

it can be that there are two (or more) living things which are not physical in case it can be that God possesses the power to bring about (in the very first instance) other living things which possess the power to do this or that freely and which are not physical ;

so, it can be that there are two (or more) living things which are not physical in case it can be that God exists and it can be that a living thing possesses the power to bring about (in the very first instance) other living things which possess the power to do this or that freely.

The conclusion follows from the first premise and the second premise and the third premise. The first premise (as we shall see in the course of the consideration of God's power) is true. The second premise is considered in the second chapter. Is it true? Well, sufficient grounds for the claim that it is untrue are to say the least not readily forthcoming. So, it is taken that the second premise is true. The third premise is true. So, the conclusion is true. It can be that there are two (or more) living things which are not physical in case it can be that God exists and it can be that a living thing possesses the power to bring about (in the very first instance) other living things which possess the power to do this or that freely.

Here is the second stage (A2.2) :

it cannot be that God does not exist in case it can be that he exists ;

it cannot be that there is some other living thing which is not known by God in case in cannot be that he does not exist ;

it cannot be that there is some other living thing which is known by God unless it is distinguishable from any other living thing (including God) ;

so, it cannot be that there is some other living thing which is not distinguishable from any other living thing (including God) in case it can be that God exists.

The conclusion follows from the first premise and the second premise and the third premise. The first premise (as we shall see in the course of the consideration of God's power) is true. The second premise is true. The third premise is true. So, the conclusion is true. It cannot be that there is some other living thing which is not distinguishable from any other living thing (including God) in case it can be that God exists.

Here is the third stage (A2.3) :

it can be that there are two (or more) living things which are not physical in case it can be that God exists and it can be that a living thing possesses the power to bring about (in the very first instance) other living things which possess the power to do this or that freely ;

it is untrue that it can be that there is some other living thing which is not distinguishable from any other living thing (including God) in case it can be that God exists ;

it is untrue that it can be that a living thing which is non-physical is distinguishable from some other such living thing unless it is so by its non-relational properties and extrinsic relational properties ;

so, it is untrue that it can be that there are two (or more) living things which are not physical and which have the same non-relational properties and extrinsic relational properties in case it can be that God exists and it can be that a living thing possesses the power to bring about (in the very first instance) other living things which possess the power to do this or that freely (and it can be accordingly that there are two (or more) living things which are not physical things).

The conclusion follows from the first premise and the second premise and the third premise. The first premise – the first premise is the conclusion of the first stage – is true. The second premise – the second premise is the conclusion of the second stage – is true. The third premise is true. So, the conclusion is true. It cannot be that there are two (or more) living things which are not physical and which have the same non-relational properties and extrinsic relational properties in case it can be that God exists and it can be that a living thing possesses the power to bring about (in the very first instance) other living things which possess the power to do this or that freely (and it can be accordingly that there are two (or more) living things which are not physical things.)

The first premise of A1.2 is accordingly untrue in case it can be that God exists and it can be that a living thing possesses the power to bring about (in the very first instance) other living things which possess the power to do this or that freely. So, A1 does *not* establish that it is untrue that it can be that there are instances of the kind *living and non-physical thing* in case it can be that that is so.

Here is an argument (A3) for the claim that it is untrue that it can be that there is a living and non-physical thing:

it can be that a living and non-physical thing exists at a time and it exists to a later time in case it can be that a living and non-physical thing exists. (It can be in other words that a living and non-physical thing *persists* from a time to a later time in case it can be that that is so.) ;

it is untrue that it can be that a living and non-physical thing exists at a time and it exists to a later time ;

so, it is untrue that it can be that a living and non-physical thing exists.

The conclusion follows from the first premise and the second premise. Sufficient grounds for the claim that the first premise is untrue are to say the least not readily forthcoming. So, let us take it that it is true. Here is the argument (A3: A - P2) for its second premise. Here are its initial premises :

it cannot be that a living and non-physical thing exists at a time and it exists to a later time unless *it* exists at that later time ;

it is untrue that it can be that a living and non-physical thing exists at that later time is *determinable.*

Let us suppose that it can be that a living and non-physical thing exists at a time and it exists to a later time.

It can be in that case that *it* exists at that later time *and* it is *not* determinable that it does so. (This initial conclusion follows from the first premise and the second premise and the supposition.) That's absurd!

So, it is untrue that it can be that a living and non-physical thing exists at a time and it exists to a later time.

The first premise is true. The second premise is true according to an advocate of this argument. The supposition is such that an absurdity follows from its addition. So, the ultimate conclusion – the ultimate conclusion is the denial of the supposition – is true. It is untrue that it can be that a living and non-physical thing exists at a time and it exists to a later time.

Is this so? Well, the second premise of the argument (A3: A – P2) for the second premise of A3 is untrue in case it can be that God exists and it can be that a living thing possesses the power to bring about (in the very first instance) other living things which possess the power to do this or that freely. Here is *an* argument (A4) for this claim:

it can be that God possesses (and exercises) the power to bring about (in the very first instance) other living and non-physical things which possesses the power to act freely and *which possess the power to lead lives* in case it can be that he exists and it can be that a living thing possesses the power to bring about (in the very first instance) other living things which possess the power to do this or that freely;

it is untrue that it can be that God does not know such a living thing exists at a time and it exists to a later time;

it is untrue that it can be that God knows it exists at that later time unless it is determinable that it does so;

so, it can be that a living and non-physical thing exists at that later time is determinable in case it can be that God exists and it can be that a living thing possesses the power to bring about (in the very first instance) other living things which possess the power to do this or that freely.

The conclusion follows from the first premise and the second premise and the third premise. The first premise (as we shall see in the course of the second chapter) is true. The second premise is true. The third premise is true. So, the conclusion is true. It can be that a living and non-physical thing exists at that later time is determinable in case it can be that God exists and it can be that a living thing possesses the power to bring about (in the very first instance) other living things which possess the power to do this or that freely. So, A3 does *not* establish that it is untrue that it can be that there is a living and non-physical thing in case it be that that is so.

Incidentally, theists claim that it can be that God brings about a change in the momentum of a physical thing and it can be in that case that he interacts with a physical thing. The claim that it can be that there is a change in the momentum of a physical thing and that change is brought about by a non-physical thing is untrue according to many analytic philosophers today. Here is an argument (A5) for this claim :

it cannot be that there is a change in the momentum of a physical thing unless there is a transfer of momentum to that physical thing from some other thing ;

it cannot be that a thing transfers momentum to some other thing unless it has momentum. (The momentum of thing is the product of its mass and its velocity.) ;

it cannot be that a non-physical thing has momentum ;

it cannot be in that case that a non-physical thing transfers momentum to a physical thing. (This initial conclusion follows from the second premise and the third premise.) ;

so, it cannot be that there is a change in the momentum of a physical thing and that change is brought about by a non-physical thing.

The ultimate conclusion follows ultimately from the first premise and the second premise and the third premise. The second premise is true. The third premise is true. (The momentum of a thing is the product of its mass and its velocity. It cannot be that a non-physical thing has mass. So, it cannot be that a non-physical thing has momentum.) So, the ultimate conclusion is true in case the first premise is true. Is it true?

Well, it can be that there is a change in the momentum of a physical thing in case there is some other physical thing and they are subject to the force of gravity. (Each of these things in that case accelerates towards the other.) The change in motion is *not* as a result of a transfer of momentum. It can be in that case that there is a change in the momentum of a physical thing even though there is no transfer of momentum to that physical from some other thing. So, the first premise is untrue. A5 does *not* establish that it cannot be that there is a change in the momentum of a physical thing and that change is brought about by a non-physical thing.

God's nature is considered in what follows. God's nature has been the subject of a great deal of analysis by analytic philosophers. Why? Well, this is so in order to determine it *and* in order to determine whether it can be that such a thing exists. This is undertaken prior to a consideration of whether such a thing does exist. (Such a prior undertaking is characteristic of the analytic tradition of philosophy.)

An all-knowing or omniscient thing and God's knowledge

Some preliminary remarks

A thing which is all-knowing or omniscient at some time is a thing which knows every fact which can be known by a thing at that time.[4]

There are kinds of fact. There are facts which have to be facts. Here is an example: *3* is greater than *2*. This is so *and* this has to be so. (This is so and this has to be so just in case the state of affairs that *3* is greater than *2* obtains and it has to obtain.)

There are facts which do not have to be facts. Here is an example: the Tate gallery is in London. This is so *and* this does not have to be so. (This is so and this does not have to be so just in case the state of affairs that the Tate gallery is in London obtains and it does not have to obtain.)

There is a tripartite or standard analysis of the following: a thing *knows* this or that. First of all, a thing does not know this or that unless (that) this or that *is* the case. Here is an example: someone does not know the gate is locked unless it *is* locked! (The gate *is* locked just in case the state of affairs that the gate is locked obtains. So, someone does not know the gate is locked unless the state of affairs that the gate is locked obtains.)

Further, a thing apprehends the state of affairs which represents this or that in case it knows (that) this or that - *it* after all represents (that) this or that. There is a (mental) relation which a thing has to this state of affairs. The relation – according to this analysis – is *believes.* So, a thing does not know this or that unless it believes that (that) this or that. In our example, someone does not know the gate is locked unless he believes that it is locked.

Finally, a thing does not know this or that unless it has sufficient grounds to hold the belief that (that) this or that. In our example, someone does not know the gate is locked unless he has sufficient grounds to hold the belief that it is locked.

The tripartite analysis is as follows: a thing knows this or that just in case (that) this or that is the case *and* it believes that (that) this or that *and* it has sufficient grounds to hold the belief that (that) this or that. The tripartite analysis requires *at least* one or two amendments. There are some amendments to it in the paragraphs which follow.

Let us consider our example again prior to the identification of these amendments. Let us suppose that someone holds the belief that the gate is locked because he sees the gate and it looks locked. He holds it because he sees the gate and it looks locked. He does not hold it because he infers it from some other belief *or* because he has some other (indirect) evidence. He holds the belief that the gate is locked in that case *directly* or *immediately.* (Let us suppose on the other hand that he holds the belief that the gate is locked because he hears someone shout that the gate is locked. He holds the belief in that case *indirectly* or *mediately.*)

Let us consider the tripartite analysis again. A thing does not know this or that unless it has sufficient grounds to hold the belief that (that) this or that according to this analysis. Here is an amendment to this requirement: a thing does not know this or that unless it has sufficient grounds to hold the belief that (that) this or that and these grounds do not have to rule out the possibility of error. In our example, someone holds the belief that the gate is locked on the grounds that he sees it and it looks locked. These grounds do not rule out the possibility of error: the gate may not be locked although it looks locked. Even so, he *is* justified in his belief that it is locked.

A further amendment is required due to an article written by the philosopher Edmund Gettier, "Is Justified True Belief Knowledge?".[5] How this amendment should be stated is a matter of some dispute among analytic philosophers.

In order to illustrate the amendment which is required, let us suppose, with our example in mind, the following: he knows no one else has a key to the gate – the gate is the back gate to his house – and he knows there is usually no one else at the house at this time of the day, *viz.* noon, and he knows a friend's bicycle is behind the gate; he knows he locks the gate; he knows he has kept the key as usual under the flower pot outside of the front of the house; he knows he has left the front door open; he knows he has left the house for a *short* while; he knows he has returned to the house.

Let us also suppose the following: the friend arrives at the house while he is not there; he finds the key; he opens the back gate to ensure that his bicycle is safe; he locks it; he leaves the key where he found it; he leaves the house before the house owner returns.

In this case, the gate is locked *and* the house owner believes that it is locked *and* he has sufficient grounds to hold the belief that it is locked. But, the state of affairs that it is locked obtains ultimately because his friend locks it. His grounds to hold the belief that it is locked are not related to why the state of affairs that it is locked obtains ultimately. So, he does *not* know that the gate is locked.

Here in that case is a further amendment to the same requirement: a thing does not know this or that unless it has sufficient grounds to hold the belief that (that) this or that (and these grounds do not have to rule out the possibility of error) *and* these grounds are related to why the state of affairs that (that) this or that obtains *ultimately.*

The amended analysis is plausible. The amended analysis is as follows: a thing knows this or that just in case (that) this or that is the case *and* it believes that (that) this or that *and* it has sufficient grounds to hold the belief that (that) this or that (and these grounds do not have to rule out the possibility of error) and these grounds are related to why the state of affairs that (that) this or that obtains ultimately. Let us take it that it is correct in what follows. Further, a thing presumably does not hold a belief unless it is *alive.* It is only living things which can know this or that.

How does a living thing know this or that fact? *How* does a living thing retain this or that fact? Well, let us consider human beings. A human being's use of some of his capacities is how he knows this or that fact and how he retains this or that fact.

He has the capacity to reason. He has that is to say a capacity to among other things apprehend abstract things and the relations between them and to deduce. Here is a human being's use of it in order to know a particular fact, *viz.* *3* is greater than *2*. (This is a fact and this has to be a fact.): he *apprehends* (directly) *3* and *2* and he apprehends that 3 *is greater than* 2; he holds as a result the belief that *3* is greater than *2*; he has sufficient grounds to hold the belief that *3* is greater than *2* and these grounds are related to why the state of affairs that *3* is greater than *2* obtains ultimately. He knows *3* is greater than *2*. This is an example of how a human being knows a fact by its use.

He has the capacity to perceive. He has that is to say the capacity to sense things. Here is a human being's use of it in order to know a particular fact, *viz.* there is a College between King's College and Trinity College in Trinity Street, Cambridge. (This is a fact and this does not have to be a fact.): he *sees* a College between King's College and Trinity College in Trinity Street, Cambridge; he holds as a result the belief that there is a College between King's College and Trinity College in Trinity Street, Cambridge; he has sufficient grounds to hold the belief that there is a College between King's College and Trinity College in Trinity Street, Cambridge and these grounds are related to why the state of affairs that there is a College between King's College and Trinity College in Trinity Street, Cambridge obtains ultimately. He knows there is a College between King's College and Trinity College in Trinity Street, Cambridge. This is an example of how a human being knows a fact by its use.

He has the capacity to memorise. He has that is to say the capacity to recall past experiences and to retain past knowledge. Here is a human being's use of it in order to know a particular fact with the example in the preceding paragraph in mind, *viz.* he saw *Caius* College. (This is a fact and this does not have to be a fact.): he *recalls* at some time he saw a

College between King's College and Trinity College in Trinity Street, Cambridge; he learns shortly after that Caius College is the College between King's College and Trinity College in Trinity Street, Cambridge; he holds as a result the belief that he saw Caius College; he has sufficient grounds to hold the belief that he saw Caius College and these grounds are related to why the state of affairs that he saw Caius College obtains ultimately. He did not know he saw *Caius* College. Now, he knows - as a result in part of what he *recalls* - he saw Caius College. This is an example of how a human being knows a fact by its use. A human being knows this or that *or* retains this or that by its use.

Finally, he has the capacity to introspect. He has that is to say the capacity to attend "from within" to the operations of his mind *or* to his mind itself. Here is a human being's use of it in order to know a particular fact, *viz.* he believes that he saw Caius College. (This is a fact and this does not have to be a fact.): he *attends* to his belief that he saw Caius College; he holds as a result the belief that he believes that he saw Caius College; he has sufficient grounds to hold the belief that he believes that he saw Caius College and these grounds are related to why the state of affairs that he believes that he saw Caius College obtains ultimately. He knows he believes that he saw Caius College. This is an example of how a human being knows a fact by its use.

An all-knowing or omniscient thing

Can it be that there is an all-knowing or omniscient thing at some time? It cannot be that there is an all-knowing or omniscient thing at some time in case *it can be that I (viz. some other living thing) believe* ________ at that time and it can be that that other living thing knows this fact at that time. Here is an argument (A6) for this claim. Its initial premise is as follows:

a thing which is all-knowing or omniscient at some time is a thing which knows every fact which can be known by a thing at that time.

Let us suppose that it can be that there is an all-knowing or omniscient thing at some time and *it can be that I (viz. some other living thing) believe* _______ at that time and it can be that that other living thing knows this fact at that time.

It can be in that case that it knows every fact which can be known at that time. (This initial conclusion follows from the first premise and the first conjunct of the supposition.)

It can be in that case that it knows that fact, *viz.* it can be that *I* (*viz.* that other living thing) believe ________ . (This further conclusion follows from the second conjunct and the third conjunct of the supposition and the initial conclusion.) That's absurd! (A living thing cannot know such a fact unless it can apprehend the state of affairs which represents such a fact; but, only that other living thing can do so and no other living thing can be that living thing; so, no other living thing can know such a fact.)

So, it is untrue that it can be that there is an all-knowing or omniscient thing at some time and *it can be that I (viz. some other living thing) believe* ________ at that time and it can be that that other living thing knows this fact at that time.

The ultimate conclusion follows ultimately from the first premise and the supposition. The first premise is true. The supposition is such that an absurdity follows from it. So, the ultimate conclusion – the ultimate conclusion is the denial of the supposition – is true. It cannot be in other words that there is an all-knowing or omniscient thing at some time in case *it can be that I (viz. some other living thing) believe* _______ at that time and it can be that that other living thing knows this fact at that time.

Can it be that there is an all-knowing or omniscient thing at some time in case it cannot be that God exists? Well, let us consider to begin with the following statement in order to address this question: it cannot be that there are living things which know this or that at that time in case it cannot be that God exists *or* it can be that there are living things which know this or that at that time in case it cannot be that God exists. This statement is true.

It cannot be that there is an all-knowing or omniscient thing at that (or some) time in case it cannot be that God exists and it cannot be that there are living things which know this or that at that time. Can it be that there is an all-knowing or omniscient thing at that (or some) time in case it cannot be that God exists and it can be (nonetheless) that there are living things which know this or that at that time?

Well, it cannot be that this is so in case that is so. Here is an argument (A7) for this claim. This argument takes it that it cannot be that God exists and it can be (nonetheless) that there are living things which know this or that at that time. Its initial premises are as follows:

an all-knowing or omniscient thing at that (or some) time is a thing which knows every fact which can be known by a thing at that time ;

it can be that I (viz. some other living thing) know ________ at that time and this fact is such that it can be that that other living thing knows it at that time.

Let us suppose that it can be that there is an all-knowing or omniscient thing at that (or some) time.

It can be in that case that it knows every fact which can be known by a thing at that time including the fact *it can be that I (viz. some other living thing) know* ________ . (This initial conclusion follows from the first premise and the second premise and the supposition.) That's absurd! (A living thing cannot know such a fact unless it can apprehend the state of affairs which represents such a fact; but, only that other living thing can do so and no other living thing can be that other thing; so, no other living thing can know such a fact.)

So, it is untrue that it can be that there is an all-knowing or omniscient thing at that (or some) time.

The first premise is true. The second premise is true. The supposition is such that an absurdity follows from it. So, the ultimate conclusion – the ultimate conclusion is the denial of the supposition – is true. It cannot be that there is an all-knowing or omniscient thing at that (or some) time. (This is so in case it cannot be that God exists and it can be that there are living things which know this or that at that time.)

Can it be that there is an all-knowing or omniscient thing other than God at some time in case it can be that God exists? Well, it cannot be that there is an all-knowing or omniscient thing other than God at some time in case it can be that God exists. Here is an argument (A8) for this claim. Its initial premises are as follows. (It takes it that it cannot be that there is more time than an eternal period of time – an eternal period of time is referred to in its second premise.) :

it cannot be that God does not exist in case it can be that he exists ;

it cannot be that God does not exist for an eternal period of time in case it can be that he exists.

(it cannot be that there is more time than an eternal period of time.) ;

it cannot be that I (*viz.* God) do not know this or that (at some time) in case it can be that he exists ;

it cannot be that God does not know I (*viz.* God) know (that) this or that in case it can be that he exists ;

a thing which is all-knowing or omniscient at some time is a thing which knows every fact which can be known by a thing at that time.

Let us suppose that it can be that there is an all-knowing or omniscient thing other than God at some time and it can be that God exists.

It cannot be in that case that God does not exist at that time. (This initial conclusion follows from the first premise and the second premise and the supposition.)

It cannot be in that case that God does not know I (*viz.* God) know (that) this or that at that time. (This further conclusion follows from the third premise and the fourth premise and the initial conclusion.)

It can be in that case that that other living thing knows I (*viz.* God) know (that) this or that, too. (This penultimate conclusion follows from the fifth premise and the first conjunct of the supposition and the further conclusion.) That's absurd!

So, it is untrue that it can be that there is an all-knowing or omniscient thing other than God at some time and it can be that God exists.

The first premise (as we shall see in the course of the consideration of God's power) is true. The second premise is true. (There is a consideration of whether God exists in time *or* God exists not in time in the course of the consideration of his knowledge.) The third premise (as we shall see in the course of the consideration of God's knowledge) is true. The fourth premise is true in case the third premise is true. The fifth premise is true. The supposition is such that an absurdity follows with its addition. So, the ultimate conclusion – the ultimate conclusion is the denial of the supposition – is true. It cannot be in other words that there is an all-knowing or omniscient thing other than God at some time in case it can be that he exists.

God's knowledge

God does not know this or that to begin with unless (that) this or that is the case *and* unless he believes that (that) this or that *and* unless he has sufficient grounds to hold it *and* these grounds are related to why the state of affairs that (that) this or that obtains ultimately.

Can it be that God is such that his grounds for this or that belief are such that they do *not* rule out the possibility of error? Well, it cannot be that God is such that his grounds for this or that belief are such that they do not rule out the possibility of error in case it can be that he exists. Here is an argument (A9) for this claim. Its initial premises are as follows:

it can be that God is such that his grounds for this or that belief *do* rule out the possibility of error in case it can be that he exists;

God is better (or greater) in case he is such that his grounds for this or that belief *do* rule out the possibility of error than in case he is such that his grounds for this or that belief do *not* rule out the possibility of error.

Let us suppose that it can be that God exists and it can be that God is such that his grounds for this or that belief do *not* rule out the possibility of error.

It can be in that case that God is better (or greater) than he can be by supposition. (This initial conclusion follows from the first premise and the second premise and the supposition.) That's absurd!

So, it is untrue that it can be that God exists *and* it can be that God is such that his grounds for this or that belief do not rule out the possibility of error.

The first premise is true. (God's capacities to know this or that are identified in what follows. God's capacities to know this or that can be such that his grounds for this or that belief *do* rule out the possibility of error in case it can be that he exists.) The second premise is true. The supposition is such that an absurdity follows with its addition. So, the ultimate conclusion – the ultimate conclusion is the denial of the supposition – is true. It cannot be in other words that God is such that his grounds for this or that belief do not rule out the possibility of error in case it can be that he exists.

God does not know this or that unless (that) this or that is the case *and* unless he believes that (that) this or that *and* unless he has sufficient grounds to hold it *and* these grounds rule out the possibility of error *and* these grounds are related to why the state of affairs that (that) this or that obtains ultimately. Further, God presumably is such that he holds this or that belief directly or immediately *or* he holds this or that belief because he deduces it (immediately) from some such belief(s).

Can it be that God does not have the capacity to apprehend abstract things and the relations which hold between them? Well, it cannot be that he does not have this capacity in case it can be that he exists. Here is an argument (A10) for this claim. Its initial premises are as follows :

it can be that God has this capacity in case it can be that he exists ;

God is better (or greater) in case he has this capacity than in case he does not have this capacity.

Let us suppose that it can be that he exists and it can be that he does not have this capacity.

It can be in that case that he is better (or greater) than he can be by supposition. (This initial conclusion follows from the first premise and the second premise and the supposition.) That's absurd!

So, it is untrue that it can be that he exists *and* it can be that he does not have this capacity.

The first premise is true. The second premise is true. The supposition is such that an absurdity follows with its addition. So, the ultimate conclusion – the ultimate conclusion is the denial of the supposition – is true. It cannot be in other words that he does not have this capacity in case it can be that he exists. (This is so whether he is in time eternally *or* whether he is not in time eternally.)

Can it be that he does not use this capacity in case it can be that he exists? Well, it cannot be that that he does not use this capacity in case it can be that he exists. Here is an argument (A11) for this claim. Its initial premises are as follows :

it can be that God uses this capacity in case it can be that he exists ;

God is better (or greater) in case he uses this capacity than in case he does not use it.

Let us suppose that it can be that he exists and it can be that he does not use it.

It can be in that case that he is better (or greater) than he can be by supposition. (This initial conclusion follows from the first premise and the second premise and the supposition.) That's absurd!

So, it is untrue that it can be that he exists *and* it can be that he does not use it.

The first premise is true. The second premise is true. The supposition is such that an absurdity follows with its addition. So, the ultimate conclusion – the ultimate conclusion is the denial of the supposition – is true. It cannot be in other words that he does not use this capacity in case it can be that he exists. (This is so whether he is in time eternally *or* whether he is not in time eternally.)

So, it cannot be that God does not (directly) apprehend abstract things and the relations between them in case it can be that he exists. It cannot be that he does not (as a result of apprehending them) hold beliefs about them in case it can be that he exists. It cannot be that he does not (as a result of apprehending them) have grounds which are sufficient to hold these beliefs about them and which are related to why the state of affairs that (that) this or that obtains ultimately in case it can be that he exists. These grounds are such that rule out the possibility of error. So, it cannot be that he does not know (directly) about abstract things and the relations which hold between them in case it can be that he exists.[6]

Can it be that God does not have the capacity to attend "from within" to his states? (His states include his capacities and his use of his capacities.) Well, it cannot be that he does not have this capacity in case it can be that he exists. The argument for this claim is (with appropriate substitutions) along the lines of A10. (This is so whether he is in time eternally *or* whether he is not in time eternally.)

Can it be that he does not use this capacity in case it can be that he exists? Well, let us to begin with consider the following use of this capacity by a living thing which knows this or that: it attends to its state that it knows (that) this or that; it attends to its state that it attends to its state that it knows (that) this or that; .... . It is not implausible that it cannot be (at least) that God uses this capacity in this way (at all times) in case it can be that he exists. Here is an argument (A12) for this claim. Its initial premises are as follows :

it cannot be that God's use of a capacity is superfluous ;

God's use of a capacity is superfluous in case his use of it is *not* such that he is better (or greater) than in case he does not use it ;

God's use of this capacity in this way (at all times) is *not* such that he is better (or greater) than in case he does not use it in this way (at all times).

Let us suppose that it can be that he exists and it can be that he uses this capacity in this way (at all times).

It cannot be in that case that God use of a capacity is superfluous and it can be that his use of a capacity is superfluous. (This initial conclusion follows from the first premise and the second premise and the third premise and the second conjunct of the supposition.) That's absurd!

So, it is untrue that it can be that he exists *and* it can be that he uses this capacity in this way (at all times).

The first premise is true. The second premise is true. The third premise is not implausible. The supposition is such that an absurdity follows with its addition. So, the ultimate conclusion – the ultimate conclusion is the denial of the supposition – is not implausible. It is not implausible in other words that it cannot be that God uses this capacity in this way (at all times) in case it can be that he exists.

Can it be in any case that God does not use this capacity to attend to his *capacities* and to *his use* of his capacities? Well, it cannot be that he does not use this capacity to attend to his capacities and to his use of his capacities in case it can be that he exists. The argument for this claim is (with appropriate substitutions) along the lines of A11. (This is so whether he is in time eternally *or* whether he is not in time eternally.)

So, it cannot be that God does not attend (directly) to his capacities and to his use of his capacities in case it can be that he exists. It cannot be that he does not (as a result of attending to his capacities and to his use of his capacities) hold beliefs about his capacities and about his use of his capacities in case it can be that he exists. It cannot be that he does not (as a result of attending to his capacities and to his use of his capacities) have grounds which are sufficient to hold these beliefs about his capacities and about his use of his capacities and which are related to why the state of affairs that (that) this or that obtains ultimately in case it can be that he exists. These grounds are such that they rule out the possibility of error. So, it cannot be that he does not know (directly) about his capacities and his use of his capacities in case it can be that he exists.

Can it be that God does not possess the capacity to bring about (in the very first instance) other living things which possess (among other powers) the power to act freely in a universe? Well, it cannot be (as we shall see in the course of the consideration of his power) that he does not have this capacity in case it can be that he exists and it can be that a living thing possesses the power to bring about (in the very first instance) other such living things. So, it cannot be that he does not know he has this capacity in case it can be that that is so.

Can it be that God does not use this capacity in case it can be that that is so? Well, it cannot be (as we shall see in the course of the consideration of his power) that he does not use this capacity it can be that that is so. So, it cannot be that he does not know he uses this capacity in case it can be that that is so.

Can it be that God does not have the capacity to "perceive" *directly* what is the case as a result of his use of this capacity in case it can be that that is so? Well, it cannot be that he does not have the capacity to "perceive" directly what is the case as a result of his use of this capacity in case it can be that that is so.[7] The argument for this claim is (with appropriate substitutions) along the lines of A10. (This is so whether he is in time eternally *or* whether he is not in time eternally.)

Can it be that he does not use this capacity in case it can be that that is so? Well, it cannot be that he does not use this capacity in case it can be that that is so. Here is *an* argument (A13) for this claim :

it cannot be that God does not care about these other living things and this universe ;

it cannot be that God cares about these other living things and this universe in case he does *not* use this capacity ;

so, it cannot be that he does not use this capacity.

The conclusion follows from the first premise and the second premise. The first premise is true. The second premise is true. So, the conclusion is true. It cannot be that God does not use this capacity. (It cannot be that he does not use this capacity to do so whether he is in time eternally *or* whether he is not in time eternally.)

So, it cannot be that God does not "perceive" directly these other living things and this universe in case it can be that that is so. It cannot be that he does not (as a result of "perceiving" directly these other living things and this universe) hold beliefs about these other living things and this universe in case it can be that that is so. It cannot be that he does not (as a result of "perceiving" directly these other living things and this universe) have grounds which are sufficient to hold these beliefs about these other living things and this universe and which are related to why the state of affairs that (that) this or that obtains ultimately in case it can be that that is so. These grounds are such that they rule out the possibility of error. So, it cannot be that he does not know (directly) about these other living things and this universe in case it can be that that is so.

Can it be that God does not have *the capacity* to retain states such as the state that he knows he uses his capacity to bring about other such living things in a universe at some time in case it can be that that is so *and* it cannot be that he is not in time? (The matter of whether God is in time *or* God is not in time is considered in what follows of this consideration of God's knowledge.) Well, it cannot be that God does not have the capacity to retain states such as the state that he knows he uses his capacity to bring about other such living things in a universe at some time in case it can be that that is so and it cannot be that he is not in time. The argument for this claim is (with appropriate substitutions) along the lines of A10.

Can it be that God does not *use* this capacity in case it can be that that is so and it cannot be that he is not in time. Well, it cannot be that he does not use this capacity in case it can be that that is so and it cannot be that he is not in time. The argument for this claim is (with appropriate substitutions) along the lines of A11. It cannot be that he does not retain such states in case it can be that that is so and it cannot be that he is not in time. So, it cannot be that he does not know at later times a fact such as the fact he brings about other such living things in a universe at some time in case it can be that that is so and it cannot be that he is not in time.[8]

Can it be that God is all-knowing or omniscient at some time in case in can be that he exists? Well, it cannot be that God is all-knowing or omniscient at some time in case in can be that he exists and it can be that a living thing possesses the power to bring about (in the very first instance) other living things which possess the power to do this or that freely. Here is an argument (A14) for this claim. It is in three stages. Here is the first stage (A14.1). (It takes it that it cannot be that there is more time than an eternal period of time – an eternal period of time is referred to in its second premise.) :

it cannot be that God does not exist in case it can be that he exists ;

it cannot be that God does not exist for an eternal period of time in case it can be that he exists.

(it cannot be that there is more time than an eternal period of time.) ;

it cannot be that God does not exercise the power to bring about (in the very first instance) other living things which possess the power to do this or that freely at *a* time (*although there is no particular time*) in case it can be that he exists and it can be that a living thing possesses this power ;

it cannot be in that case that there is a time and it cannot be that God exercises this power at that time in case it can be that that is so. (This initial conclusion follows from the first premise and the second premise and the third premise.) ;

it cannot be that he exercises it unless he possesses the power to do so ;

so, it cannot be that there is a time and it cannot be that God does not possess the power to do so at that time in case it can be that that is so.[9]

The ultimate conclusion follows ultimately from the first premise and the second premise and the third premise and the fifth premise. The first premise (as we shall see in the course of the consideration of God's power) is true. The second premise is true. (There is a consideration of whether God exists in time *or* God exists not in time recall in the course of this consideration of God's knowledge.) The third premise (as we shall see in the course of the consideration of God's power) is true. The fifth premise is true. So, the ultimate conclusion is true. It cannot be that there is a time and it cannot be that God does not possess the power to do so at that time in case it can be that that is so.

Let us re-state the conclusion of the first stage more briefly: for any time, it can be that God possesses the power to do so at that time in case it can be that that is so. Here is the second stage (A14.2) :

for any time, it can be that I (*viz.* some other such living thing) know this or that at that time in case it can be that there are other such living things at that time ;

it can be that there are other such living things at that time in case it can be that God possesses the power to bring about other such living things at that time ;

it can be that God possesses the power to bring about other such living things at that time in case it can be that that is so ;

so, for any time, it can be that I (*viz.* some other such living thing) know this or that at that time in case it can be that that is so.

The conclusion follows from the first premise and the second premise and the third premise. The first premise is true. (There is a consideration of these other living things in the second chapter.) The second premise is true. The third premise is true. (The third premise is the conclusion of the first stage.) So, the conclusion is true. For any time, it can be that I (*viz.* some other such living thing) know this or that at that time in case it can be that that is so.

Here is the third stage (A14.3) :

a thing which is all-knowing or omniscient at some time is a thing which knows every fact which can be known by a thing at that time ;

for any time, there is a fact, *viz.* it can be that I (*viz.* some other such living thing) know this or that, at that time in case it can be that that is so ;

it can be that that other living thing knows this fact at that time.

Let us suppose that it can be that God exists *and* it can be that a living thing possesses the power to bring about (in the very first instance) other living things which possess (among other powers) the power to do this or that freely *and* it can be that he is all-knowing or omniscient at some time.

It can be in that case that God knows every fact which can be known by a thing at that time. (This initial conclusion follows from the first premise and the third conjunct of the supposition.)

It can be in that case that God knows every fact which can be known by a living thing at that time including the fact it can be that I (*viz.* some other such living thing) know this or that. (This further conclusion follows from the second premise and the third premise and the supposition and the initial conclusion.) That's absurd!

So, it is untrue that it can be that he exists *and* it can be that a living thing possesses the power to bring about (in the very first instance) other living things which possess (among other powers) the power to do this or that freely *and* it can be that he is all-knowing or omniscient at some time.

The first premise is true. The second premise is true. (The second premise is the conclusion of the second stage.) The third premise is true. The supposition is such that an absurdity follows with its addition. So, the ultimate conclusion – the ultimate conclusion is the denial of the supposition – is true. It cannot be in other words that God is all-knowing or omniscient at some time in case it can be that he exists and it can be that a living thing possesses the power to bring about (in the very first instance) other living things which possess (among other powers) the power to do this or that freely.

Ought a theist who maintains that it can be that a living thing possesses this power to be concerned that this is so? (All theists maintain that it can be that he exists. Most theists maintain that it can be that a living thing, *viz.* God himself, possesses this power.) Well, he ought not to be concerned that this is so. Why? Well, the third premise of the first stage is true and the third premise is in accord with God being worthy of worship as we shall see in the course of the consideration of God's power. (That this is so in that case is in accord with God being worthy of worship.) So, such a theist ought not to be concerned that this is so.

Can it be that God has always known a living thing, X, exercises a power to do this or that freely at a particular time?

Well, it cannot be that God has always known a living thing, X, exercises a power to do this or that *freely* at a particular time in case it can be that X exercises it at that time. A living thing's power to do this or that freely is such that it cannot be that it possesses it unless it is *not* brought to exercise it by something else. It is such that it cannot be that it possesses it unless it possesses the power to *not* do (that) this or that. (The great theistic religions of the Middle East in the main also maintain that this is so.[10])

Here is an argument (A15) for the claim that it cannot be that God has always known a living thing, X, exercises a power to do this or that freely at a particular time in case it can be that X exercises it at that time. It is in two stages. Here is the first stage (A15.1). Its initial premises are as follows :

it is untrue that it can be that what is (already) the case at some time is not the case thereafter ;

it is untrue that it can be that something which *has* to be the case as a consequence of what is (already) the case is not the case thereafter, too ;

it is untrue that it can be that a living thing possesses the power to not do this or that at some time in case *it does (that) this or that at that time* has to be the case as a consequence of what is (already) the case ;

it is untrue that it can be that a living thing exercises a power to do this or that *freely* at some time although it does not possess the power to not do it at that time.

Let us suppose that it can be that God has always known a living thing, X, exercises a power to do this or that at a particular time.

It is untrue that it can be that this (is the case and it) is not the case thereafter. (This initial conclusion follows from the first premise and the supposition.)

Something which *has* to be the case as a consequence of *God has always known a living thing, X, exercises a power to do this or that at a particular time* is *X does (that) this or that at that time.* (This further conclusion follows from the analysis of *God knows this or that* and the supposition.)

It is untrue that it can be that this is not the case thereafter, too. (This still further conclusion follows from the second premise and the supposition and the initial conclusion and the further conclusion.)

It is untrue that it can be that thereafter X has the power to *not* do it at that time. (This penultimate conclusion follows from the third premise and the still further conclusion.)

So, it untrue that it can be that thereafter X exercises the power to do it freely at that time.

The ultimate conclusion follows ultimately from the first premise and the second premise and the third premise and the fourth premise and the supposition (and the analysis of *a thing knows this or that.*) The first premise is true. The second premise is true. The third premise is true. The fourth premise is true. (The analysis of *God knows this or that* is correct.) So, the ultimate conclusion is true in case the supposition is true. It is untrue in other words that it can be that God has always known a living thing, X, exercises a power to do this or that at a particular time *and* X exercises it freely at that time.

Here is the second stage (A15.2). Its initial premise is as follows:

it is untrue that it can be that God has always known a living thing, X, exercises a power to do this or that at a particular time *and* X exercises it freely at that time.

Let us suppose that it can be that a living thing, X, exercises a power to do this or that freely at a particular time.

So, it is untrue that it can be that God has always known X exercises it freely at that time.

The conclusion follows from the first premise and the supposition. The first premise is true. So, the conclusion is true in case the supposition is true. It is untrue that it can be that God has always known a living thing, X, exercises a power to do this or that freely at a particular time in case it can be that X exercises it freely at that time.

Let us consider some objections to this argument. The first objection is the result of the work of William of Ockham (c. 1285 - 1349).[11] The objection is that the initial conclusion of the first stage of this argument is untrue. The initial conclusion of the first stage is effectively the following: *God has always known a living thing, X, exercises a power to do this or that at a particular time* once it is the case is unchangeable. The objection is that this once it is the case is *not* unchangeable. The objection is in effect that the first premise of the first stage is untrue.

There is a consideration of past facts in the course of this objection. Past facts which are just about the past are distinguished from past facts which are not just about the past. Past facts which are just about the past are unchangeable. Some past facts which are not just about the past are *not* unchangeable.

Here is an illustration. Let us suppose that the following are facts and that it is after 12.00pm today: someone begins an act, *viz.* the act of locking a gate, at 11.59am today; he begins an act, *viz.* the act of locking it, at 11.59am today and he completes it at 12.00pm today. These facts are past facts. Further, these past facts are just about the past after 12.00pm or noon today. They are *unchangeable* after 12.00pm today.

But, these past facts are not both just about the past in case a time between 11.59am today and 12.00pm today – say, 11.59.59am today - is considered. The first fact is just about the past at that time. The second fact is about the past for 11.59am today is in the past at that time. The second fact is also about the future for 12.00pm is in the future at that time.

Further, he had the power to not to complete the act which he began at 11.59am today up to 11.59.59am today. (He had the power to determine the following up to 11.59.59am today: he begins an act, *viz.* the act of locking the gate, at 11.59am today and he does not complete the act.) The fact he begins an act, *viz.* the act of locking it, at 11.59am today and he completes it at 12.00pm today would not have been a fact (about the past) in case he had exercised this power between 11.59am today and 12.00pm today. So, there is a past fact which is not just about the past and which is changeable at 11.59.59am today according to an advocate of this objection.

Is this right? Well, it is right to say that the fact he begins an act, *viz.* the act of locking it, at 11.59am today and he completes it at 12.00pm today is not just about the past in case a time between 11.59am today and 12.00pm today – say, 11.59.59am today - is considered.

Further, let us take it that it is right to say that he had the power to not to complete the act which he began at 11.59am today up to 11.59.59am today. Finally, it is right to say that the fact he begins an act, *viz.* the act of locking it, at 11.59am today and he completes it at 12.00pm today *would not have been a fact* (about the past) in case he *had* exercised this power.

But, it is not right to say that in that case there is a past fact which is not just about the past and which is changeable at 11.59.59am today. It is not right to say this for there is *no* such fact at that time! There is *no* such fact *until* after 12.00pm today!

Let us suppose that the following is a fact and that it is after 12.00pm today with this illustration in mind: God has always known he begins an act, *viz.* the act of locking it, at 11.59am today and he completes it at 12.00pm today. This fact is a past fact. This past fact is not just about the past in case a time between 11.59am today and 12.00pm today – say, 11.59.59am today - is considered. He had the power to not to complete the act which he began at 11.59am today up to 11.59.59am today. (He had the power to determine the following up to 11.59.59am today: he begins an act, *viz.* the act of locking the gate, at 11.59am today and he does not complete the act.) The fact God has always known he begins an act, *viz.* the act of locking it, at 11.59am today and he completes it at 12.00pm today would not have been a fact (about the past) in case he had exercised this power between 11.59am today and 12.00pm today. So, there is a past fact which is not just about the past and which is changeable at 11.59.59am to-day according to an advocate of this objection.

Is this right? Well, it is right to say that the fact God has always known he begins an act, *viz.* the act of locking it, at 11.59am today and he completes it at 12.00pm today is not just about the past in case a time between 11.59am today and 12.00pm today – say, 11.59.59am today - is considered. Further, let us take it that it is right to say that he had the power to not to complete the act which he began at 11.59am today up to 11.59.59am today. Finally, let us take it that the fact God has always known he begins an act, *viz.* the act of locking it, at 11.59am today and he completes it at 12.00pm today *would not have been a fact* (about the past) in case he *had* exercised this power.

But, it is not right to say that in that case there is a past fact which is not just about the past and which is changea-ble11.59.59am today. It is not right to say this for there is *no* such fact at that time! There is *no* such fact *until* after 12.00pm today! So, the first objection does *not* establish that the initial conclusion of the first stage of this argument (A15.1) is untrue.

The second objection is about the supposition of the first stage of the argument. The supposition of the first stage is that it can be that God has always known a living thing, X, ex-ercises a power to do this or that at a particular time. It can be in that case that God is in time. The objection is that God does not exist in time and indeed God cannot exist in time. So, the supposition is untrue.

Are there grounds for this objection? Well, here is an argument (A16) for at least the claim that it can be that God is not in time in case it can be that he exists :

it cannot be that God exists and there is something, *viz.* time, and it is not brought about by him ;

it cannot be that God exists and he does not possess the power to bring about something, *viz.* time, *and* the power to *not* bring it about.

Let us suppose that it can be that God exists.

So, it can be that he is not in time.

The conclusion follows from the first premise and the second premise and the supposition. (The first and second premises are true for an advocate of this argument. So, the conclusion is true in case the supposition is true. It can be that God is not in time in case it can be that he exists.) Is the first premise true? Is instead the following statement true: it cannot be that God exists and there is something, *viz.* time *in terms of other things*, and it is not brought about by him? (There are comments on this statement – in particular, the part of the statement that there is time in terms of other things – in the course of what follows.)

Here is another argument (A17). It is an argument for at least the claim that it can be that God is alive not in time in a permanent (or eternal) "present" in case it can be that he is alive (or exists). The argument is in four stages. Here is the first stage (A17.1). Its initial premises are as follows :

it cannot be that there is something which is alive for a duration of time and it does not have temporal parts - a part up to a present moment in its life and a part after this present moment in its life ;

it cannot be that something which is alive for a duration of time relives a temporal part of its life up to a present moment in its life ;

for such a thing, a temporal part which is good and which cannot be relived is a loss of some good ;

any temporal parts of God's life are good.

Let us suppose that it can be that God is alive for a duration of time.

It can be in that case that God's life has temporal parts and some temporal part cannot be relived. (This initial conclusion follows from the first premise and the second premise and the supposition.)

It can be in that case that God's life includes a loss – the loss of a good. (This further conclusion follows from the third premise and the fourth premise and the initial conclusion.) That's absurd!

So, it cannot be that God is alive for a duration of time.

The ultimate conclusion follows from the initial premises and the supposition.

Here is the second stage (A17.2) :

it cannot be that something is alive in time unless it is alive for a moment (or moments) in time *or* for a duration of time ;

it cannot be that God is alive for a moment (or moments) in time ;

it cannot be God is alive for a duration of time ;

so, it cannot be that God is alive in time.

The conclusion follows from the premises.

Here is the third stage (A17.3) :

it cannot be that God is alive in time.

Let us suppose that it can be that God is alive (or exists).

So, it can be that God is alive not in time.

The conclusion follows from the first premise and the supposition. It can be in other words that God is alive not in time in case it can be that God is alive (or exists).

Here is the fourth stage (A17.4) :

it can be that God is alive not in time in case it can be that God is alive (or exists) ;

it is untrue that it can be that God is alive not in time unless he is so permanently or eternally ;

anything which is so is in a "present" ;

so, it can be that God is alive not in time in a permanent (or eternal) "present" in case it can be that he is alive (or exists).

The conclusion follows from the premises.

Let us consider the first stage of this argument. It identifies an absurdity in case he is alive for a duration of time and (in that case) his life has temporal parts which cannot be relived and these parts are good: God's life includes the loss of a good. Is this right? Does God's life include the loss of a good in case that is so? Well, it does not do so in case that is so. The good of *any* temporal part of God's life is (ultimately) nothing other than the good of being a living thing which is worthy of worship in case that is so. There is in that case *no* loss of a good in case that is so. So, this argument does not establish its ultimate conclusion, *viz.* it can be that God is alive not in time in a permanent (or eternal) "present" in case it can be that he is alive (or exists).

Boethius (480 - 524), a Christian philosopher, claims that God does not exist in time.[12] (He sets out the most influential statement of this claim.) For Boethius, God's life is in a permanent *present* and what occurs in it is in a permanent present. (God's life is *eternal* for what occurs in it is in a *permanent* present.) What occurs in time is in the present and then it is no longer in the present. So, God's life is not in time.

For Boethius, it can be that something is present and it is not in time. But, isn't it the case that something which is *present* exists at *a present time*? Well, let consider the following argument (A18) :

there is a time series which is other than our time series ;

the times in that series do not have a temporal relation to the times in our time series. (They do not occur before *or* at the same time *or* after any time in our time series.) ;

so, something which exists in the present in that time series does *not* exist in the present in our time series.

The conclusion follows from the first premise and the second premise. Let us disregard any doubts about the coherence of another time series.[13] Let us take it that the first premise is true. The second premise is true. So, the conclusion is true. Something which exists in the present in another time series does *not* exist in the present in our time series. Still, it exists in *that* time and in *that* present. It is in time!

Here is a line of argument (A19) for the claim that it cannot be that God is not timeless in case it can be that he exists. (It is a line of argument which may well have influenced Boethius.[14]) :

it cannot be that God is not immutable in case it can be that he exists ;

it cannot be that God is immutable *and* not timeless ;

so, it cannot be that God is not timeless in case it can be that he exists.

The conclusion follows from the first premise and the second premise. Are the premises true? Well, here is the argument (A19: A – P1) for the first premise. Its initial premises are as follows :

it can be that God is immutable in case it can be that he exists ;

God is better (or greater) in case he is immutable than in case he is not immutable.

Let us suppose that it can be that he exists and it can be that he is not immutable.

It can be in that case that God is better (or greater) than he can be by supposition. (This follows from the first premise and the second premise and the supposition.) That's absurd!

So, it is untrue that it can be that he exists and it can be that he is not immutable. (In other words, it cannot be that he is not immutable in case it can be that he exists.)

Can it be that God is immutable in case it can be that he exists? Is God better (or greater) in case he is immutable than in case he is not immutable? Well, let us consider the second question. The consideration of God's nature in this chapter includes an argument (*viz.* A31) for the claim that it is *untrue* that it can be that God is immutable in case it can be that he exists *and* it can be that a living thing possesses the power to bring about (in the very first instance) other living things which possess the power to do this or that freely. (The first premise of this argument is that it cannot be that God does not exist for an eternal period of time in case it can be that he exists.) There are *no* grounds for the claim that God is not a living thing which is worthy of worship in this case. (There are *no* grounds for the claim that God is not a living thing which is better or greater than any other thing in this case.) There are *no* grounds for the claim that God better (or greater) in case he is immutable than in case he is not immutable at least in the course of the consideration of God's nature in this chapter.

Finally, there is a difficulty for Boethius as a Christian. The Bible uses the word *olam* (Hebrew) in relation to God's life. It means for a *never ending duration of time* or *forever* in relation to God's life. It does not mean that God's life begins and it is for a never ending duration of time or forever. It does not mean that God's life ends and it has been for a never ending duration of time or forever.

Instead, it means that God is alive and God has been alive throughout the whole of a never ending duration of time or forever *and* God will be alive throughout the whole of a never ending duration of time or forever. Hence, God's life is "from everlasting to everlasting".[15] (Further, it is taken tacitly here that there is no time other than this time. So, there is no time when God does not exist.)

The second objection to A15 is the following: the supposition of the first stage of A15 is that it can be that God has always known a living thing, X, exercises a power to do this or that at a particular time;[16] it can be in that case that God is in time; but, God does not exist in time and indeed God cannot exist in time; so, the supposition is untrue. This objection has been considered in the last few pages. Grounds for this objection are to say the least not readily forthcoming.

God exists in time. Can it be that God does not exist *eternally* in time in case it can be that he exists? (God exists eternally in time just in case he is alive and he has been alive throughout the whole of a never ending duration of time or forever and he will be alive throughout the whole of a never ending duration of time or forever.) Well, it cannot be that God does not exist eternally in time in case it can be that he exists. Here is an argument (A20) for this claim. Its initial premises are as follows:

it can be that God exists eternally in time in case it can be that he exists;

God is better (or greater) in case he exists eternally in time than in case he does not exist eternally in time.

Let us suppose that it can be that he exists and it can be that he does not exist eternally in time.

It can be in that case that God is better (or greater) than he can be by supposition. (This follows from the first premise and the second premise and the supposition.) That's absurd!

So, it is untrue that it can be that he exists *and* it can be that he does not exist eternally in time.

The first premise is true. The second premise is true. The supposition is such that an absurdity follows with its addition. So, the conclusion – the conclusion is the denial of the supposition – is true. It cannot be in other words that he does not exist eternally in time in case it can be that he exists.

A theist ought to maintain that it cannot be that God does not exist in time *eternally*. But, the Bible, for example, refers to a "beginning of time".[17] How is this to be understood? Well, let us consider to begin with the following argument (A21). It is in three stages. Here is the first stage (A21.1) :

it cannot be that there is time (other than a moment, or moments, of time) unless it passes ;

it cannot be that time passes unless there is a now and then later there is a later now... (There is a distinct sub-period of time until now and then later a distinct sub-period until a later now...) ;

it cannot be that there is a now and then later there is a later now... unless there are distinct sub-periods of time ;

so, it cannot be that there is time (other than a moment, or moments, of time) unless there are distinct sub-periods of time.

The conclusion follows from the first premise and the second premise and the third premise. The first premise is true. The second premise is true. The third premise is true. So, the conclusion is true. It cannot be that there is time (other than a moment, or moments, of time) unless there are distinct sub-periods of time.

Here is the second stage (A21.2) :

it cannot be that there is time (other than a moment, or moments, of time) unless there are distinct sub-periods of time ;

it cannot be that there are distinct sub-periods of time unless for example the now which is the end of a sub-period *is earlier than* a then later now which is the end of another sub-period ;

so, it cannot be that that there is time (other than a moment, or moments, of time) unless it is extended.

The conclusion follows from the first premise and the second premise. The first premise is true. (The first premise is the conclusion of the first stage.) The second premise is true. So, the conclusion is true. It cannot be that there is time (other than a moment, or moments, of time) unless it is extended.

Here is the third stage (A21.3) :

it cannot be that there is time (other than a moment, or moments, of time) unless it is extended ;

it cannot be that time is extended unless there are things to bear relations such as *earlier than* ;

so, it cannot be that there is time (other than a moment, or moments, of time) unless there are things to bear relations such as *earlier than.*

The conclusion follows from the first premise and the second premise. The first premise is true. (The first premise is the conclusion of the second stage.) The second premise is true. So, the conclusion is true. It cannot be that there is time (other than a moment, or moments, of time) unless there are things to bear relations such as *earlier than.*

Now, it cannot be that there is time (other than a moment, or moments, of time) in terms of things which are physical unless there are things which are physical to bear relations such as *earlier than.* Let us suppose that time has passed until a "now" and that there have been no physical things. So, there is *no* time in *such* terms. Further, let us suppose that there is a time when for the first time there are physical things and there is time in these terms. (Time passes in these terms.) The "beginning of time" refers plausibly to that time.

God's life is measurable in these terms from that time. God's life is not measurable in these terms before this time and it is not measurable in these terms at any time after there are physical things. Let us take it plausibly that we have no other measure. So, God's life before and after there are physical things is beyond our ability to measure. (This is a plausible explanation of what the authors of the Bible had in mind in stating that God's life is beyond our ability to measure.[18])

What is taken in what follows following the consideration of whether it can be that God has always known a living thing, X, exercises a power to do this or that freely at a particular time.

It is taken in what follows that it cannot be that God has always known a living thing, X, exercises a power to do this or that freely at a particular time in case it can be that it, X, exercises it freely at that time.

It cannot be (as we shall see in the course of the consideration of his power) that God does not exercise the power to bring about other living things which possess (among other powers) the power to act freely at a time in case it can be that he exists and it can be that a living thing possesses the power to bring about (in the very first instance) living things which possess the power to act freely. It cannot be that God has always known this or that such living thing exercises a power to do this or that freely at a particular time.

Most theists in the great religions of the Middle East maintain *strongly* that human beings *are* free. They maintain, for example, the following: there is a Day of Judgement – God on this Day judges what a human being has done during his life on earth and God rewards *or* punishes him accordingly; God does not possess the power to do so unless a human being possesses the power to act freely during his time on earth; a human being in that case possesses the power to act freely during his time on earth. They maintain that there are passages in the Bible and the Qur'an which state that this is so: *eg,* Deuteronomy 30:19; Qur'an 2:158. Given this, these theists should maintain that it cannot be that God has always known this or that human being exercises a power to do this or that freely at a particular time. God knows what a human being does freely at a particular time when he does it.

An all-powerful or omnipotent thing and God's power

Some preliminary remarks

A thing which is all-powerful or omnipotent at some time is a thing which possesses every power which can be possessed by a thing at that time.[19]

A power of a thing is the power to bring about this or that. A thing possesses the power to bring about this or that at some time just in case it possesses the capacity and opportunity to bring it about at that time. (A thing which possesses the power to bring about this or that at some time exercises it at that time *or* it does not exercise it at that time.)

A thing which possesses the power to bring about this or that at some time possesses the power to bring about the state of affairs that (that) this or that at that time. Here is an example. Let us suppose that there is a thing which possesses the power to bring about a mechanical watch at some time and which exercises this power at that time. There is a mechanical watch. The state of affairs that there is a mechanical watch obtains. The thing possesses the power to bring about the state of affairs that there is a mechanical watch at that time. (A thing possesses the power to bring about a state of affairs at some time just in case it possesses the power to bring about the thing(s) which are included in it at that time.) Concrete things alone can possess powers.

Can it be that a thing possesses the power to bring about just *any* state of affairs at some time? Well, it cannot be that a thing possesses the power to bring about just any state of affairs at some time. This power is not a power which can be possessed by a thing at some time. Here is an argument (A22) for this claim :

states of affairs include states of affairs which cannot obtain ;

it cannot be that a thing possesses the power to bring about a state of affairs at some time *unless* it possesses the power to bring about the thing(s) which are included in it at that time ;

it cannot be that a thing possesses the power to bring about the thing(s) which are included in a state of affairs at some time *unless* it has the opportunity to bring about the thing(s) which are included in it at that time ;

it cannot be that a thing has the opportunity to bring about the thing(s) which are included in a state of affairs at some time *unless* the thing(s) which are included in it can be the case ;

it cannot be that the thing(s) which are included in states of affairs which cannot obtain are the case ;

it cannot be in that case that a thing possesses the power to bring about states of affairs which cannot obtain at some time. (This initial conclusion follows from the second premise and the third premise and the fourth premise and the fifth premise.) ;

so, it cannot be that a thing possesses the power to bring about just *any* state of affairs at some time.

The ultimate conclusion follows from the first premise and the initial conclusion. The first premise is true. The initial conclusion is true. (The initial conclusion follows from the second premise and the third premise and the fourth premise and the fifth premise. These premises are true. So, the initial conclusion is true.) So, the ultimate conclusion is true. It cannot be that a thing possesses the power to bring about just any state of affairs at some time.[20]

Can it be that a thing possesses the power to bring about just *any* state of affairs which can obtain at some time? Well, it cannot be that a thing possesses the power to bring about just any state of affairs which can obtain at some time. This power is not a power which can be possessed by a thing at some time. (Saint Thomas Aquinas (1225 - 1274) maintains effectively that a thing which is all-powerful or omnipotent is a thing which possesses the power to bring about just any state of affairs which can obtain.[21]) Here is an argument (A23) for this claim:

states of affairs which can obtain include states of affairs which can obtain and which have to obtain;

it cannot be that a thing possesses the power to bring about a state of affairs at some time *unless* it possesses the power to bring about the thing(s) which are included in it at that time;

it cannot be that a thing possesses the power to bring about the thing(s) which are included in a state of affairs at some time *unless* it has the opportunity to bring about the thing(s) which are included in it at that time;

it cannot be that a thing has the opportunity to bring about the thing(s) which are included in a state of affairs at some time *unless* the thing(s) which are included in it can *not* be the case;

it cannot be that the thing(s) which are included in states of affairs which can obtain and which have to obtain are *not* the case;

it cannot be in that case that a thing possesses the power to bring about states of affairs which can obtain and which have to obtain at some time. (This initial conclusion follows from the second premise and the third premise and the fourth premise and the fifth premise.);

so, it cannot be that a thing possesses the power to bring about just *any* state of affairs which can obtain at some time.

The ultimate conclusion follows from the first premise and the initial conclusion. The first premise is true. The initial conclusion is true. (The initial conclusion follows from the second premise and the third premise and the fourth premise and the fifth premise. These premises are true. So, the initial conclusion is true.) So, the ultimate conclusion is true. It cannot be that a thing possesses the power to bring about just any state of affairs which can obtain at some time.

Can it be that a thing possesses the power to bring about just *any* state of affairs which does not have to obtain although it can obtain at some time or some now? Well, it cannot be that a thing possesses the power to bring about a state of affairs which does not have to obtain although it can obtain *and* which is a past state of affairs at some time or some now. This power is not a power which can be possessed by a thing at some time or some now.

Here is an example of such a state of affairs: that Magna Carta is written at a time prior to now. Here is an argument (A24) to illustrate that it cannot be that a thing possesses the power to bring about such a state of affairs at some time or some now. Here is its initial premise:

it cannot be that a thing possesses the power to bring about the state of affairs that Magna Carta is written at a time prior to now at some time (or some now) unless it possesses the power to bring it about that Magna Carta is written at a time prior to now at that time (or that now).

Let us suppose it can be that a thing possesses the power to bring it about that Magna Carta is written at a time prior to now at that time (or that now).

It can be in that case that Magna Carta is written at a time prior to now and what brings this about – that thing exercising its power at that time or that now – is not by that time the case.

(This initial conclusion follows from the supposition.) That's absurd!

It cannot be in that case that a thing possesses the power to bring it about that Magna Carta is written at a time prior to now at that time (or that now). (An absurdity follows with the addition of the supposition. This further conclusion – this further conclusion is the denial of the supposition – in that case follows.)

So, it cannot be that a thing possesses the power to bring about the state of affairs that Magna Carta is written at a time prior to now at some time (or some now).

The ultimate conclusion follows from the initial premise and the further conclusion. The initial premise is true. The further conclusion is true. So, the conclusion is true. It cannot be that a thing possesses the power to bring about the state of affairs that Magna Carta is written at a time prior to now at some time (or some now).

Can it be that a thing possesses the power to bring about just *any* state of affairs which does not have to obtain although it can obtain and which is *not* a past state of affairs at some time? Well, it cannot be that this is so in case there is such a state of affairs which can be brought about *only* by something *other* than that thing at that time.

Let us suppose that it can be that something other than that thing possesses the power to act *freely* at that time in order to illustrate that this is so. It can be that that something exercises that power at that time. It can be in that case that that something brings about the state of affairs that it exercises that power at that time. But, it cannot be that a thing other than it brings it about at that time. (It cannot be that a thing other than it brings it about at that time even though it is a state of affairs which does not have to obtain although it can obtain at that time and which is not a past state of affairs.)

The power which can be possessed by a thing at some time is related to states of affairs which do not have to obtain although they can obtain *and* which are not past states of affairs *and* which are not such that only something other than thing can bring them about at that time.

An all-powerful or omnipotent thing

Can it be that there is an all-powerful or omnipotent thing at some time? Well, it cannot be that there is an all-powerful or omnipotent thing at some time in case it can be that some other thing possesses the power to act freely at that time. There is a power which can only be possessed by that other thing at that time in case this is so, *viz.* the power to bring about the state affairs that it exercises that power at that time. So, it cannot be that it possesses every power which can be possessed by a thing at that time in case this is so.

Can it be that there is a thing which is all-powerful or omnipotent at some time in case it cannot be that God exists? Well, let us consider to begin with the following statement in order to address this question. (Concrete things alone can possess powers.): it cannot be that there are concrete things (which possess powers) at that time in case it cannot be that God exists *or* it can be that there are concrete things (which possess powers) at that time in case it cannot be that God exists. This statement is true.

It cannot be that there is an all-powerful or omnipotent thing at that (or some) time in case it cannot be that God exists and it cannot be that there are concrete things (which possess powers) at that time. Can it be that there is an all-powerful or omnipotent thing at that (or some) time in case it cannot be that God exists and it can be (nonetheless) that there are concrete things (which possess powers) at that time? Well, it cannot be that there is an all-powerful or omnipotent thing at that (or some) time in case it cannot be that God exists and it can be (nonetheless) that there are concrete things (which possess powers) at that time. Here is an argument (A25) for this claim. This argument takes it that it cannot be that God exists and it can be (nonetheless) that there are concrete things at that time. Its initial premises are as follows :

an all-powerful or omnipotent thing at that (or some) time is a thing which possesses every power which can be possessed by a thing at that time ;

it can be that there is a concrete thing which possesses the power to lift any stone at that time ;

it can be that there is a concrete thing which possesses the power to bring about a stone which nothing possesses the capacity to lift at that time ;

it cannot be that there is a concrete thing which possesses the power to bring about a stone which nothing possesses the capacity to lift at some time unless there is nothing which possesses the capacity to lift just any stone at that time.

Let us suppose that it can be that there is a thing which is an all-powerful or omnipotent thing at that (or some) time.

It can be in that case that there is a thing which possesses every power can be possessed by a thing at that time including the power to bring about a stone which nothing possesses the capacity to lift. (This initial conclusion follows from the first premise and the third premise and the supposition.)

There is in that case nothing which possesses the capacity (and in that case the power) to lift just any stone at that time. (This further conclusion follows from the fourth premise and the initial conclusion.)

It can be in that case that there is a thing which possesses every power which can be possessed by a thing at that time (including the power to bring about a stone which nothing possesses the capacity to lift) *and* which does *not* possess a power which can be possessed by a thing at that time, *viz.* the power to lift any stone. (This pen-ultimate conclusion follows from the second premise and the initial conclusion and the further conclusion.) That's absurd!

So, it is untrue that it can be that there is a thing which is an all-powerful or omnipotent thing at that (or some) time.

The first premise is true. The second premise is true. The third premise is true. The fourth premise is true. The supposition is such that an absurdity follows with its addition. So, the ultimate conclusion – the ultimate conclusion is the denial of the supposition – is true. It cannot be in other words that there is a thing which is an all-powerful or omnipotent thing at that (or some) time in case it cannot be that God exists and it can be (nonetheless) that there are concrete things at that time.

Can it be that there is a thing which is all-powerful or omnipotent and which is other than God at some time in case it can be that God exists? Well, it cannot be that this is so in case it can be that God exists and it can be that a living thing possesses the power to bring about (in the very first instance) other living things which possess the power to do this or that freely. Here is an argument for this claim (A26). (It takes it that it cannot be that there is more time than an eternal period of time – an eternal period of time is referred to in its second premise.) Its initial premises are as follows :

it cannot be that God does not exist in case it can be that he exists ;

it cannot be that he does not exist for an eternal period of time in case it can be that he exists.

(it cannot be that there is more time than an eternal period of time.) ;

it cannot be that God does not exercise the power to bring about (in the very first instance) other living things which possess the power to do this or that freely at *a* time (*although there is no particular time*) in case it can be that he exists and it can be that a living thing possesses the power to bring about (in the very first instance) other living things which possess the power to do this or that freely ;

for any time, it can be God possesses the power to do so at that time in case it can be that that is so ;

an all-powerful or omnipotent thing at some time is a thing which possesses every power which can be possessed by a thing at that time.

Let us suppose that it can be that there is a thing which is all-powerful or omnipotent and which is other than God at some time *and* it can be that God exists *and* it can be that a living thing possesses the power to bring about (in the very first instance) other living things which possess the power to do this or that freely.

It cannot be in that case that God does not exist and it cannot be that God does not exist at that time. (This initial conclusion follows from the first premise and the second premise and the first conjunct and the second conjunct of the supposition.)

It can be in that case that God possesses the power to bring about (in the very first instance) other living things which possess the power to do this or that freely at that time. (This further conclusion follows from the third premise and the fourth premise and the supposition and the initial conclusion.)

It can be in that case that that thing possesses the power to bring about (in *the* very first instance) other living things which possess the power to do this or that freely at that time *and* God has exercised this power *or* is exercising it *or* will exercise it. (This pen-ultimate conclusion follows from the third premise and the fifth premise and the supposition and the initial conclusion and the further conclusion.) That's absurd!

So, it is untrue that it can be that there is a thing which is other than God and which is all-powerful or omnipotent at some time *and* it can be that God exists *and* it can be that a living thing possesses the power to bring about (in the very first instance) other living things which possess the power to do this or that freely.

The first premise (as we shall see in the course of what follows) is true. The second premise is true. The third premise (as we shall see in the course of what follows) is true. The fourth premise is true. The fifth premise is true. The supposition is such that an absurdity follows with its addition. So, the ultimate conclusion – the ultimate conclusion is the denial of the supposition – is true. It cannot be in other words that there is a thing which is all-powerful or omnipotent and which is other than God at some time in case it can be that he exists and it can be that a living thing possesses the power to bring about (in the very first instance) other living things which possess the power to do this or that freely.

God's power

God's power at any time is related to states of affairs which do not have to obtain although they can obtain.[22] God's power at any time is related to such states which are not past states of affairs and which are not such that they can only be brought about by some other thing at that time. Can it be that God possesses the power to bring about just *any* such state of affairs at some time in case it can be that he exists? (The states of affairs at issue are states of affairs which do not have to obtain although they can obtain *and* which are not past states of affairs *and* which are not such that they can only be brought about by some other thing at that time.)

Well, it cannot be that he possesses the power to bring about just *any* such state of affairs at some time in case it can be that he exists and it can be that a living thing possesses power to bring about (in the very first instance) other living things which possess the power to do this or that freely. Here is an example of such a state of affairs in case it can be that that is so: that there are unsuitable conditions for other living things. It cannot be that he possesses the power to bring about this state of affairs at some time in case it can be that that is so. Why? Well, this is so because (among other things) it cannot be that he is not morally perfect.

God's power at any time is related to any such state of affairs which is *not* such that he cannot bring it about because of one of his properties. Can it be that God possesses the power to bring about just *any* such state of affairs *eternally* in time in case it can be that he exists? (The states of affairs at issue are states of affairs which do not have to obtain although they can obtain *and* which are not past states of affairs *and* which are not such that they can only be brought about by some other thing *and* which are not such that he cannot bring them about because of one of his properties.)

Well, it cannot be that God possesses the power to bring about any such state of affairs eternally in time in case it can be that he exists and it can be that a living thing possesses power to bring about (in the very first instance) other living things which possess the power to do this or that freely. Here is an example of such a state of affairs in case it can be that that is so: that he interacts with some other concrete thing. Let us consider to begin with the following argument (A27). It is in three stages. Here is the first stage (A27.1) :

it cannot be that a concrete thing possesses the power to interact with some other concrete thing at some time unless it has the opportunity to do so at that time ;

it cannot be that a concrete thing has the opportunity to do so at some time unless there is some other concrete thing at that time ;

so, it cannot be that a concrete thing possesses the power to interact with some other concrete thing unless there is some other concrete thing at that time.

The conclusion follows from the first premise and the second premise. The first premise is true. The second premise is true. So, the conclusion is true. It cannot be that a concrete thing possesses the power to interact with some other concrete thing unless there is some other concrete thing at that time.

Here is the second stage (A27.2). Its initial premises are as follows. (It takes it that it cannot be that there is more time than an eternal period of time – an eternal period of time is referred to in its second premise.) :

it cannot be that God does not exist in case it can be that he exists ;

it cannot be that God does not exist for an eternal period of time in case it can be that he exists.

(it cannot be that there is more time than an eternal period of time.) ;

it cannot be that there are concrete things other than God eternally in time in case it can be that he exists.

Let us suppose that it can be that God exists.

So, it cannot be that God does not exist *and* it cannot be that he does not exist eternally in time *and* it cannot be that there are concrete things other than God eternally in time.

The conclusion follows from the first premise and the second premise and the third premise and the supposition. The first premise (as we shall see in the course of what follows) is true. The second premise is true. The third premise is true. Here is an argument for this claim (A27.2: A – P3). Its initial premises are as follows. (It takes it that it cannot be that there is more time than an eternal period of time – an eternal period of time is referred to in its second premise.) :

it cannot be that God does not exist in case it can be that he exists ;

it cannot be that God does not exist for an eternal period of time in case it can be that he exists.

(it cannot be that there is more time than an eternal period of time.) ;

it cannot be that there are concrete things other than God without God willing (in the first instance) at some time that this is so in case it cannot be that God does not exist.

Let us suppose that it can be that God exists and it can be that there are concrete things other than God for an eternal period of time.

It cannot be in that case that God does not exist.

It cannot be in that case that God does not exist for an eternal period of time. (These initial conclusions follow from the first premise and the second premise and the first conjunct of the supposition.)

It can be in that case that, for any time, there is a time which is earlier and which is such that some other concrete things *already* exist at that time. (This further conclusion follows from the second conjunct of the supposition.)

It can be in that case that that time – that time is just *any* time - is *not* the time when God wills (in the first instance) that there are such things. (This still further conclusion follows from the third premise and the first initial conclusion and the further conclusion.)

It can be in that case that there is *no* time when God wills (in the first instance) the existence of such things. (This penultimate conclusion follows from the still further conclusion.) That's absurd!

So, it is untrue that it can be that God exists and it can be that there are concrete things other than God for an eternal period of time.

The first premise (as we shall see in the course of what follows) is true. The second premise is true. The third premise is true. The supposition is such that an absurdity follows with its addition. So, the ultimate conclusion – the ultimate conclusion is the denial of the supposition – is true. It cannot be in other words that there are concrete things other than God eternally in time in case it can be that God exists.[23]

The conclusion of A27.2 follows from its first premise and its second premise and its third premise and its supposition. Its first premise (as we shall see in the course of what follows) is true. Its second premise is true. Its third premise is true. So, its conclusion is true in case its supposition is true. It cannot be that God does not exist and it cannot be that he does not exist eternally in time and it cannot be that there are concrete things other than God eternally in time in case it can be that he exists.

Here is the third stage (A27.3). Its initial premises are as follows :

it cannot be that God does not exist *and* it cannot be that he does not exist eternally in time *and* it cannot be that there are concrete things other than God eternally in time in case it can be that he exists ;

it cannot be that a concrete thing possesses the power to interact with some other concrete thing unless there is some other concrete thing at that time.

Let us suppose that it can be that God exists.

So, it cannot be that God possesses the power to interact with some other concrete thing eternally in time.

The conclusion follows from the first premise and the second premise and the supposition. The first premise is true. (The first premise is the conclusion of the second stage.) The second premise is true. (The second premise is the conclusion of the first stage.) So, the conclusion is true in case the supposition is true. It cannot be that God possesses the power to interact with some other concrete thing in time eternally in case it can be that he exists.

So, it cannot be that God possesses the power to bring about the state of affairs *that he interacts with some other concrete thing* eternally in time in case it can be that he exists and it can be that a living thing possesses power to bring about (in the very first instance) other living things which possess the power to do this or that freely. (This is an example of a states of affairs which does not have to obtain although it can obtain *and* which is not a past states of affairs *and* which is not such that it can only be brought about by some other thing at that time *and* which is not such that he cannot bring it about because of one of his properties in case it can be that that is so.)

Can it be that God is all-powerful or omnipotent at all times in case it can be that exists? Well, it cannot be that God is all-powerful or omnipotent at all times in case it can be that he exists *and* it can be that a living thing possesses the power to bring about (in the very first instance) other living things which possess the power to do this or that freely. Here is an argument (A28) for this claim:

it cannot be that God is all-powerful or omnipotent at all times in case it cannot be that there are *no* other living things which possess the power to do this or that freely at all times ;

it cannot be that there are no other living things which possess the power to do this or that freely at all times in case it can be that God exists *and* it can be that a living thing possesses the power to bring about (in the very first instance) other living things which possess the power to do this or that freely ;

so, it cannot be that God is omnipotent or all-powerful at all times in case it can be that he exists and it can be that a living thing possesses the power to bring about (in the very first instance) other living things which possess the power to do this or that freely.

The conclusion follows from the first premise and the second premise. The first premise is true. Is the second premise true? Well, it is true. Here is an argument (A28: A - P2) for the claim that the second premise is true. The argument is in three stages. Here is the first stage of the argument (A28: A - P2.1). Its initial premise is as follows :

God is greater in case it can be that he exists and it cannot be that he does not exist than in case it can be that he exists and it can be that he does not exist.

Let us suppose that it can be that he exists and it can be that he does not exist.

God is greater in case it can be that he exists and it cannot be that he does not exist than he is by supposition. (This initial conclusion follows from the first premise and the supposition.) That's absurd!

So, it is untrue that it can be that he exists and it can be that he does not exist.

The first premise is true. (Here is an argument for this claim: God is a living thing which among other things is such that he possesses among other powers the power to bring about other things and the power to affect them; any living thing which possesses such powers is greater in case in can be that it exists *and* it cannot be that it does not exist than in case it can be that it exists *and* it can be that it does not exist; so, God is greater in case in can be that he exists and it cannot be that he does not exist than in case it can be that he exists and it can be that he does not exist. The conclusion follows from the first premise and the second premise. The first premise is true. The second premise is true. So, the conclusion is true.) The supposition is such that an absurdity follows with its addition. So, the ultimate conclusion – the ultimate conclusion is the denial of the supposition – is true. It cannot be in other words that God does not exist in case it can be that he exists.

Prior to a consideration of the second stage, let us consider the following question: is there an explanation of God's existence in case it can be that he exists? Well, let us suppose that it can be that God exists *and* there is an explanation of God's existence. (God does not exist without it and it is enough for God to exist. An explanation is something which is the case, *viz.* a fact.) It cannot be in that case (as we have seen in the previous paragraph) that God does not exist. So, it cannot be that *it* is not the case.[24]

What is the explanation? Well, it is God himself *or* it is something which is other than God and which is such that it cannot be that it is not the case. Let us suppose that a thing is the explanation of itself. It has an explanation (*viz.* itself).... . This is a *vicious* infinite regress. It is in that case something which is other than God and which is such that it cannot be that it is not the case. What is it? Well, an answer to this question is to say the least not readily forthcoming. So, let us take it that God's existence is without explanation in case it can be that he exists. *God exists* is *a brute fact* in case it can be that he exists.

Here is the second stage of the argument (A28: A - P2.2). Its initial premises are as follows. (It takes it that it cannot be that there is more time than an eternal period of time – an eternal period of time is referred to in its first premise.) :

it cannot be that God does not exist for an eternal period of time in case it can be that he exists.

(it cannot be that there is more time than an eternal period of time.) ;

it cannot be that God does not possess (at any time) the power to bring about (in the very first instance) other living things which possess the power to do this or that freely in case it can be that he exists and it can be that a living thing possesses this power ;

it cannot be that God does not exercise this power at a time in case he possesses it (at least at some times).

Let us suppose that it can be that he exists and it can be that a living thing possesses this power.

It cannot be in that case that he does not exist eternally in time and it cannot be that he does not possess (at any time) the power to bring about (in the very first instance) other living things which possess the power to do this or that freely. (This initial conclusion follows from the first premise and the second premise and the supposition.)

So, it cannot be that God does not exercise this power at a time.

The ultimate conclusion follows ultimately from the first premise and the second premise and the third premise and the supposition. The first premise is true. The second premise is true. Here is an argument (A28: A - P2.2: A – P2) for this claim :

it cannot be that God does not exist for an eternal period of time in case it can be that he exists ;

it can be that God possesses (at least at some times) this power in case it can be that he exists and it can be that a living thing possesses this power ;

God is better (or greater) in case he possesses (at least at some times) this power than in case he does not possess (at any time) this power.

Let us suppose that it can be that he exists and it can be that a living thing possesses this power and it can be that he does *not* possess (at any time) this power.

It can be in that case that he is better (or greater) than he can be by supposition. (This initial conclusion follows from the first premise and the second premise and the third premise and the supposition.) That's absurd!

So, it is untrue that it can be that he exists *and* it can be that a living thing possesses this power *and* it can be that he does not possess (at any time) this power.

The first premise is true. The second premise is true. The third premise is true. The supposition is such that an absurdity follows with its addition. So, the ultimate conclusion – the ultimate conclusion is the denial of the supposition – is true. It cannot be in other words that God does not possess (at any time) this power in case it can be that he exists and it can be that a living thing possesses this power.

The third premise is true. Here is an argument (A28: A - P2.2: A – P3) for this claim :

it cannot be that God does not exercise a power which he possesses at a time in case it is unworthy of him to not exercise it at a time ;

it is unworthy of God to not exercise this power at a time and thereby to not afford such an opportunity to other living things in case he possesses it (at least at some times) ;

so, it cannot be that God does not exercise this power at a time in case he possesses it (at least at some times).

The conclusion follows from the first premise and the second premise. The first premise is true. The second premise is true. So, the conclusion is true. It cannot be that God does not exercise this power at a time in case he possesses it (at least at some times). (There is a consideration of the matter of God's exercise of this power in the second chapter.)

The ultimate conclusion of A28: A - P2.2 follows ultimately from its first premise and its second premise and its third premise and its supposition. Its first premise is true. Its second premise is true. Its third premise is true. So, its ultimate conclusion is true in case its supposition is true. It cannot be that God does not exercise the power to bring about (in the very first instance) other living things which possess the power to do this or that freely at a time in case it can be that he exists and it can be that a living thing possesses this power. (It cannot be that God possesses the power to *not* exercise this power at a time in case it can be that that is so. So, it cannot be that God is free in relation to *this* matter.)

Here is the third stage of the argument (A28: A - P2.3). The initial premises of the argument of this stage are as follows. (It takes it that it cannot be that there is more time than an eternal period of time – an eternal period of time is referred to in its second premise.) :

it cannot be that God does not exist in case it can be that he exists ;

it cannot be that God does not exist for an eternal period of time in case it can be that he exists.

(it cannot be that there is more time than an eternal period of time.) ;

it cannot be that God does not exercise the power to bring about (in the very first instance) other living things which possess the power to do this or that freely at a time in case it can be that he exists and it can be that a living thing possesses this power.

Let us suppose that it can be that he exists and that it can be that a living thing possesses this power.

It cannot be in that case that God does not exist. (This initial conclusion follows from the first premise and the first conjunct of the supposition.)

It cannot be in that case that God does not exist for an eternal period of time. (This further conclusion follows from the second premise and the first conjunct of the supposition.)

It cannot be in that case that God does not exercise the power to bring about (in the very first instance) other living things which possess the power to do this or that freely at a time. (This pen-ultimate conclusion follows from the third premise and the supposition.)

So, it cannot be that there are no other living things which possess the power to do this or that freely at all times.

The ultimate conclusion follows ultimately from the first premise and the second premise and the third premise and the supposition. The first premise is true. (The first premise is the conclusion of the first stage.) The second premise is true. The third premise is true. (The third premise is the conclusion of the second stage.) So, the ultimate conclusion is true in case the supposition is true. It cannot be that there are no other living things which possess the power to do this or that freely at all times in case in can be that God exists and it can be that a living thing possesses the power to bring about (in the very first instance) other living things which possess the power to do this or that freely.

The arguments of these three stages establish the truth of the second premise of the original argument (A28). Here once more is the original argument (A28) :

it cannot be that God is all-powerful or omnipotent at all times in case it cannot be that there are no other living things which possess the power to do this or that freely at all times ;

it cannot be that there are no other living things which possess the power to do this or that freely at all times in case it can be that God exists and it can be that a living thing possesses the power to bring about (in the very first instance) other living things which possess the power to do this or that freely ;

so, it cannot be that God is all-powerful or omnipotent at all times in case it can be that he exists and it can be that a living thing possesses the power to bring about (in the very first instance) other living things which possess the power to do this or that freely.

The conclusion follows from the first premise and the second premise. The first premise is true. The second premise is true. So, the conclusion is true. It *cannot* be that God is all-powerful or omnipotent *at all times* in case it can be that he exists and in case it can be that a living thing possesses (at least at some times) the power to bring about (in the very first instance) such living things.

Can it be that God is all-powerful or omnipotent at some time in case it can be that he exists? Well, it cannot be that God is all-powerful or omnipotent at some time in case it can be that he exists and it can be that a living thing possesses the power to bring about (in the very first instance) other living things which possess the power to do this or that freely. Here is an argument for this claim (A29). Its initial premises are as follows. (It takes it that it cannot be that there is more time than an eternal period of time – an eternal period of time is referred to in its second premise.) :

it cannot be that God does not exist in case it can be that he exists ;

it cannot be that God does not exist for an eternal period of time in case it can be that he exists.

(it cannot be that there is more time than an eternal period of time.) ;

it cannot be that God does not exercise the power to bring about (in the very first instance) other living things which possess the power to do this or that freely at *a* time (*although there is no particular time*) in case it can be that he exists and it can be that a living thing possesses this power ;

it cannot be that God possesses every power which can be possessed by a thing at some time unless it cannot be that there are other such living things at that time ;

a thing which is all-powerful or omnipotent at some time is a thing which possesses every power which can be possessed by a thing at that time.

Let us suppose that it can be that God exists and it can be that a living thing possesses this power.

It cannot be in that case that there is a time and it cannot be that there are other such living things at that time. (This initial conclusion follows from the first premise and the second premise and the third premise and the supposition.)

So, it cannot be that God is all-powerful or omnipotent at some time. (This ultimate conclusion follows from the fourth premise and the fifth premise and the initial conclusion.)

The ultimate conclusion follows ultimately from the first premise and the second premise and the third premise and the fourth premise and the fifth premise and the supposition. The first premise is true. The second premise is true. The third premise is true. The fourth premise is true. The fifth premise is true. So, the conclusion is true in case the supposition is true. It *cannot* be that God is all-powerful or omnipotent *at some time* in case it can be that he exists and it can be that a living thing possesses the power to bring about (in the very first instance) other living things which possess the power to do this or that freely.

Ought a theist who accepts that it can be that a living thing possesses this power to be concerned about the ultimate conclusion of this argument and the ultimate conclusion of the pen-ultimate argument? (All theists maintain that it can be that he exists. Most theists maintain that it can be that a living thing, *viz.* God himself, possesses this power.) Well, he ought not to be concerned about these conclusions. Why? Well, he ought not to be concerned about these conclusions because they are as we have seen - in particular, in A28: A - P2.2: A – P3 - in accord with God being worthy of worship.

It cannot be that God possesses the property of *being simple* in case it can be that he exists and it can be that a living thing possesses the power to bring about (in the very first instance) other living things which possess the power to do this or that freely. Here is an argument (A30) for this claim. Its initial premises are as follows :

it cannot be that God does not exist in case it can be that he exists ;

it cannot be that God does not exist for an eternal period of time in case it can be that he exists.

(it cannot be that there is more time than an eternal period of time.) ;

it cannot be that God does not exercise the power to bring about (in the very first instance) other (concrete) living things which possess the power to do this or that freely at a time in case it can be that he exists and it can be that a living thing possesses this power ;

it cannot be that there are concrete things other than God eternally in time in case it can be that God exists ;

it cannot be that God possesses the property of *being simple* unless he and his life do *not* have temporal parts.

Let us suppose that it can be that God exists and it can be that a living thing possesses power to bring about (in the very first instance) other living things which possess the power to do this or that freely.

It cannot be in that case that God does not exist.

It cannot be in that case that God does not exist for an eternal period of time. (These initial conclusions follow from the first premise and the second premise and the first conjunct of the supposition.)

It cannot be in that case that God does not exercise the power to bring about (in the very first instance) other living things which possess the power to do this or that freely at a time. (This further conclusion follows from the third premise and the supposition.)

It cannot be in that case that God's life does not include a (temporal) part which is such that there are such other living things. (This still further conclusion follows from the further conclusion.)

It cannot be in that case that God's life does not include a (temporal) part which is such that there are *no* such other living things. (This pen-ultimate conclusion follows from the second premise and the fourth premise and the first conjunct of the supposition.)

So, it cannot be that God possesses the property of *being simple.* (This ultimate conclusion follows from the fifth premise and the still further conclusion and the pen-ultimate conclusion.)

The ultimate conclusion follows ultimately from the first premise and the second premise and the third premise and the fourth premise and fifth premise and the supposition. The first premise is true. The second premise is true. The third premise is true. The fourth premise is true. The fifth premise is true. So, the conclusion is true in case the supposition is true. It cannot be that God possesses the property of *being simple* in case it can be that he exists and it can be that a living thing possesses the power to bring about (in the very first instance) other living things which possess the power to do this or that freely.

Indeed, it cannot be that God possesses the property of *being immutable* in case it can be that he exists and it can be that that a living thing possesses the power to bring about (in the very first instance) other living things which possess the power to do this or that freely. Here is an argument (A31) for this claim. Its initial premises are as follows :

it cannot be that God does not exist for an eternal period of time in case it can be that he exists.

(for any time in this period, there is a time which is earlier than it.) ;

it cannot be that God does not use the capacity to bring about (in the very first instance) other living things which possess the power to do this or that freely at *a* time in case it can be that he exists and it can be that a thing possesses this power ;

it cannot be that God does not possess this capacity at a time prior to it ;

it cannot be that God has used this capacity at such a time ;

God undergoes intrinsic change in case he does not use this capacity at some time(s) and he uses it at a later time ;

God is not immutable in case he undergoes an intrinsic change.

Let us suppose that it can be that God exists and it can be that a living thing possesses the power to bring about (in the very first instance) other living things which possess the power to do this or that freely.

It cannot be in that case that God does not exist for an eternal period of time. (This initial conclusion follows from the first premise and the first conjunct of the supposition.)

It cannot be in that case that God does not use the capacity to bring about (in the very first instance) other living things which possess the power to do this or that freely at a time. (This further conclusion follows from the second premise and the supposition.)

It cannot be in that case that God has used this capacity at the time(s) prior to it. (This still further conclusion follows from the third premise and the fourth premise and the initial conclusion and the further conclusion.)

It cannot be in that case that God does not undergo intrinsic change. (This pen-ultimate conclusion follows from fifth premise and the further conclusion and the still further conclusion.)

So, it cannot be that God is immutable.

The ultimate conclusion follows ultimately from the first premise and the second premise and the third premise and the fourth premise and the fifth premise and the sixth premise and the supposition. The first premise is true. The second premise is true. The third premise is true. The fourth premise is true. The fifth premise is true. The sixth premise is true. So, the ultimate conclusion is true in case the supposition is true. It cannot be in other words that God is immutable in case it can be that he exists and it can be that a living thing possesses power to bring about (in the very first instance) other living things which possess the power to do this or that freely.[25]

Ought a theist who accepts that it can be that a living thing possesses this power to be concerned that God cannot be simple and he cannot be immutable in case it can be that that is so? (All theists maintain that it can be that he exists. Most theists maintain that it can be that a living thing, *viz.* God himself, possesses this power.) Well, a theist ought not to be concerned that this is so because this is in accord with God being worthy of worship. (Recall the argument, *viz.* A28, for among other things the third premise of A30 and the second premise of A31.)

Finally, let us consider the following question: can it be that there are two Gods, X and Y, in case it can be that (a) God exists and it can be that a living thing possesses the power to bring about (in the very first instance) other living things which possess the power to do this or that freely? Well, it is untrue that it can be that this is so in case in can be that that is so. Here is an argument (A32) for this claim. Its initial premises are as follows. (It takes it that it cannot be that there is more time than an eternal period of time – an eternal period of time is referred to in its second premise.) :

it cannot be that (a) God does not exist in case it can be that he exists ;

it cannot be that (a) God does not exist for an eternal period of time in case it can be that exists.

(it cannot be that there is more time than an eternal period of time.) ;

it cannot be that (a) God does not exercise the power to bring about (in the very first instance) other living things which possess the power to do this or that freely at a time in case it can be that (a) God exists and it can be that a living thing possesses this power ;

it cannot be that (a) God exercises this power at some time unless it is *the* very first instance that there are other such living things ;

it cannot be that it is *the* very first instance that there are other such living things unless this power has *not* already been exercised by something, including some other God ;

it cannot be that it is *the* very first instance that there are other such living things unless some other thing, including some other God, is *not* exercising this power at that time.

Let us suppose that it can be that (a) God exists *and* it can be that a living thing possesses this power *and* it can be that there are two Gods, X and Y.

It cannot be in that case that X and Y do not exist *and* it cannot be that X and Y do not exist in time eternally *and* it cannot be that X and Y do not exercise the power to bring about (in the very first instance) other living things which possess the power to do this or that freely at a time. (This initial conclusion follows from the first premise and the second premise and third premise and the supposition.)

It cannot be in that case that X exercises this power after *or* before Y. (This further conclusion follows from the fourth premise and the fifth premise and the initial conclusion.)

It cannot be in that case that X exercises this power at the same time that Y exercises it. (This still further conclusion follows the fourth premise and the sixth premise and the initial conclusion.)

It cannot be in that case that X does not exercise it at a time *and* it cannot be that X exercises it at a time. (This pen-ultimate conclusion follows from the initial conclusion and the further conclusion and the still further conclusion.) That's absurd!

So, it is untrue that it can be that (a) God exists *and* it can be that a thing possesses this power *and* it can be that there are two Gods, X and Y.

The first premise is true. The second premise is true. The third premise is true. The fourth premise is true. The fifth premise is true. The sixth premise is true. The supposition is such that an absurdity follows with its addition. So, the ultimate conclusion – the ultimate conclusion is the denial of the supposition - is true. It is untrue in other words that it can be that there are two Gods, X and Y, in case it can be that (a) God exists and it can be that a living thing possesses the power to bring about (in the very first instance) other living things which possess the power to do this or that freely.

Notes

1. Some of God's traditional properties have been the subject of a great deal of analysis by analytic philosophers. These properties include being all-knowing and being all-powerful.

Some of God's traditional properties on the other hand have *not* been the subject of a great deal of analysis by analytic philosophers. These properties include being just and being merciful.

This is in part so because the former lend themselves to analysis and the latter do not do so.

2. Can it be that a living thing possesses this power? Well, this is a question which is not considered in this work for it is beyond its scope.

3. There are a number of particular claims in the course of what follows and there are arguments to establish that these claims are true in the course of what follows and these claims are a way to begin to establish that this is so.

These claims include the following:

it cannot be that there is some other thing which is all-knowing at some time in case in can be that that is so ;

it cannot be that there is some other thing which is all-powerful at some time in case in can be that that is so.

These claims include the following, too:

it cannot be that God does not exist in case it can be that he exists ;

it cannot be that there is some other concrete thing which exists eternally (in time) in case it can be that that is so. (God alone exists eternally in time in case it can be that that is so.) ;

it cannot be that there is some other thing which possesses the power to bring about (in the very first instance) other living things which possess the power to do this or that freely it case it can be that that is so. (God alone possesses this power in case it can be that that is so.)

4. It knows every fact just in case every fact can be known by a thing at that time.

Here is another understanding of such a thing, *viz.* a thing which is all-knowing or omniscient: a thing which is all-knowing or omniscient is a thing which is such that it cannot be that there is some other thing which knows more than it.

Is this so? Well, it is not so for it is all-knowing or omniscient although it can be that there is a thing which knows this or that and it does not know (that) this or that and that's absurd!

This is one of a number of misunderstandings of such a thing.

5. *Analysis*, 1963.

6. For René Descartes (1595 - 1650), God knows facts such as the fact 2 + 2 = 4. God knows these facts because he wills them and he knows whatever he wills. (Letter to Mersenne, 6.5.1630, Cottingham, J., (ed.), *The Philosophical Writings of Descartes*, Cambridge, 1994.)

These facts accordingly are *not* independent of him.

See the 22nd note, too.

7. Traditionally, God does not have eyes, ears,...: references to such parts of God's body at least in the Bible and Qur'an are not understood literally; instead, they are understood metaphorically.

8. So, it cannot be that God is such that there is a need to "jog" this capacity in case it can be that that is so and it cannot be that he is not in time.

There is a need to "jog" such a capacity of a human being sometimes.

9. God possesses the power to exercise it *and* the power to not exercise it at any time he exercises this power.

This is contrary to the account of God's power of Peter Abelard (1079 - 1142). (*Introduction to Theology,* Chapter 5, Book 3 in J. Migne's *Patroligina Latina,* vol.178, Paris, no date.) For Abelard, God does *not* possess the power to not exercise it at any time he exercises it. God does not possess this power at any time he exercises it for it is "right and just" to exercise it at that time. (It is "right and just" to exercise it at that time for God exercises it at that time.)

But, what are the grounds for the claim that it is "right and just" to do so at that time? These grounds are to say the least not readily forthcoming.

Abelard adds among other things that, although it is "right and just" for God to exercise a power to do this or that at any time he exercises the power to do (that) this or that, this is not to say that God does not possess the power to do (that) this or that at other times. (Here is an example of a power which he considers in his consideration of this matter: the power to bring it about that it is raining.) He does so in order to deny the claim that God's power changes.

But, God does *not* possess the power to do (that) this or that at other times in case it is "right and just" to do so at that time *and* it is not a power which can be exercised more than once.

Further, it is "right and just" to exercise the power to bring about (in the very first instance) other living things which possess the power to do this or that freely at any time God exercises it for Abelard. The power to bring about (in the very first instance) other living things which possess the power to do this or that freely is not a power which can be exercised more than once. So, God does not possess the power to exercise this power other than at that time – this conclusion is an implication of Abelard's account of God's power. (It cannot be that God exercises this power at some time and he possesses it other than at that time – this is an implication of Abelard's account of God's power.) This is a further difficulty for Abelard.

10. For example, Deuteronomy 30:19 and Qur'an 2:158.

11. See, for example, Joshua Hoffman and Gary S. Rosenkrantz, *The Divine Attributes* (Blackwell, 2002), pp.134–135.

12. Boethius, *The Consolation of Philosophy*, 6, translated by S. J. Tester (Harvard, 1973).

13. Presumably, it is untrue that there are two time series, X and Y. Here is an argument for this claim. Its initial premises are as follows :

it can be that there is someone who learns at some time in a time series, X, that another time series, Y, exists *and* that it is some time in Y *and* that an event can occur in the future in Y in case there are two time series, X and Y. (A time in Y is not related to – it is not before *or* at the same time as *or* after - any time in X.) ;

in relation to such an event in Y, he is not able to say at all times (in X) that it does not occur (in case it occurs) ;

in relation to such an event in Y, he is not able to say at a particular time (in X) that it occurs in case it occurs (for times in Y are not related to times in X) ;

in relation to such an event in Y, he is not able to say at all times (in X including that time) that it occurs (in case it does not occur).

Let us suppose that there are two time series, X and Y.

It can be in that case that there is someone who learns at some time in X that Y exists and that it is some time in Y and that an event can occur in the future in Y. (This initial conclusion follows from the first premise and the supposition.)

In relation to such an event in Y, he is not able in that case to say (at all times that it does not occur *or*) at a particular time that it occurs *or* at all times (including that time) that it occurs in case it occurs. (This further conclusion follows from the second premise and the third premise and the fourth premise and the initial conclusion.) That's absurd!

So, it is untrue that there are two time series, X and Y.

Presumably, the first premise is true. The second premise is true. The third premise is true. The fourth premise is true. The supposition is such that an absurdity follows with its addition. So, the ultimate conclusion – the ultimate conclusion is the denial of the supposition – is presumably true. Presumably, it is untrue that there are two time series, X and Y.

14. Boethius is among the early Christian theologians and philosophers who are influenced considerably by the thought of Plato (428 - 347 BCE).

For Plato, there are non-perceptible things – in particular, Forms and the Form of the Good - and there are perceptible things. (See, in particular, the *Republic*, 471c *ff.*)

Forms and the Form of the Good are greater in value than perceptible things and they are (among other things) immutable.

It may well be that, for Boethius, God is immutable because of the influence of the thought of Plato.

15. For example, Psalms 90:2.

16. For Luis de Molina's (1536 - 1600), God has always known a living thing exercises a power to bring about this or that freely in particular conditions at some time in case it does so.

Let us consider Molina's claim. Let us keep the following in mind in the course of our consideration of his claim. First of all, a power of a thing is the power to bring about this or that. A thing possesses the power to bring about this or that at some time just in case it possesses the capacity and opportunity to do so at that time. Secondly, particular conditions exist at any time a living thing possesses the power to do this or that.

For Molina, God has always known a living thing exercises a power to bring about this or that freely in particular conditions at some time in case it does so. How? Well, God has always known it *would* do so in case it *were* in them at that time *and* he has always known it is in these particular conditions at that time. (God has always known it is in these particular conditions at that time because he has always known he brings it about that it is in these particular conditions at that time.) So, God has always known it exercises a power to bring about this or that freely in them at that time in case it does so. This is Molina's claim. (Incidentally, *God has always known it would do so in case it were in them at that time* is an instance of God's *middle knowledge* according to Molina. It has a "middle" status between what is the case and what is not the case although it can be the case. Alfred J. Freddosso trans., *On Divine Foreknowledge: Part IV of "The Concordia"*, Cornell, 1998.)

Let us consider the claim that it *would* do so in case it *were* in them at that time. It is untrue in that case that it can be that it exercises a power to not bring it about in these particular conditions at that time. It does not in that case exercise a power to bring about this or that freely in them at that time. Why? Well, it cannot be that it possesses (and exercises) the power to bring about this or that freely in them at that time in case it is untrue that it can be that it exercises a power to not bring it about in them at that time. Here is an argument to establish grounds for this claim. (Its first premise is true for Molina.) :

it cannot be that a living thing possesses the power to bring about this or that *freely* in particular conditions at some time unless it possesses the power to not bring it about in them at that time ;

it cannot be that a living thing possesses the power to not bring about this or that in particular conditions at some time unless it has the opportunity to not bring about this or that in them at that time;

it cannot be that a living thing has the opportunity to not bring about this or that in particular conditions at some time unless it can be that it exercises the power to not bring about this or that in them at that time.

Let us suppose that it is untrue that it can be that a living thing exercises a power to not bring about this or that in particular conditions at some time.

It cannot be in that case that it has the opportunity to not bring about this or that in them at that time. (This initial conclusion follows from the third premise and the supposition.)

It cannot be in that case that it possesses the power to not bring about this or that in them at that time. (This further conclusion follows from the second premise and the initial conclusion.)

So, it cannot be that it possesses the power to bring about this or that freely in them at that time.

The ultimate conclusion follows ultimately from the first premise and the second premise and the third premise and the supposition. The first premise is true. The second premise is true. The third premise is true. So, the conclusion is true in case the supposition is true. It cannot be that it possesses the power to bring about this or that freely in them at that time in case it is untrue that it can be that it exercises a power to not bring about this or that in them at some time.

So, it, *viz.* the living thing which is referred to in the paragraphs prior to this argument, does *not* exercise a power to bring about this or that freely in the particular conditions at that time *and* it does exercise a power to bring about this or that freely in them at that time. That's absurd! The absurdity follows Molina's claim. So, the claim is untrue.

17. For example, 2 Timothy 1:9.

18. For example, Job 36:26.

19. Here is another understanding of such a thing, *viz.* a thing which is all-powerful or omnipotent: a thing which is all-powerful or omnipotent is a thing which is such that it cannot be that there is some other thing which possesses more powers than it.

Is this so? Well, it is not so for it is all-powerful or omnipotent although it can be that there is a thing which possesses the power to do this or that and it does not possess it and that's absurd!

This is one of a number of misunderstandings of such a thing.

20. Here is another argument for this claim. Its initial premise is as follows :

states of affairs include states of affairs which cannot obtain.

Let us suppose that it can be that a thing possesses the power to bring about just any state of affairs at some time.

It can be in that case that it brings about a state of affairs which cannot obtain at some time. (This initial conclusion follows from the initial premise and the supposition.) That's absurd!

So, it cannot be that a thing possesses the power to bring about just any state of affairs at some time.

The initial premise is true. The addition of the supposition is such that an absurdity follows with its addition. So, the ultimate conclusion – the ultimate conclusion is the denial of the supposition – is true. It cannot be that a thing possesses the power to bring about just any state of affairs at some time.

21. *Summa Theologiae*, 1a., 25.3.

22. Let us consider Descartes' view about states of affairs which can obtain *and* which have to obtain such as the state of affairs that $2 + 2 = 4$.

For Descartes, *2 + 2 = 4* because God wills it to be so. This is not so unless God wills it to be so. (Letter to Mersenne, 6.5.1630, Cottingham, J., (ed.), *The Philosophical Writings of Descartes*, Cambridge, 1994.)

Further, it can be that God wills otherwise. (For example, Letter to Mersenne, 27.5.1630, *ibid.* So, it can be that the interior angles of a triangle are not equal 180°.)

Finally, human beings do not possess the capacity to apprehend that $2 + 2 \neq 4$. Human beings do not possess the capacity to apprehend that this is so because their capacities are constituted in this way by God. (For example, Letter to Arnauld, 29.7.1648, *ibid.*) What human beings do not possess the capacity to apprehend can nonetheless be something which God has the power to bring about.

There are a number of difficulties for Descartes. Here is one of these difficulties: our understanding is that it *has* to be that 2 + 2 =

4; but, our understanding is at fault in this regard; our understanding (according to Descartes) has been brought about by God; so, God has brought it about that our understanding is at fault – that's absurd! (God as a being worthy of worship *cannot* bring it about that this is so.)

23. Here is another and less formal argument :

let us suppose that there are concrete things other than God eternally in time and God exists eternally in time ;

for *any* time, there is in that case an earlier time when concrete things *already* exist ;

that time in that case is *not* the time when God wills (in the first instance) the existence of such things ;

but, that time is just *any* time ;

there is no time in that case when God wills (in the first instance) the existence of such things. That's absurd! (Such things do not exist without such a time.) ;

so, it is untrue that there are concrete things other than God eternally in time in case God exists eternally in time.

24. Here is an argument for this claim. Its initial premise is as follows :

it cannot be that God does not exist in case it can be that he exists.

Let us suppose that it *can* be that it (*viz.* the explanation of God's existence) is not the case in case it can be that God exists.

It can be in that case that it is not the case and (without it) God does not exist in case it can be that God exists. (This initial conclusion follows from the supposition.)

It cannot be in that case that God does not exist in case it can be that he exists *and* it can be that God does not exist in case it can be that he exists. (This further conclusion follows from the first premise and from the initial conclusion.) That's absurd!

So, it is untrue that it can be that it (*viz.* the explanation of God's existence) is not the case in case it can be that God exists.

The first premise is true. The supposition is such that an absurdity follows with its addition. So, the ultimate conclusion – the ultimate conclusion is the denial of the supposition – is true. It *cannot* be that it (*viz.* the explanation of God's existence) is not the case in case it can be that God exists.

25. Incidentally, it cannot be that God does not undergo a relational change in case it can be that he exists and it can be that a living thing possesses (at least at some times) this power, too. Here is an argument for this claim :

it cannot be that there is no time when God exercises this power in case it can be that he exists and it can be that a living thing possesses (at least at some times) this power ;

prior to the time he exercises this power, God is the only concrete thing (or one of a particular number of concrete things) co-existing with abstract things ;

God is not so once he has exercised this power ;

God does not have such a relation once he has exercised this power ;

so, it cannot be that God does not undergo a relational change in case it can be that he exists and it can be that a living thing possesses (at least at some times) this power.

The conclusion follows from the premises. The premises are true. So, the conclusion is true. It cannot be that God does not undergo a relational change in case it can be that he exists and it can be that a thing possesses (at least at some times) this power.

Chapter 2

Evil being overridden & God bringing about a particular kind of universe

Evil states of affairs and an evil state of affairs being overridden

Bad states of affairs include *evil* states of affairs. Here are some examples of evil states of affairs: that a living thing is in pain *or* suffering; that a living thing is unable to function properly; that someone exercises his power to *not* to relieve the suffering of someone else; that someone exercises its power to *not* to be considerate of some other living thing and its life and its powers. (Bad states of affairs include states of affairs which are *not* evil. Here are some examples: that something which is made by a human being is not functioning altogether properly; that something which is made by a human being is not altogether well-proportioned.)

An evil state of affairs which is being overridden consists in the following : there is an evil state of affairs; it is a (temporally immediate) part of a good state of affairs; the degree of value of the good state of affairs is *greater than* the degree value of the evil state of affairs; the degree of value of the good state of affairs is *greater than* the value of any good state of affairs which is a (temporally immediate) part of it; it is *not* the case that the value of the good state of affairs is determined by its parts and it is *not* the case the relation of its degree of value to the degree of value of a part is determined by its parts.[1]

An example

Here is an example of an evil state of affairs *being overridden*: that someone wills – and acts as a result of his will - to overcome something, *viz.* his suffering. It is an example of *someone being noble.*

There is an evil state of affairs, *viz.* that he is suffering. It is a (temporally immediate) part of a (whole) good state of affairs, *viz.* that he wills – and acts as a result of his will - to overcome something, *viz.* his suffering. The degree of value of the good state of affairs is *greater than* the degree of it.

There is a good state of affairs, *viz.* that he wills – and acts as a result of his will - to overcome something. It is a (temporally immediate) part of the (whole) good state of affairs, *viz.* that he wills – and acts as a result of his will - to overcome something, *viz.* his suffering. The degree of value of the (whole) good state of affairs is *greater than* the degree of it.

Further, it is *not* the case that this relation is determined by its parts. Let us consider the good part in order to illustrate that this is so. Let us suppose that this relation *is* determined by its parts. The part which is evil in that case is *good.* (The whole good state of affairs is not greater than its good part otherwise.) That's absurd! So, the supposition is untrue. It is *not* the case that this relation is determined by its parts.

Finally, the value – the degree of value - of the whole good state of affairs is not determined by its parts. Let us suppose that its value – its degree of value - *is* determined by its parts. The degree of value of its good part is in that case greater than the degree of value of its evil part. (It is not good otherwise.) Further, its degree of value is the degree of value of its good part *minus* the degree of value of its evil part. Its degree is *less than* the degree of value of its good part. It is greater than the degree of value of its good part *and* it is less than the degree of value of its good part. That's absurd! Its value – its degree of value – is *not* determined by its parts. So, the evil state of affairs that he is suffering is being overridden in the good state of affairs that he wills – and acts as a result of his will - to overcome something, *viz.* his suffering.

God bringing about a particular kind of universe

It cannot be that God (does not possess at any time and) does not exercise the power to bring about (in the very first instance) some other living things which possess the power to act freely at a time in case it can be that he exists and it can be that a living thing possesses this power. This is so as we have seen in the course of A28: A - P2.

Incidentally, it cannot be that a thing possesses the power to act freely unless it possesses (among other powers) the following powers: the power to will or choose or desire to do this or that; the power to bring about (that) this or that.

It cannot be that God (does not possess at any time and) does not exercise the power to bring about (in the very first instance) some other living things which possess the power to act freely and *independently* of him at a time in case it can be that he exists and it can be that a living thing possesses the power to bring about (in the very first instance) some other living things which possess the power to act freely. (The opportunity to act freely *and* independently of him is even better (or greater) than the opportunity afforded by the power merely to act freely.) The argument for this claim is (with appropriate substitutions) along the lines of A28: A - P2.2.

What is it for some other living thing to possess the power to act freely and *independently* of God? Well, it cannot be to begin with that some other living thing possesses the power to act freely and *independently* of God unless it is *not* immediately aware of God. So, it cannot be to begin with that such a living thing is immediately aware of God. (A living thing which is *not* immediately aware of God is at least in this way *separated* from him.)

It cannot be that God (does not possess at any time and) does not exercise the power to bring about (in the very first instance) some other living things which possess the power to act freely and independently of him and which possess the power *to lead in that way a life* at a time in case it can be that he exists and it can be that a living thing possesses the power to bring about (in the very first instance) other living things which possess the power to act freely. The argument for this claim once more is (with appropriate substitutions) along the lines of A28: A - P2.2.

Further, it cannot be that God (does not possess at any time and) does not exercise the power to imbue other such living things with powers such as the following in case it can be that that is so: the power to know in that way it leads a life; the power to know in that way about what is the case and its value and its relations to what else is the case; the power to reason in that way. The argument for this claim once more is (with appropriate substitutions) along the lines of A28: A - P2.2.

Further still, it cannot be that God does not possess the power to bring about other such living things - *viz.* other living things which possess the power to act freely and independently of him and which possess the power to lead in that way lives and which possesses such powers - which are *non-physical* and which possess *the power to interact in that way with some physical thing(s)* in case in can be that that is so. Here is an argument (A33) for this claim. Its initial premises are as follows:

it can be that God possesses the power to bring about other such living things which are non-physical and which possess the power to interact in that way with some physical thing(s) in case in can be that that is so;

God is better (or greater) in case he possesses this power than in case he does not do so.

Let us suppose that that is so, *viz.* it can be that God exists and it can be that a living thing possesses the power to bring about (in the very first instance) other living things which possess the power to act freely, *and* it can be that he does not possess this power.

It can be in that case that God is better (or greater) than he can be by supposition. (This initial conclusion follows from the first premise and the second premise and the supposition.) That's absurd!

So, it is untrue that it can be that that is so *and* it can be that he does not possess this power. (It cannot be in other words that he does not possess this power in case it can be that that is so.)

Is the first premise true? Well, an argument is to say the least not readily forthcoming for the claim that it is untrue. It can be to begin with that there is a living thing which is non-physical in case it can be that God exists. (The introduction of the first chapter includes a consideration of whether it can be that there are living things which are non-physical.)

There is a consideration of the following claim (of theists) in the introduction of the first chapter: it can be that a thing which is non-physical, *viz.* God, brings about a change in the momentum of a physical thing and it can be in that case that a thing which is non-physical, *viz.* God, interacts with a physical thing. An argument (A5) for the claim that it is *untrue* that it can be that a thing which is non-physical brings about a change in the momentum of a physical thing is considered in that introduction. This argument does *not* establish it is untrue that it can be that this is so. Let us take it that the first premise is true.

The second premise is true. The supposition is such that an absurdity follows with its addition. So, the ultimate conclusion – the ultimate conclusion is the denial of the supposition – is true. It is untrue in other words that it can be that God does not possess the power to bring about other such living things which are non-physical and which possess the power to interact in that way with some physical thing(s) in case it can be that that is so. (Any other such living thing which is *non-physical* and which is brought about by God is let us say *a soul.*) Finally, let us refer to any whole which includes other such living things and which is brought about by God as *a universe.*

Now, it is plausible that it cannot be that these other such living things are *not* liable to experience evil due to the conditions which prevail in a whole which includes them in case it can be that that is so. Here is an argument (A34) for this claim. Its initial premises are as follows :

it cannot be that God does not exist in case it can be that he exists ;

it cannot be that some other living thing is not liable to experience any evil due to the conditions which prevail in a whole which includes it *unless* it is immediately aware of God in case it cannot be that God does not exist ;

it cannot be that God (does not possess at any time and) does not exercise the power to bring about (in the very first instance) some other such living things at a time in case it can be that he exists and it can be that a living thing possesses the power to bring about (in the very first instance) other living things which possess the power to act freely ;

it cannot be that these other such living things are immediately aware of God. (A living thing which is not immediately aware of him is at least in this way *separated* from him.)

Let us suppose that it can be that God exists and it can be that a living thing possesses the power to bring about (in the very first instance) other living things which possess the power to act freely.

It cannot be in that case that God does not exist. (This initial conclusion follows from the first premise and the first conjunct of the supposition.)

It cannot be in that case that some other living thing is not liable to experience any evil due to the conditions which prevail in a whole which includes it unless it is immediately aware of God. (This further conclusion follows from the second premise and the initial conclusion.)

But, it cannot be that he does not exercise the power to bring about (in the very first instance) some other such living things which are not immediately aware of him at a time. (This penultimate conclusion follows from the third premise and the fourth premise and the supposition.)

So, it cannot be that these other living things are not liable to experience any evil due to the conditions which prevail in a whole which includes them.

The ultimate conclusion follows ultimately from the first premise and the second premise and the third premise and the fourth premise and the supposition. The first premise is true. The second premise is plausible. (Here in any case is an argument for this claim: some other living thing which is not immediately aware of God is at least in this way separated from him in case it cannot be that he does not exist; it cannot be that some other living thing which is at least in this way separated from him is not liable to experience any evil due to the conditions which prevail in a whole which includes it in case it cannot be that he does not exist; so, it cannot be that some other living thing is not liable to experience any evil due to the conditions which prevail in a whole which includes it unless it is immediately aware of him in case it cannot be that he does not exist. The conclusion follows from the first premise and the second premise. The first premise is true. The second premise is plausible. So, the conclusion is plausible. It is plausible that it cannot be that some other living thing is not liable to experience any evil due to the conditions which prevail in a whole which includes it unless it is immediately aware of him in case it cannot be that he does not exist.) The third premise is true. The fourth premise is true. So, it is plausible that the conclusion is true in case the supposition is true. It is plausible that it cannot be that these other living things are not liable to experience any evil due to the conditions which prevail in a whole which includes them in case it can be that God exists and it can be that a living thing possesses the power to bring about (in the very first instance) other living things which possess the power to act freely. (The whole at issue is the universe which includes them and which is brought about by God.)

Any liability of these other living things to experience evil due to the conditions in that whole and any evil which they experience due to conditions in that whole is a matter of degree. The degree of any liability of these other living things to experience evil due to the conditions in that whole and the degree of any evil which they experience due to the conditions in that whole is to the degree that they are independent of God. (This degree cannot be a certain degree: for example, it cannot be to the degree that they are *only* liable to experience such evil; God is not worthy of worship otherwise.)

Let us suppose that it cannot be that they are not liable to experience any evil due to the conditions which prevail in a whole which includes them in case it can be that God exists and it can be that a living thing possesses the power to bring about (in the very first instance) other living things which possess the power to act freely. It does *not* follow that it cannot be that they possess powers such as the power to relieve any evil which they are experiencing. Indeed, it cannot be that God (does not possess at any time and) does not exercise the power to imbue them with other powers such as the power to relieve any evil which they are experiencing and which is due to the conditions in that universe in case it can be that that is so. The argument for this claim once more is (with appropriate substitutions) along the lines of A28: A - P2.2.[2]

It cannot be that they do not possess the power to *not* exercise such a power for they possess the power to exercise them *freely*. So, it cannot be that they do not possess a power such as the power to *not* relieve any evil which they are experiencing and which is due to the conditions in that universe in case in can be that that is so.

It cannot be in any case that they do not possess a power such as the power to *not* relieve any evil which they are experiencing and which is due to the conditions in that universe in case it can be that that is so. Why? Well, it cannot be that God (does not possess at any time and) does not exercise the power to imbue other such living things with the power to not do what he would instruct *or* command them to do in case it can be that that is so. Why? Well, this is so for it cannot be that there are other such living things – living thing which possess (among other powers) the power to act freely and *independently* of him – unless they possess the power to not do what he would instruct *or* command them to do.

What would God instruct *or* command them to do? Well, here are some examples of what he would instruct *or* command them to do: to use their power to know about their conditions; to use their power to reason; to use their power to relieve any evil which they are experiencing and which is due to the conditions in that universe.[3]

It cannot be in that case that God (does not possess at any time and) does not exercise the power to imbue other such living things with powers such as the power to not exercise the power to know about its conditions and the power to not exercise the power to reason and the power to not exercise the power to relieve any evil which they are experiencing and which is due to the conditions in that universe in case it can be that that is so.

So, it cannot be in any case that they do not possess a power such as the power to not relieve any evil which they are experiencing and which is due to the conditions in that universe in case it can be that that is so. (It cannot be in any case that they do not possess a power such as the power to not exercise the power to know about its conditions and the power to not exercise the power to reason in case it can be that that is so.)

Further still, it cannot be that God (does not possess at any time and) does not exercise the power to imbue other such living things with other powers in case it can be that that is so. Here are some examples of these other powers: the power to diminish that power to not exercise that power to know about its conditions; the power to diminish that power to not exercise its power to reason; the power to diminish that power to not exercise that power to relieve any the evil which they are experiencing and which is due to the conditions in that universe. The argument for this claim once more is (with appropriate substitutions) along the lines of A28: A - P2.2.

It cannot be that they do not possess the power to *not* exercise such a power for they possess the power to exercise them *freely*. So, it cannot be that they do not possess a power such as the power to *not* diminish that power to not exercise that power to know about its conditions in case it can be that that is so.

It cannot be in any case that they do not possess the power to *not* exercise such a power for they possess the power to act freely and *independently* of him and they do not possess this power unless they possess the power to not do what he would instruct *or* command them to do and what he would instruct *or* command them to do is to exercise such powers. So, it cannot be in any case that they do not possess a power such as the power to *not* diminish that power to not exercise that power to know about its conditions in case it can be that that is so.

Incidentally, it can be that they exercise their power to diminish their power to know the value of what is the case and its relations to whatever else is the case. It can be that God possesses and exercises the power to instruct them about the value of what is the case and its relations to whatever else is the case at such a time. Let us consider an argument (A35) for the claim that it cannot be that God exercises the power to instruct them about their value at some time (including such a time) **:**

it cannot be that God does not exercise the power to bring about other living things which possess (among other powers) the power to act freely and independently of him at a time in case it can be that he exists and it can be that a living thing possesses the power to bring about (in the very first instance) other living things which possess the power to act freely **;**

it cannot be that they do not possess this power thereafter ;

it cannot be that they possess this power in case he instructs .... them about their value at some time ;

so, it cannot be that he instructs .... them about their value at some time.

The conclusion follows from the first premise and the second premise and the third premise. The first premise is true. The third premise is true. Is the second premise true? Well, it is *not* true. So, this argument does *not* establish that it cannot be that he instructs them about their value at some time.

Can it be that God brings about (in the very first instance) these other living things which possess (among other powers) the power to act freely and independently of him in complete isolation from each other in case it can be that he exists and it can be that a living thing possesses the power to bring about (in the very first instance) other living things which possess the power to act freely? Well, it cannot be that this is so in case it can be that that is so. Here is an argument (A36) for the claim that it cannot be that God does not exercise the power to bring it about that these other such livings (in the very first instance) do not live in complete isolation from each other in case in can be that that is so :

it cannot be that God does not possess (at any time) the power to bring it about that these other such living things (in the very first instance) do not live in complete isolation from each other in case it can be that that is so ;

it cannot be that God (does not possess at any time and) does not exercise the power to bring about (in the very first instance) some other such living things in a universe at a time *and* it cannot be that these other such living things (in the very first instance) do not possess powers such as the power to be considerate of other such living things and their powers and their lives in case in can be that that is so ;

it cannot be that these other such living things (in the very first instance) possess powers such as the power to be considerate of other such livings things and their powers and their lives unless they (in the very first instance) do *not* live in complete isolation from other such living things ;

so, it cannot be that God does not exercise the power to bring it about that these other such livings (in the very first instance) do not live in complete isolation from each other in case it can be that that is so.

The conclusion follows from the first premise and the second premise and the third premise. The first premise is true. The second premise is true. (The first conjunct of the second premise is true in case it can be that God exists and it can be that a living thing possesses the power to bring about (in the very first instance) some other living things which possess the power to act freely. The second conjunct is also true in case it can be that that is so. Otherwise, it can be that these other such living things are not considerate of each other and their powers and their lives because they in the very first instance do not possess the power to be so in a universe which is brought about by God. That's absurd! So, it is true.) The third premise is true. So, the conclusion is true. It cannot be that God does not exercise the power to bring it about that these other such livings (in the very first instance) do not live in complete isolation from each other in case it can be that that is so.

The second conjunct of the second premise states that it cannot be that these other such living things (in the very first instance) do not possess powers such as the power to be considerate of other such living things and their powers and their lives in case in can be that that is so. It cannot be in that case that they do not possess powers such as the power to *not* be considerate of other such living things and their powers and their lives for they possess the power to exercise them *freely.*

It cannot be in any case that they do not possess powers such as the power to *not* be considerate of other such living things and their powers and their lives in case it can be that that is so for they possess the power to act freely and *independently* of God and they do not possess this power unless they possess the power to *not* do what he would instruct *or* command them to do and what he would instruct *or* command them to do is to exercise powers such as the power to be considerate of other such living things and their powers and their lives.

Further, it can be that God possesses and exercises the power to imbue these other such living things with powers such as the power to relieve any evil which some *other* such living thing is experiencing and which is due to the conditions in the universe which includes them in order that they possess the power to be considerate of some other such living thing and its powers and its life in case it can be that that is so. It can be in that case that they possess powers such as the power to *not* relieve any evil which some other such living thing is experiencing and which is due to the conditions in the universe which includes them for they possess the power to exercise their powers *freely.*

It can be in that case that they possess powers such as the power to *not* relieve any evil which some other such living thing is experiencing and which is due to the conditions in the universe which includes them for they possess the power to act freely and *independently* of God and they do not possess this power unless they possess the power to *not* do what he would instruct *or* command them to do and what he would instruct *or* command them to do is to exercise powers such as the power to relieve any evil which some other such living thing is experiencing and which is due to the conditions in the universe which includes them.

These powers are examples of powers which are *morally* significant. One of these other such living things which for example exercises its power to relieve any evil which some other such living thing is experiencing and which is due to the conditions in the universe which includes them brings about a state of affairs which is *morally* good. One of these other such living things which for example exercises its power to *not* relieve any evil which some other such living thing is experiencing and which is due to the conditions in the universe which includes them brings about a states of affairs which is *morally* evil. So, their powers include powers which are *morally* significant.

Their powers include powers which are *not* morally significant. Here is an example of a power which is not morally significant: to know about its conditions. (One of these other such living things which exercises its power to know about its conditions does not bring about a state of affairs which is morally good *or* morally evil.) So, their powers include powers which are morally significant *and* powers which are not morally significant.

Finally, it cannot be that they are not such that they hold the belief that it is better that a state of affairs which they know is (morally) good obtains rather than it does not obtain and they possess as a result the desire (to some degree) to bring it about. It cannot be that this is so in case it can be that God exists and it can be that a living thing possesses the power to bring about (in the very first instance) some other living things which possess the power to act freely. Here is an argument (A37) for this claim. It is in three stages. Here is the first stage (A37.1). Its initial premises are as follows :

it can be that God possesses the power to bring it about that other such living things are such that they hold the belief that it is better that a state of affairs which they know is (morally) good obtains rather than it does not obtain and they possess as a result the desire (to some degree) to bring it about in case it can be that he exists and it can be that a living thing possesses the power to bring about (in the very first instance) some other living things which possess the power to act freely ;

God is better (or greater) in case he possesses this power than in case he does not possess it.

Let us suppose that it can be that he exists and it can be that a living thing possesses the power to bring about (in the very first instance) some other living things which possess the power to act freely and it can be that he does not possess this power.

It can be in that case that God is better (or greater) than he can be by supposition. (This initial conclusion follows from the first premise and the second premise and the supposition.) That's absurd!

So, it is untrue that it can be that he exists *and* it can be that a living thing possesses the power to bring about (in the very first instance) some other living things which possess the power to act freely *and* it can be that he does not possess this power.

The first premise is true. The second premise is true. The supposition is such that an absurdity follows with its addition. So, the ultimate conclusion – the ultimate conclusion is the denial of the supposition – is true. It cannot be in other words that he does not possess this power in case it can be that he exists and it can be that a living thing possesses the power to bring about (in the very first instance) some other living things which possess the power to act freely.

Here is the second stage (A37.2) :

it cannot be that God brings about other such living things which are debased ;

other such living things *are* debased in case they are *not* such that they hold the belief that it is better that a state of affairs which they know is (morally) good obtains rather than it does not obtain and they possess as a result the desire (to some degree) to bring it about ;

so, it cannot be that God brings about other such living things which are not such that they hold the belief that it is better that a state of affairs which they know is (morally) good obtains rather than it does not obtain and they possess as a result the desire (to some degree) to bring it about.

The conclusion follows from the first premise and the second premise. The first premise is true. The second premise is true. So, the conclusion is true. It cannot be that God brings about other such living things which are not such that they hold the belief that it is better that a state of affairs which they know is (morally) good obtains rather than it does not obtain and they possess as a result the desire (to some degree) to bring it about.

Here is the third stage (A37.3) :

it cannot be that God (does not possess at any time and) does not exercise the power to bring about (in the very first instance) some other such living things in a universe at a time in case it can be that he exists and it can be that a living thing possesses the power to bring about (in the very first instance) some other living things which possess the power to act freely ;

it cannot be that God does not possess the power to bring it about that other such living things are such that they hold the belief that it is better that a state of affairs which they know is (morally) good obtains rather than it does not obtain and they possess as a result the desire (to some degree) to bring it about in case it can be that that is so ;

it cannot be that God brings about other such living things which are *not* such that they hold the belief that it is better that a state of affairs which they know is (morally) good obtains rather than it does not obtain and they possess as a result the desire (to some degree) to bring it about ;

so, it cannot be that God (does not possess the power and) does not exercise the power to bring it about that other such living things are such that they hold the belief that it is better that a state of affairs which they know is (morally) good obtains rather than it does not obtain and they possess as a result the desire (to some degree) to bring it about in case it can be that that is so.

The conclusion follows from the first premise and the second premise and the third premise. The first premise is true. The second premise is true. (The second premise is the conclusion of the first stage.) The third premise is true. (The third premise is the conclusion of the second stage.) So, the conclusion is true. It cannot be that God (does not possess the power and) does not exercise the power to bring it about that other such living things are such that they hold the belief that it is better that a state of affairs which they know is (morally) good obtains rather than it does not obtain and they possess as a result the desire (to some degree) to bring it about in case it can be that he exists and it can be that a living thing possesses the power to bring about (in the very first instance) some other living things which possess the power to act freely.

God bringing about this particular kind of universe and evil being overridden in it

Let us consider the following whole state of affairs: there are living things other than God *and* they possess the power to lead lives *and* they possess other powers such as the power to know about what is the case and its value and its relations to what else is the case and the power to *not* do so and the power to reason and the power to *not* do so *and* they are not immediately aware of God (and they are liable to experience evil due to their conditions) *and* they possess powers such as the power to be considerate of other such living things and their lives and their powers and the power to *not* be so *and* they are such that they hold the belief that it is better that a state of affairs which they know is (morally) good obtains rather than it does not obtain and they possess as a result the desire (to some degree) to bring it about. It is a state of affairs of *other livings things (which are not debased and) which possess the power to lead (rationally) lives (which are morally significant and) which are free and independent of God.*

There is an evil state of affairs, *viz.* that living things possess powers such as the power to *not* know about what is the case and its value and its relations to what else is the case and the power to *not* reason *and* they are *not* immediately aware of God (and they are liable to experience evil due to their conditions) *and* they possess powers such as the power to *not* be considerate of other such living things and their powers and their lives. It is a (temporally immediate) part of a good state of affairs, *viz.* that whole state of affairs. The degree of value of the whole good state of affairs is *greater than* the degree of it.

There is a good state of affairs, *viz.* that there are other living things *and* they possess the power to lead lives *and* they possess other powers such as the power to know about what is the case and its value and its relations to what else is the case and the power to reason *and* they possess powers such as the power to be considerate of other such living things and their lives and their powers *and* they are such that they hold the belief that it is better that a state of affairs which they know is (morally) good obtains rather than it does not obtain and they possess as a result the desire (to some degree) to bring it about. It is a (temporally immediate) part of that whole good state of affairs. The degree of value of the whole good state of affairs is *greater than* the degree of it.

Further, it is *not* the case that this relation is determined by its parts. Let us consider the good part in order to illustrate that this is so. Let us suppose that this relation *is* determined by its parts. The part which is evil in that case is *good.* (The whole good state of affairs is not greater than its good part otherwise.) That's absurd! So, the supposition is untrue. It is *not* the case that this relation is determined by its parts.

Finally, the value – the degree of value - of the whole good state of affairs is not determined by its parts. Let us suppose that its value – its degree of value - *is* determined by its parts. The degree of value of its good part is in that case greater than the degree of value of its evil part. (It is not good otherwise.) Further, its degree of value is the degree of value of its good part *minus* the degree of value of its evil part. Its degree is *less than* the degree of value of its good part. It is greater than the degree of value of its good part *and* it is less than the degree of value of its good part. That's absurd! Its value – its degree of value – is *not* determined by its parts. So, the evil state of affairs is overridden in the whole good state of affairs.

An observation on God bringing about this particular kind of universe and a moral theory

It cannot be that God does not exercise the power to bring about other such living things in a universe at a time in case it can be that he exists and it can be that a living thing possesses the power to bring about (in the very first instance) other living things which possess the power to act freely. The value of this universe is *good.* The degree of value of this universe increases *or* decreases depending on among other things *the number* of these other living things.

Consequentialism is a moral theory. Here is a statement of its claim at least in its most common form: it is untrue that it can be that a thing exercises a power to bring about something which is good at a time *and* it possesses the power to bring about some other thing which is good and which is greater in value at that time *and* its exercise of its power is morally appropriate. So, it is untrue that it can be that God exercises the power to bring about other such living things in a universe at a time *and* he possesses the power to bring about some other such universe which is greater in value at that time *and* his exercise of this power is morally appropriate in case it can be that that is so. Is this so? Well, this is not so. Here is an argument (A38) for the claim that it is not so :

it is untrue that it can be that God exercises a power at a time and it is morally inappropriate to do so ;

it can be that God (possesses and) exercises the power to bring about such a universe at a time in case it can be that he exists and it can be that a living thing possesses the power to bring about (in the very first instance) some other living things which possess the power to act freely ;

it can be that God exercises this power to bring about such a universe at a time *and* he possesses the power to bring about such a universe which is greater in value at that time in case it can be that that is so ;

so, it can be that God exercises this power to bring about such a universe at a time *and* it is *not* morally inappropriate to do so *and* he possesses the power to bring about such a universe which is greater in value in case it can be that that is so.

The conclusion follows from the first premise and the second premise and the third premise. The first premise is true. The second premise is true. Is the third premise true? Well, let us observe to begin with the following: the number of livings things in such a universe is finite *or* infinite; whether that number is finite *or* infinite, there is a number which is greater. (For any finite number, there is a finite number which is greater. Further, the standard view in mathematics is that, for any infinite number, there is an infinite number which is greater.[4] Let us take it that this is so.) With this in mind, here is an argument (A38: A - P3) for the claim that the third premise is true :

it can be that God (possesses and) exercises the power to bring about a number of living things in such a universe at a time in case it can be that he exists and it can be that a living thing possesses the power to bring about (in the very first instance) some other living things which possess the power to act freely ;

it can be that God possesses the power to bring about *a greater number* of other living things in such a universe at that time in case it can be that that is so ;

such a universe which has a greater number of living things than some other such universe is better (or greater) than it.

Let us suppose that it can be that he exists and it can be that a living thing possesses the power to bring about (in the very first instance) some other living things which possess the power to act freely.

So, it can be that God exercises this power to bring about such a universe at some time *and* he possesses the power to bring about such a universe which is greater in value at that time.

The conclusion follows from the first premise and the second premise and the third premise and the supposition. The first premise is true. The second premise is true. The third premise is true. So, the conclusion is true in case the supposition is true. It can be that God exercises this power to bring about such a universe at a time and he possesses the power to bring about such a universe which is greater in value at that time in case it can be that he exists and it can be that a living thing possesses the power to bring about (in the very first instance) some other living things which possess the power to act freely.

The third premise (of A38) is true. (The other premises of A38 are true and its conclusion follows from its premises.) So, its conclusion is true. It can be that God exercises this power to bring about such a universe at a time *and* it is *not* morally inappropriate to do so *and* he possesses the power to bring about such a universe which is greater in value in case it can be that that is so. Consequentialism at least in its most common form implies that this conclusion is untrue. So, it is at least in its most common form *untrue.*

Notes

1. *Cf.* R. M. Chisholm, "The Defeat of Good and Evil", *Proceedings of the American Philosophical Association*, 42, 1968-1969, pp.21-38.

This paper is reprinted, and *revised* for publication, in M. M. Adams and R. M. Adams (eds.), *The Problem of Evil* (Oxford, 1990), pp.53-68.

Chisholm states a definition of the "evil" of a state of affairs being "totally defeated". Here is his definition of the "evil" of a state of affairs being "totally defeated" :

there is a "bad" state of affairs which is *a part of* some other state of affairs which is *not bad*;

it is *worse than* that other state of affairs ;

any good state of affairs which is a part of that other state of affairs and which is *better than* that other state of affairs is a part of that bad state of affairs. (See *The Problem of Evil*, p.62, D5 *and* D7.)

See also, for example, R. M. Chisholm, *Brentano and Intrinsic Value* (Cambridge, 1986), p.59 *ff.*

2. It cannot be that God exercises a power such as the power to relieve any evil which they are experiencing and which is due to the conditions in that universe unless he undermines their powers such as the power to relieve freely any evil which they are experiencing and which is due to the conditions in that universe in case it can be that that is so.

3. This is so in case there are no other matters to consider.

4. This series begins with the infinite number which is constituted by the natural numbers: 1, 2, 3,.... .

The standard view is due to the work of mathematicians in the late 19th century. It is due in particular to the work of Gregor Cantor. Incidentally, the area of mathematics which is concerned with such numbers is *trans-finite arithmetic.*

Chapter 3

The Existence of God

Are there sufficient grounds for the claim that God does not exist?

God and Evil

The principal arguments for the claim that God does not exist

The evil which exists is the principal grounds for the claim that God does not exist. The evil which exists and which is related to human beings in particular is the principal grounds for the claim that God does not exist. Here is a statement of an argument (A39) for the claim that God does not exist :

it cannot be that God exists *and* evil exists ;

evil exists ;

so, God does not exist.

The conclusion follows from the first premise and the second premise. The second premise is true. So, the conclusion is true in case the first premise is true. Is the first premise true? Well, here is a statement of the principal argument (A39: A - P1) for the claim that it is true :

it cannot be that a living thing, *viz.* God, does not exercise a (or his) power to not permit any evil in case he knows about it *and* he possesses the power to do so *and* he is morally perfect ;

it cannot be that God (as an all-knowing or omniscient living thing) does not know about any evil ;

it cannot be that God (as an all-powerful or omnipotent living thing) does not possess the power to not permit any evil ;

it cannot be in addition that God is not morally perfect ;

it cannot be in that case that God does not exercise a power which he possesses, *viz.* a power to not permit any evil. (This initial conclusion follows from the first premise and the second premise and the third premise and the fourth premise.) ;

so, it cannot be that God exists *and* evil exists.

Here is a statement of another argument (A40) for the claim that God does not exist :

it cannot be that God exists *and* there is *the degree of evil* of (in particular) the state of affairs that some other living thing which possesses the power to lead a life and which possesses other powers such as the power to know about its conditions and the power to reason and the power to be considerate of some other such living thing(s) and its life and its powers, *viz.* a human being, exercises a power to *not* be considerate *at all* of some other such living thing(s) and its life and its powers **;**

there is the degree of evil of this state of affairs **;**

so, God does not exist**.**

The conclusion follows from the first premise and the second premise. The second premise is true. (Here is an example of such a state of affairs: that a human being kills some other human beings without reason.) So, the conclusion is true in case the first premise is true. Is the first premise true? Well, the principal argument for the first premise is (with the appropriate substitutions) along the lines of the principal argument for the first premise of the preceding argument. (There is to begin with reference in this case to God's power to not permit *the degree of evil* of in particular *this* state of affairs.)

Here is a statement of another argument (A41) for the claim that God does not exist **:**

it cannot be that God exists *and* there is the evil of states of affairs such as the state of affairs that living things which possess the power to lead a life and which possess other powers such as the power to know about their conditions and the power to reason, *viz.* human beings, experience pain and suffering brought about by a major earthquake due to their conditions **;**

there is the evil of such states of affairs **;**

so, God does not exist.

The conclusion follows from the first premise and the second premise. The second premise is true. So, the conclusion is true in case the first premise is true. Is the first premise true? Well, the principal argument for the first premise is (with the appropriate substitutions) along the lines of the principal argument for the first premise of the pen-ultimate argument. (There is to begin with reference in this case to God's power to not permit the evil of *such* states of affairs.)

Here is a statement of another argument (A42) for the claim that God does not exist:

it cannot be that God exists *and* there is the *amount* of evil there is;

there is the amount of there is;

so, God does not exist.

The conclusion follows from the first premise and the second premise. The second premise is true. So, the conclusion is true in case the first premise is true. Is the first premise true? Well, the principal argument for the first premise is (with the appropriate substitutions) along the lines of the principal argument for the first premise of the initial argument. (There is to begin with reference in this case to God's power to not permit the *amount* of evil there is.)

Alvin Plantinga's response in *The Nature of Necessity*

Alvin Plantinga is a contemporary analytic philosopher. Here is a statement of the argument in his work *The Nature of Necessity* for the claim that it can be that God exists and evil exists and for the claim that it can be that God exists and there is the evil there is.[1] It is in effect an argument for the claim that the first premise of each of the arguments for the claim that God does not exist in the preceding section is untrue and the claim that these arguments in that case do not establish their conclusions. (It is in effect an argument for among other things the claim that the third premise of the principal argument for the first premise of each of these arguments is untrue.)

Some preliminary remarks

The argument's premise refers to *significantly free* creatures. A creature is not *free* unless he possesses the power to do this or that *and* the power to not do it. (Antecedent conditions and causal laws do not determine that he does not do this or that *or* that he does it.)

A creature is *significantly* free in case his power to do this or that and his power to not do it is on occasion *morally* significant. It is morally significant in case it is *right* for him to exercise his power to do this or that and it is *wrong* for him to exercise his power to not do it *or vice versa.* Here is an example: it is right for him to exercise his power to keep a promise which he makes and it is wrong for him to exercise his power to not keep it.

The argument's premise refers to *evil*. *Moral evil* is the evil which occurs when a significantly free human creature acts wrongly. Here is an example of a moral evil: a significantly free human creature who exercises his power to bring about suffering in others. *Natural evil* is any other evil. Here is an example of a natural evil: such creatures' suffering which is brought about by an earthquake.

A possible world which includes significantly free creatures who do more good than evil is *better* (or "more valuable") than a possible world without free creatures. (A possible world to begin with is a state of affairs which represents things as a whole or a "world" and which is such that it can obtain.[2]) This is so in case there are no other matters to consider.

The argument's premise also refers to *God's power to bring about (or "actualise")* ________ . This power is in relation to a possible world. This power does *not* include the power to bring about a possible world which does *not* include his existence. (His power does *not* include the power to bring about the state of affairs that he exists in a possible world which includes his existence.) This power *at some time* does *not* include the power to bring about a possible world which includes his existence *and* which includes a contingent state of affairs which is the negation of a contingent state of affairs which already obtains. Here is an example: God's power *now* does *not* include the power to bring about a possible world which includes his existence and which includes the contingent state of affairs that the Magna Carta is *not* written in 1215 for this state of affairs is the negation of a contingent state of affairs which already obtains, *viz.* the state of affairs that the Magna Carta is written in 1215.[3]

Still, perhaps this power at an earlier time includes the power to bring about a possible world which includes his existence and which includes the negation of that state of affairs. This power even then does *not* include the power to bring about every state of affairs in a possible world which includes his existence: it does not include the power to bring about necessary states of affairs in it for there is no time when they do not obtain.

Further, this power even then does not include the power to bring about every contingent state of affairs in it in case it includes a contingent state of affairs which includes a creature which acts *freely* in particular circumstances in it.

But, this power includes the power to (at least) bring about this creature in them. (This creature possesses the power to bring about this or that freely in them *and* the power to not bring it about freely in them.) Let us say that God knows it would bring it about freely in them in case he were to bring it about in them. This power in that case includes the power to bring it about that it does so by bringing it about in them. God "weakly" brings it about (or "weakly actualises") that it does so in case he brings it about that it does so in this way. (He "weakly" brings about or "weakly actualises" the contingent state of affairs that it does so in case he brings it about that it does so in this way.)

Even so, this power even then does not include the power to "weakly" bring about every possible world which includes his existence. This power does not include for example the power to "weakly" bring about the possible world which includes his existence and which includes this creature and it exercises its power to *not* bring about that this or that in those circumstances.

Finally, it can be that this power even then does not include the power to "weakly" bring about a possible world which includes his existence and which is morally perfect. This is so for it can be that even then God knows each and every significantly free human creature (which he possesses the power to bring about) would act wrongly at least once. (Such a creature has "trans-world depravity".) This power even then in that case does not include the power to "weakly" bring about a possible world which includes his existence and which is morally perfect.

A statement of Plantinga's argument

Here is a statement of Plantinga's argument with these preliminary remarks in mind **:**

it can be that

(i) God possesses the power to bring about significantly free (human and non-human) creatures (who do more good than evil) and they are responsible for any evil.[4] (It can be that significantly free human beings are responsible for some evil and significantly free non-human creatures are responsible for any other evil[5] - evil of the natural kind there is.)

and

(ii) God even then knows there would be moral evil and (among other things) at least the degree of moral evil and the amount of moral evil there is[6] and (among other things) the amount of natural evil there is[7] (and among other things the degree of moral good there is and the amount of moral good there is and among other things the amount of natural good there is) *whichever* significantly free (human and non-human) creatures he brings about. (It can be in that case that even then he does not possess the power to "weakly" bring about such a possible world which does not include at least some moral evil *or* which does not include at least the degree and the amount of moral evil there is *or* at least the amount of natural evil there is.) ;

so, it can be that God exists *and* there is the evil there is.[8]

A consideration of Plantinga's argument

The conclusion follows the premise. Is the premise true? Well, it is not true unless it can be that God exists. Can it be that God exists? Well, let us suppose, for the sake of argument, that it can be that God exists. (There are no grounds for the claim that it is untrue that it can be that God exists in the course of the consideration of God's nature. Still, it does not follow that it can that God exists.)

It is not true unless it can be that a thing possesses the power to bring about significantly free creatures. Can it be that a thing possesses this power? Well, let us suppose, for the sake of argument, that it can be that a thing possesses this power.

It is not true unless the power to bring about significantly free creatures (who do more good than evil) is compatible with God having the property of being worthy of worship. Is it compatible with God having the property of being worthy of worship? Well, let us suppose, for the sake of argument, that this power is compatible with God having the property of being worthy of worship.

It is not true unless it can be that God knows what a significantly free creature would do in particular circumstances. But, this is untrue as we have seen in the course of the first chapter – in particular, in the sixteenth note of the first chapter. Still, let us suppose, for the sake of argument, that it can be that this is so. Is the premise true? Well, it is not true. Here is an argument (A43) for this claim. Its initial premises are as follows :

it can be that

(i) God possesses the power to bring about significantly free (human and non-human) creatures (who do more good than evil) and they are responsible for any evil

and

(ii) God even then knows there would be *no* evil (and some moral and natural good) *or* there would be at least the evil there is (and the moral and natural good there is) depending on which significantly free (human and non-human) creatures he brings about ;

God is better (or greater) in case he possesses the power to "weakly" bring about such a possible world which includes no evil (and some moral and natural good) *and* the power to "weakly" bring about such possible worlds which include at least the evil there is (and the moral and natural good there is) than he is in case he possesses only the power to "weakly" bring about such possible worlds which include at least the evil there is (and the moral and natural good there is).

Let us suppose that it can be that (God possesses the power to bring about significantly free human and non-human creatures and they are responsible for any evil and) God even then knows there would be at least the evil there is (and the moral and natural good there is) *whichever* significantly free (human and non-human) creatures he brings about.

It can be in that case that God even then possesses only the power to "weakly" bring about such possible worlds which include at least the evil there is (and the moral and natural good there is). (This initial conclusion follows from the supposition and the statements in the preliminary remarks about the possible world(s) which God can "weakly" bring about or "weakly actualise".)

It can be that God even then possesses the power to "weakly" bring about such a possible world which includes no evil (and some moral and natural good) *and* the power to "weakly" bring about such possible worlds which include at least the evil there is (and the moral and natural good there is). (This further conclusion follows from the first premise and the statements in the preliminary remarks about the possible world(s) which God can "weakly" bring about or "weakly actualise".)

It can be in that case that God is better (or greater) than he can be in the initial conclusion which follows from the supposition. (This pen-ultimate conclusion follows from the second premise and the initial conclusion and the further conclusion.) That's absurd!

So, the supposition, *viz.* it can be that (God possesses the power to bring about significantly free human and non-human creatures and they are responsible for any evil and) God even then knows there would be at least the evil there is (and the moral and natural good there is) whichever significantly free (human and non-human creatures) he brings about, is untrue.

The first premise is true. The second premise is true. The supposition is such that an absurdity follows with its addition. So, the ultimate conclusion – the ultimate conclusion is the denial of the supposition – is true. It is untrue that it can be that (God possesses the power to bring about significantly free human and non-human creatures and they are responsible for any evil and) God even then knows there would be at least the evil there is (and the moral and natural good there is) whichever significantly free (human and non-human) creatures he brings about.

The premise (in the statement) of Plantinga's argument in that case is not true. So, his argument does *not* establish its conclusion, *viz.* it can be that God exists and there is the evil there is. His argument does *not* establish in effect that the first premise of each of the arguments in the preceding section is untrue and the claim that these arguments in that case do not establish their conclusions.

Another response

Each of the arguments in the pen-ultimate section is an argument for the claim that God does not exist. The first premise of the first argument is that it cannot be that God exists *and* evil exists. The first premise of the second argument is that it cannot be that God exists *and* there is *the degree of evil* of (in particular) the state of affairs that some other living thing which possesses the power to lead a life and which possesses other powers such as the power to know about its conditions and the power to reason and the power to be considerate of some other such living thing(s) and its life and its powers, *viz.* a human being, exercises a power to *not* be considerate *at all* of some other such living thing(s) and its life and its powers. (The principal argument for each of these premises is *not* that this is so because it cannot be that God exists.)

But, it can be as we have seen that God brings about other living things which possess the power to lead a life and which possess other powers such as the power to know about their conditions and the power to reason and the power to be considerate of some other such living thing(s) and its life and its powers and the power to not be considerate at all of some other such living thing(s) and its life and its powers in a universe in case it can be that he exists and it can be that a thing possesses the power to bring about (in the very first instance) other living things which possess the power to act freely. So, it can be that God exists and evil exists and there is the degree of evil of this state of affairs in case it can be that that is so. (An advocate of the first argument in the pen-ultimate section and an advocate of the second argument in the pen-ultimate section in that case are at least required to provide sufficient grounds for the claim that it cannot be that that is so.)

The third argument of the pen-ultimate section is an argument for the claim that God does not exist. Its first premise is that it cannot be that God exists *and* there is the evil of states of affairs *such as* the state of affairs that living things which possess the power to lead a life and which possess other powers such as the power to know about their conditions and the power to reason, *viz.* human beings, experience pain and suffering such as the pain and suffering brought about by a major earthquake due to their conditions. (The principal argument for the claim that it is true is not that it is true because it cannot be that God exists.)

But, it can be as we have seen that God brings it about that there are other living things which possess the power to act freely and independently of him and which possess the power to lead a life and which possess other powers such as the power to know about their conditions and the power to reason and which possess the power to interact with some physical thing(s) in a universe *and* they are liable to experience evil due to the conditions which prevail in it in case it can be that he exists and it can be that a living thing possesses the power to bring about (in the very first instance) other living things which possess the power to act freely. (The degree of their liability to experience evil and the degree of that evil is determined by the degree of their independence of God.)

Is it true that it cannot be that there is the evil of states of affairs such as this state of affairs in case it can be that that is so? Well, sufficient grounds for the claim that this is true are not readily forthcoming. (An advocate of the third argument in the pen-ultimate section in that case is at least required to provide sufficient grounds for the claim that it cannot be that that is so.)

The last argument of the pen-ultimate section is an argument for the claim that God does not exist. Its first premise is that it cannot be that God exists *and* there is the *amount* of evil there is. (The principal argument for the claim that it is true is not that it is true because it cannot be that God exists.)

But, it can be as we have seen that God brings it about that there are other living things which possess the power to act freely and independently of him and which possess the power to lead a life and which possess other powers such as the power to know about their conditions and the power to reason and which possess other powers such as the power to be considerate of some other such living thing(s) and its life and its powers and the power to not be considerate at all of some other such living thing(s) and its life and its powers in a universe *and* they are liable to experience evil due to the conditions which prevail in it in case it can be that he exists and it can be that a living thing possesses the power to bring about (in the very first instance) other living things which possess the power to act freely.

Is it true that it cannot be that there is the amount of evil there is in case it can be that that is so? Well, sufficient grounds for the claim that this is true are not readily forthcoming. (An advocate of the fourth argument in the pen-ultimate section in that case is at least required to provide sufficient grounds for the claim that it cannot be that that is so.)

So, the arguments in the pen-ultimate section for the claim that God does not exist do not establish that this claim is true *or* do not provide sufficient grounds for this claim in case it can be that God exists and it can be that a living thing possesses the power to bring about (in the very first instance) other living things which possess the power to act freely.

Notes

1. Alvin Plantinga, *The Nature of Necessity* (Oxford, 1974), pp.164-193.

These pages are re-printed in M. M. Adams and R. M. Adams (eds.), *The Problem of Evil* (Oxford, 1990).

2. *The Nature of Necessity*, p.44.

Here is another account of (the endless number of) possible worlds: they are all concrete and they are causally isolated; an individual thing which exists in a possible world exists only in it - it does not exist in any other possible world; but, it has "counter-parts" in at least some other possible worlds. See, for example, David Lewis, "Counter-part Theory and Quantified Modal Logic", *Journal of Philosophy*, 65 (1968), pp.113–126.

Here is an argument for the claim that this is an improper account of possible worlds. Its initial premise is as follows. (Its supposition is an implication of this account.) :

it is untrue that it can be that God does not exist in case it can be that he exists.

Let us suppose that it is true that it can be that God does not exist in case it can be that he exists.

It is untrue in that case that it can be that God does not exist in case it can be that he exists and it is true that it can be that God does not exist in case it can be that he exists. (This initial conclusion follows from the first premise and the supposition.) That's absurd!

So, the supposition is untrue.

The first premise is true. The supposition is such that an absurdity follows with its addition. So, the ultimate conclusion – the ultimate conclusion is the denial of the supposition – is true. The supposition is untrue.

The supposition is an implication of this account of possible worlds; but, the supposition is untrue; so, this is an improper account of possible worlds.

3. This is not the example given by Plantinga.

4. This power is compatible with God having the property of being morally perfect for Plantinga.

5. The evil in that case is "broadly moral evil". *The Nature of Necessity,* p.193.

6. *The Nature of Necessity,* pp.190-191.

Plantinga refers to "the vast amount and variety of [moral] evil".

7. *The Nature of Necessity,* pp.191–193.

8. It is an assumption of this argument that the significantly free creatures in the actual world do more good than evil. Is this so?

Chapter 4

The Existence of God

Are there sufficient grounds for the claim that God exists?

Some Ontological arguments
Anselm

Introduction

There are a number of traditional arguments for the existence of God. They are as follows: ontological arguments; design arguments; cosmological arguments. Ontological arguments include a reference to particular properties of God in order to establish that he exists. Here is an example of such a property: being such that nothing greater can be conceived.

The most famous and most widely discussed ontological argument *or* ontological arguments is *or* are the argument *or* arguments of Saint Anselm (1033 - 1109). (It is a matter of some dispute whether there is a single argument *or* more than a single argument.) It *or* they are included in a work written in the period 1063 - 1078. (He was Prior of the Benedictine monastery at Bec in this period. His works of this period are of a contemplative nature. He says that they are written for someone who is "striving to elevate his own mind to the contemplation of God".) The work is entitled *Proslogion.*[1] The argument *or* arguments are the result of a combination which is considered authoritative at the time: a vision of God in meditation *and* logical rigour.

Proslogion Second Chapter

Some preliminary remarks

(i) Anselm states that God is a thing than which nothing greater can be conceived. Here is an appropriate re-statement in the first instance of this statement: there is a thing, *viz.* God, which is such that it cannot be that there is a thing which is greater than it.[2]

Is this so for him because it cannot be that that thing, *viz.* God, exists? Well, it need hardly be said that this is not so for him because this is so. So, here is an appropriate re-statement in the second instance: there is a thing, *viz.* God, which can exist (in reality) and which is such that it cannot be that there is a thing which is greater than it.

Is this so for him because it cannot be that that thing, *viz.* God, has a degree of value? Well, it need hardly be said that this is not so for him because this is so. The things which are at issue are good things. So, here is a re-statement of Anselm's statement in the third instance: there is a thing, *viz.* God, which can exist (in reality) and which is good and which is such that it cannot be that there is a thing which is greater than it.[3, 4]

Finally, can it be that there is a thing which is other than that thing, *viz.* God, and which is at least equal to (even though it is not greater than) that thing, *viz.* God, for Anselm? Well, it need hardly be said that it cannot be that this is so for Anselm.[5] So, here is a re-statement of Anselm's statement in the fourth instance: there is a thing, *viz.* God, which can exist (in reality) and which is good and which is such that it cannot be that there is a thing which is greater than it and which is such that it cannot be that there is some other thing which is equal to it.

Let us re-state more briefly this re-statement in the fourth instance of Anselm's statement: there is a thing, *viz.* God, which can exist (in reality) and which is good and which is such that it cannot be that there is a thing which is greater than it *or* some other thing which is equal to it. (In other words, it can be that God exists (in reality) and he is good and it cannot be that there is a thing which is greater than him *or* some other thing which is equal to him.)

Here is a re-statement of this re-statement in terms of states of affairs. (The values of the states of affairs in question are determined by the thing(s) which they include.) There is a state of affairs which includes that thing, *viz.* God, and which can obtain and which is good and which is greater than any state of affairs which includes some other thing and which can obtain and which is good (*or* bad). These are the re-statements in the final instance of Anselm's statement.

Incidentally, here is an objection to Anselm's original statement, *viz.* God is a thing than which nothing greater can be conceived: it implies that there *is* such a thing. It need hardly be said that this statement does *not* imply that there is such a thing for Anselm. These re-statements do *not* imply that that there *is* such a thing.

(ii) Anselm states that even the Fool[6] understands what he hears when he hears "a thing than which nothing greater can be conceived [*viz.* God]" *and* what he hears exists in the understanding *and* even the Fool understands that this is so even in case he does not understand that it exists in reality.

It cannot be that someone (such as the Fool) understands what he hears when he hears "a thing than which nothing greater can be conceived [*viz.* God]" unless it can be that someone understands "a thing than which nothing greater can be conceived [*viz.* God]" at some time. So, it can be that someone understands "a thing than which nothing greater can be conceived [*viz.* God]" at some time for Anselm.

Further, it can be in that case that "a thing than which nothing greater can be conceived [*viz.* God]" exists in someone's understanding at some time for Anselm for "a thing than which nothing greater can be conceived [*viz.* God]" exists in someone's understanding at some time when someone understands "a thing than which nothing greater can be conceived [*viz.* God]" at some time.

(iii) Anselm states that "a thing than which nothing greater can be conceived [*viz.* God]" cannot exist in the mind alone. Anselm states to begin with that "a thing than which nothing greater can be conceived [*viz.* God]" can be conceived to exist in reality as well as in the understanding in order to demonstrate that this is so. Here is an appropriate re-statement of this statement: it can be that "a thing than which nothing greater can be conceived [*viz.* God]" exists in reality *and* in someone's understanding at some time.

(iv) Finally, Anselm states effectively, with the second statement referred to in *(iii)* in mind, that that thing, *viz.* God, is greater in case it exists in reality and in the understanding than in case it exists only in the understanding.

A statement in the first instance of Anselm's argument in the second chapter of the Proslogion

Here is a statement in the first instance of Anselm's argument. It is in two stages. With *(i)*, *(iii)*, and *(iv)* to begin with in mind, here is the first stage. Its initial premises are as follows:

there is a thing, *viz.* God, which can exist (in reality) and which is good and which is such that it cannot be that there is a thing which is greater than it *or* some other thing which is equal to it;

it can be that that thing, *viz.* God, exists in reality *and* it exists in someone's understanding at some time ;

that thing, *viz.* God, is greater in case it exists in reality and in the understanding than in case it exists only in the understanding.[7]

Let us suppose that it can be that that thing, *viz.* God, exists only in someone's understanding at some time.

It can be in that case that there is a thing, *viz.* that thing *itself,* which is greater than that thing can be by supposition and it cannot be that this is so. (This initial conclusion follows from the first premise and the second premise and the third premise and the supposition.) That's absurd!

So, it is untrue that it can be that that thing, *viz.* God, exists only in someone's understanding (and not in reality) at some time.

The first premise and the second premise and the third premise are true for Anselm. The supposition is such that an absurdity follows with its addition. So, the ultimate conclusion – the ultimate conclusion is the denial of the supposition - is true for Anselm.

With *(ii)* in particular in mind, here is the second stage :

it is not the case that that thing, *viz.* God, does not exist in reality and it exists in someone's understanding at some time ;

it exists in someone's understanding at some time.

so, it exists in reality.

The conclusion follows from the first premise and the second premise. The first premise follows from the conclusion of the first stage of the argument. The second premise is true according to Anselm. So, the conclusion is true according to Anselm.

A statement in the final instance of Anselm's argument and a consideration of it

Let us keep *(ii)* in mind: in particular, the claim that someone understands "a thing than which nothing greater can be conceived [*viz.* God]" at some time and as a result that thing, *viz.* God, exists in someone's understanding at that time. With it in mind, here is a re-statement of the statement in the first instance of Anselm's argument. Here are the initial premises of the first stage :

there is a thing, *viz.* God, which can exist (in reality) and which is good and which is such that it cannot be that there is a thing which is greater than it *or* some other thing which is equal to it ;

it can be that that thing, *viz.* God, exists in reality *and* someone understands that (*viz.* the first premise) at some time ;

that thing, *viz.* God, is greater in case it exists in reality and someone understands that (*viz.* the first premise) than in case someone understands that (*viz.* the first premise) only.

Let us suppose that it can be that someone understands that (*viz.* the first premise) only at some time.

It can be in that case that there is a thing, *viz.* that thing *itself*, which is greater than that thing can be by supposition and it cannot be that this is so. (This initial conclusion follows from the first premise and the second premise and the third premise and the supposition.) That's absurd!

So, it is untrue that it can be that someone understands that (*viz.* the first premise) only (and that thing does not exist in reality) at some time.

Here is the second stage :

it is not the case that that thing, *viz.* God, does not exist in reality and someone understands that (*viz.* that first premise) at some time ;

someone understands that (*viz.* that first premise) at some time ;

so, it exists in reality.

Is the argument as it is re-stated finally sound? Well, let us begin with a consideration of its second stage. Its conclusion follows from its first premise and its second premise. Its first premise follows from the ultimate conclusion of the first stage.

Let us consider the first stage. The following follows from its first premise and its second premise: it can be that that thing, *viz.* God, exists in reality and someone understands that there is a thing, *viz.* God, which can exist (in reality) and which is good and which is such that it cannot be that there is a thing which is greater than it *or* some other thing which is equal to it at some time. (Can it be that God exists in reality? Well, there are no grounds for the claim that it is untrue that it can be that this is so at least in the course of this work. Still, it does not follow that it can be that this is so.)

The following follows with the addition of its third premise and the supposition: God in such a case is greater than in case it can be that someone understands that there is a thing, *viz.* God, which can exist (in reality) and which is good and which is such that it cannot be that there is a thing which is greater than it *or* some other thing which is equal to it only at some time.

What "God" refers to in the first case, *viz.* in the pen-ultimate paragraph, is a thing, *viz.* God, which can exist (in reality). There is a thing which can exist (in reality) just in case there is a state of affairs which includes that thing *and* which can obtain. A state of affairs which includes a thing and which can obtain has a value and that value is the value of that thing in case it includes no other thing.[8] The value of the state of affairs which includes a thing and which can obtain in this case, *viz.* the state of affairs that God exists (in reality), is the value of that thing, *viz.* God.

What "God" refers to in the second case, *viz.* in the second case in the pen-ultimate paragraph, is once more a thing, *viz.* God, which can exist (in reality). The value of the state of affairs which includes a thing and which can obtain in this case, *viz.* the state of affairs that God exists (in reality), is the value of that thing, *viz.* God. Since the value is the same in both cases, it is untrue that God is greater in the first case than in the second case.[9] The first stage of Anselm's argument as it is re-stated in the final instance in that case does not establish that its initial conclusion is true. So, it does not establish that its ultimate conclusion is true and accordingly it does not establish that the first premise of the second stage is true.

Proslogion Third Chapter

Some preliminary remarks

(i) Anselm refers once more to "that than which nothing greater can be conceived", *viz.* God. This is re-stated in the consideration of Anselm's argument in the second chapter. This re-statement (in the final instance) includes the following statement: .... a thing, *viz.* God, ... which is such that it cannot be that there is a thing (including itself) which is greater than it. So, God is *not* greater in case this or that than he is.

(ii) Anselm states that a thing can be conceived to exist and cannot be conceived not to exist. Here is an appropriate re-statement of this statement: it can be that there is a thing which exists (in reality) and it cannot be it does not exist (in reality).

(iii) Anselm states that a thing which can be conceived to exist and cannot be conceived not to exist is greater than a

thing which (can be conceived to exist and) can be conceived not to exist. Here is an appropriate re-statement of this statement: a thing which is such that it can be that it exists (in reality) and it cannot be it does not exist (in reality) is greater than a thing (including itself) which is such that it can be that it exists (in reality) and it can be it does not exist (in reality). So, God is greater in case it can be that he exists (in reality) and it cannot be he does not exist (in reality) than in case it can be that he exists (in reality) and it can be he does not exist (in reality).

A statement of an ontological argument which is identifiable in the third chapter of the Proslogion and a consideration of it

Here is an argument which is identifiable in the third chapter of the *Proslogion* with these preliminary remarks in mind. It is in two stages. Here is the first stage. Its initial premises are as follows:

God is not greater in case this or that than he is;

God is greater in case it can be that he exists (in reality) and it cannot be he does not exist (in reality) than in case it can be that he exists (in reality) and it can be he does not exist (in reality).

Let us suppose that it can be that God exists (in reality) *and* it can be he does not exist (in reality).

God in that case is not greater in case this or that than he is by supposition and he is greater in case it can be that he exists and it cannot be that he does not exist than he is by supposition. (This initial conclusion follows from the first premise and the second premise and the supposition.) That's absurd!

So, it is untrue that it can be that God exists (in reality) and it can be he does not exist (in reality).

The first premise is true. The second premise is true. The supposition is such that an absurdity follows with its addition. So, the ultimate conclusion – the ultimate conclusion is the denial of the supposition – is true. It is untrue that it can be that God exists (in reality) and it can be he does not exist (in reality).

Here is the second stage:

it is untrue that it can be that God exists (in reality) and it can be he does not exist (in reality);

it can be that God exists (in reality);

so, it is untrue that it can be that he does not exist (in reality).

The conclusion follows from the first premise and the second premise. The first premise is true. (The first premise is the conclusion of the first stage.) Is the second premise true? Well, there are no grounds for the claim that it is untrue at least in the course of this work. Still, it does not follow that it is true.

Some final remarks

There is an ontological argument for the claim that God exists in reality in the second chapter of Anselm's *Proslogion.* This argument does not establish that this claim is true. Further, there is an ontological argument for the claim that it is untrue that it can be that God does not exist in reality in the third chapter of his *Proslogion.* This argument does not establish that this claim is true. So, there are not sufficient grounds for the claim that God exists in these chapters of Anselm's *Proslogion.*

Some Design arguments

Introduction

Design arguments in the main have referred to the following in order to establish that God exists: individual things in the physical universe *or* to the physical universe itself; and, the properties of having an end or purpose *or* having order *or* having an end or purpose *and* having order. David Hume (1711 - 1776) considers a design argument which is an argument by analogy.[10] Here is an example of an argument which he considers :

there are things which have been brought about to fulfil particular ends and which have been brought about by the intelligent design of something(s), *viz.* human beings,[11] *and* there are things which are such that they fulfil particular ends and which are in nature ;

the things in each of these groups are just like each other in that they fulfil particular ends ;

since things in the first of these groups have been brought about by the intelligent design of something(s), it is probable that things in the second of these groups, *viz.* natural things or the whole (or "world") of natural things, have been brought about by the intelligent design of something which is somewhat similar and which has considerably greater faculties.[12]

Incidentally, this is a *teleological* argument for it is an explanation of ends, *viz.* the ends of things which are in nature. (The word *teleological* is derived from two Greek words: τελος or *telos*; λογος or *logos*. The translation of τελος in English is "end". The translation here of λογος in English is "an explanation of".)

He refers instead to the property of *order* (of natural things or the whole of natural things) in places in his consideration of this argument.[13] (The order at issue is a *persistent* order. Things in the second group have a persistent order above all for they abide by natural laws.) Finally, he refers instead to the properties of end or purpose *and* order (of natural things or the whole of natural things) in places in his consideration of this argument.[14]

But, Hume argues that natural things are *not sufficiently similar* to the things which have ends *or* order *or* both and which have been brought about by human beings in order to argue by analogy in this way.[15] They are not sufficiently similar for there are just one *or* two properties at issue and there is a considerable difference between the degree of the properties – for example, the degree of order - of the things in each group.

Further, he argues that a claim that something is the *cause* of something else is incorrect unless we have experienced that that these two things are frequently conjoined *and* accordingly we should have “experience of the origins of worlds” in order to claim correctly that it is probable that the intelligent design of something is the *cause* of natural things or the whole (or “world”) of natural things *and* we have no such experience.[16]

Further still, he argues that in any case any such intelligent designer(s) does *not* possess more power, intelligence, and moral goodness than the power, intelligence, and moral goodness which is required to bring about natural things[17] *and* that in any case the natural evil in the world is such that any such intelligent designer does *not* have the moral properties which are attributed to God[18] *and* that in any case (and among other things) it can be and indeed it is probable that - contrary to the principal claim of a theist - there are *a number* of any such intelligent designers.[19] Finally, he argues that any such intelligent designer itself requires an explanation.[20]

Some preliminary remarks

The design arguments which follow use a principle. The principle is the principle of likelihood. The principle states the following about something which is observed and two hypotheses about it : that something which is observed supports one of these hypotheses more than it supports the other hypothesis just in case its probability in case one of these hypotheses is true is greater than its probability in case the other hypothesis is true. That something which is observed is such that one of these hypotheses is *likelier* than the other hypothesis just in case this is so according to the principle of likelihood.

Further, the support of that something which is observed for a hypothesis is a matter of degree and its degree of support for a hypothesis is in line with its probability in case that hypothesis is true. Here is an example to illustrate this principle. Let us suppose that a visitor to the Tate observes the following: there are paintings in the rooms of the Tate gallery *and* they are organised. Here are two hypotheses about what he observes: there are paintings in the rooms of the Tate gallery because of the curators of the Tate; there are paintings in the rooms of the Tate gallery because of intruders in the night and these intruders do not know how to organise these paintings.

It is highly probable that there are paintings in the rooms of the Tate gallery *and* they are organised in case the first hypothesis is true. It is not highly probable that there are paintings in the rooms of the Tate gallery *and* they are organised in case the second hypothesis is true. So, what he observes supports the first hypothesis more than it supports the second hypothesis according to the principle of likelihood. What he observes is such that the first hypothesis is *likelier* than the second hypothesis according to the principle of likelihood. Further, what he observes supports the first hypothesis to a high degree. The principle of likelihood is plausible. It is taken in what follows that it is true.

The following should be kept in mind in the use of this principle. A satisfactory statement of the probability of an observation in case a particular hypothesis is true includes a statement of any assumption which is made. Let us consider the following statement in relation to our example in order to illustrate that this is so: it is not highly probable that there are paintings in the rooms of the Tate gallery *and* these paintings are organised in case the hypothesis that there are paintings in the rooms of the Tate because of intruders in the night and these intruders do not know how to organise them is true. This statement of the probability of what is observed in case that hypothesis is true is satisfactory for it includes a statement of the assumption which is made, *viz.* these intruders do not know how to organise these paintings. (The statement that it is not highly probable that there are paintings in the rooms of the Tate gallery *and* these paintings are organised in case the hypothesis that the paintings are in the rooms of the Tate because of intruders in the night is true is not satisfactory for it does not include a statement of the assumption which is made.)

It need hardly be added that it does not follow that a hypothesis *is* true in case an observation supports it rather than some other hypothesis. It does not follow in the case of our example that the hypothesis that the paintings are in the rooms of the Tate gallery because of the curators of the Tate *is* true even though what he observes supports it rather than the hypothesis that the paintings are in the rooms of the Tate gallery because of intruders in the night and these intruders do not know how to organise them. Further, it does not follow that there are *sufficient grounds* for someone to believe that a hypothesis is true in case an observation supports it rather than some other hypothesis.

It need hardly be added also that it does not follow that a hypothesis *itself* is highly probable[21] in case an observation supports it rather than some other hypothesis. Here is an example to illustrate that this is so. Let us suppose once more that a visitor to the Tate observes the following: there are paintings in the rooms of the Tate gallery *and* they are organised. Here are two hypotheses about what he observes: there are paintings in the rooms of the Tate gallery because of intruders in the night and these intruders know how to organise them and these intruders intend to organise them; there are paintings in the rooms of the Tate gallery because of intruders in the night and these intruders know how to organise them and these intruders do *not* intend to organise them.

It is highly probable that there are paintings in the rooms of the Tate gallery and they are organised in case the first hypothesis is true. It is not highly probable that he observes there are paintings in the rooms of the Tate gallery and they are organised in case the second hypothesis is true. So, what he observes supports the first hypothesis more than it supports than the second hypothesis according to the principle of likelihood. But, it does *not* follow that that hypothesis *itself* is highly probable.

Further, it does *not* follow that it is highly probable that a hypothesis is true in case this or that is observed[22] in case it is highly probable that (that) this or that is observed in case this hypothesis is true. Let us consider the example in the penultimate paragraph in order to illustrate that this is so: it is highly probable that there are paintings in the rooms of the Tate gallery *and* they are organised in case the hypothesis that there are paintings in the rooms of the Tate gallery because of intruders in the night and these intruders know how to organise them and these intruders intend to organise them is true.

But, it does not follow that it is highly probable that this hypothesis is true in case there are paintings in the rooms of the Tate gallery and they are organised.

Finally, someone's degree of belief in a hypothesis should increase and his degree of belief in another hypothesis should decrease in case he has a degree of belief in each hypothesis *and* he observes this or that and this supports the first of these hypotheses more than it supports the other hypothesis. Let us consider once more the same example in order to illustrate that this is so. Let us suppose that the visitor to the Tate has a degree of belief in the hypothesis that there are paintings in the rooms of the Tate gallery because of intruders in the night and these intruders know how to organise them and these intruders intend to organise them *and* a degree of belief in the hypothesis that there are paintings in the rooms of the Tate gallery because of intruders in the night and these intruders know how to organise them and these intruders do *not* intend to organise them. He observes there are paintings in the rooms of the Tate gallery and they are organised and this supports the first of these hypotheses more than it supports the second of these hypotheses. So, his degree of belief in the first of these beliefs should increase and his degree of belief in the second of these hypotheses should decrease.

A design argument

Some preliminary remarks

Let us consider the following argument (A44) :

it cannot be that there are no other living things which possess the power to act freely and to lead in that way lives.... in a universe at all times in case it can be that God exists and it can be that a living thing possesses the power to bring about (in the very first instance) other living things which possess the power to act freely ;

it cannot be that there are other living things which possess the power to act freely and the power to lead in that way lives.... *and* it does *not* appear to these livings things that they possess these powers in case it can be that that is so ;

so, it cannot be that it does not appear to these other living things that they possess these powers in case it can be that that is so.

The conclusion follows from the first premise and the second premise. The first premise (as we have seen in the course of the consideration of God's nature) is true. The second premise is true. (It cannot be that God does not exist and it cannot be that God (does not possess at any time and) does not exercise the power to bring about in the very first instance some other living things which possess the power to act freely...in a universe at a time in case it can be that he exists and it can be that a living thing possesses the power to bring about in the very first instance other living things which possess the power to act freely. Can it be that he exercises this power and it does *not* appear to these livings things that they possess these powers? Well, that's absurd! Hence, the second premise is true.) So, the conclusion is true. It cannot be that it does not appear to these other living things that they possess these powers in case it can be that God exists and it can be that a living thing possesses the power to bring about (in the very first instance) other living things which possess the power to act freely.

The argument

In the second premise of the argument which follows, there is a reference to a probability. The probability is *unitary* that it appears to some other living things that they possess these powers in case the hypothesis that it can be that God exists and it can be that a living thing possesses the power to bring about (in the very first instance) other living things which possess the power to act freely is true. This is the result of a consideration of an argument *or* arguments and there is no requirement that we should have "experience of the origins of worlds" (in case in can be that that is so) in order to determine it.

In the third premise of the argument which follows, there is a reference to "a uniform chance process". A uniform chance process is a process which can have a number of outcomes and which is such that these outcomes are equally probable.

Here is an example of a process which is more or less a uniform chance process: the toss of a coin. It is a process and it can have the outcome "tails" *or* the outcome "heads" and these outcomes are more or less equally probable.

Here is the argument (A45). Its initial premises are as follows:

some living things, *viz.* human beings, observe it appears to some living things, *viz.* human beings, that they possess the power to act freely and the power to lead in that way lives... in a universe (or "world");

the probability that it appears to some living things that they possess these powers in a universe in case the hypothesis that it can be that God exists and it can be that a living thing possesses the power to bring about (in the very first instance) other living things which possess the power to act freely is true is *unitary*;

the probability that it appears to some living things that they possess these powers in a universe in case instead the hypothesis that there is a uniform chance process in operation *or* there is a process which includes a uniform chance process in operation is true is *less than* unitary;

with regard to something which is observed and two hypotheses about it, what is observed supports one of these hypotheses more than it supports the other hypothesis just in case its probability in case one of these hypotheses is true is greater than its probability in case the other hypothesis is true.

Let us suppose that there are two hypotheses about the observation it appears to some living things that they possess the power to act freely and the power to lead in that way lives ... in a universe: it can be that God exists and it can be that a living thing possesses the power to bring about (in the very first instance) other living things which possess the power to act freely; there is a uniform chance process in operation *or* there is a process which includes a uniform chance process in operation.

So, the observation it appears to some living things (other than God, *viz.* human beings) they possess the power to act freely and the power to lead in that way lives ... in a universe supports the first of these hypotheses more than it supports the second of these hypotheses.

The conclusion follows from the first premise and the second premise and the third premise and the fourth premise and the supposition. The first premise is true. The second premise is true. The third premise is true. The fourth premise is true. So, the conclusion is true in case the supposition is true. The observation it appears to some living things that they possess the power to act freely and the power to lead in that way lives... in a universe supports the hypothesis that it can be that God exists and it can be that a living thing possesses the power to bring about (in the very first instance) other living things which possess the power to act freely more than it supports the hypothesis that there is a uniform chance process in operation *or* there is a process which includes a uniform chance process in operation in case these are the two hypotheses about this observation.

Another design argument

Here is another design argument (A46). Its initial premises are as follows:

some living things, *viz.* human beings, observe there are living things which are liable (to a significant degree) to experience evil (to a significant degree) in a universe (or "world");

the probability that there are living things which are liable (to a significant degree) to experience evil (to a significant degree) in a universe in case the hypothesis that it can be that God exists and it can be that a living thing possesses the power to bring about (in the very first instance) other living things which possess the power to act freely is true is *unitary*;

the probability that there are living things which are liable (to a significant degree) to experience evil (to a significant degree) in a universe in case instead the hypothesis that there is a uniform chance process in operation *or* there is a process which includes a uniform chance process in operation is true is *less than* unitary;

with regard to something which is observed and two hypotheses about it, what is observed supports one of these hypotheses more than it supports the other hypothesis just in case its probability in case one of these hypotheses is true is greater than its probability in case the other hypothesis is true.

Let us suppose that there are two hypotheses about the observation there are living things which are liable (to a significant degree) to experience evil (to a significant degree) in a universe: it can be that God exists and it can be that a living thing possesses the power to bring about (in the very first instance) other living things which possess the power to act freely; there is a uniform chance process in operation *or* there is a process which includes a uniform chance process in operation.

So, the observation there are living things which are liable (to a significant degree) to experience evil (to a significant degree) in a universe supports the first of these hypotheses more than it supports the second of these hypotheses.

The conclusion follows from the first premise and the second premise and the third premise and the fourth premise and the supposition. The first premise is true. The second premise (as we have seen in the course of the second chapter) is plausible. The third premise is true. The fourth premise is true. So, the conclusion is plausible in case the supposition is true. It is plausible that the observation there are living things which are liable (to a significant degree) to experience evil (to a significant degree) in a universe supports the hypothesis that it can be that God exists and it can be that a living thing possesses the power to bring about (in the very first instance) other living things which possess the power to act freely more than it supports the hypothesis that there is a uniform chance process in operation *or* there is a process which includes a uniform chance process in operation in case these are the two hypotheses about this observation.

Another design argument

Here is another design argument (A47). Its initial premises are as follows:

some living things, *viz.* human beings, observe there are living things which are such that they hold the belief that it is better that a state of affairs which they believe is (morally) good obtains rather than it does not obtain and they possess as a result the desire (to some degree) to bring it about ;

the probability that there are living things which are such that they hold the belief that it is better that a state of affairs which they believe is (morally) good obtains rather than it does not obtain and they possess as a result the desire (to some degree) to bring it about in case the hypothesis that it can be that God exists and it can be that a living thing possesses the power to bring about (in the very first instance) other living things which possess the power to act freely is true is *unitary*;

the probability that there are living things which are such that they hold the belief that it is better that a state of affairs which they believe is (morally) good obtains rather than it does not obtain and they possess as a result the desire (to some degree) to bring it about in case instead the hypothesis that there is a uniform chance process in operation *or* there is a process which includes a uniform chance process in operation is true is *less than* unitary ;

with regard to something which is observed and two hypotheses about it, what is observed supports one of these hypotheses more than it supports the other hypothesis just in case its probability in case one of these hypotheses is true is greater than its probability in case the other hypothesis is true.

Let us suppose that there are two hypotheses about the observation there are living things which are such that they hold the belief that it is better that a state of affairs which they believe is (morally) good obtains rather than it does not obtain and they possess as a result the desire (to some degree) to bring it about: it can be that God exists and it can be that a living thing possesses the power to bring about (in the very first instance) other living things which possess the power to act freely; there is a uniform chance process in operation *or* there is a process which includes a uniform chance process in operation.

So, the observation there are living things which are such that they hold the belief that it is better that a state of affairs which they believe is (morally) good obtains rather than it does not obtain and they possess as a result the desire (to some degree) to bring it about supports the first of these hypotheses more than it supports the second of these hypotheses.

The conclusion follows from the first premise and the second premise and the third premise and the fourth premise and the supposition. The first premise is true. The second premise (as we have seen in the course of the second chapter) is true. The third premise is true. The fourth premise is true. So, the conclusion is true in case the supposition is true. The observation there are living things which are such that they hold the belief that it is better that a state of affairs which they believe is (morally) good obtains rather than it does not obtain and they possess as a result the desire (to some degree) to bring it about supports the hypothesis that it can be that God exists and it can be that a living thing possesses the power to bring about (in the very first instance) other living things which possess the power to act freely more than it supports the hypothesis that there is a uniform chance process in operation *or* there is a process which includes a uniform chance process in operation in case these are the two hypotheses about this observation.

Some remarks on these design arguments[23]

The second hypothesis in each of these arguments about what is observed is the hypothesis that there is a uniform chance process in operation *or* there is a process which includes a uniform chance process in operation. It is a plausible claim that this is the principal non-theistic hypothesis about what is observed.

With the preliminary remarks in mind, let us make the following remarks: it does *not* follow from each of these arguments that the hypothesis that it can be that God exists and it can be that a living thing possesses the power to bring about (in the very first instance) other living things which possess the power to act freely *is* true; it does *not* follow from each of these arguments that there are *sufficient grounds* for someone to hold the belief that it is true; it does *not* follow from each of these arguments that that hypothesis *itself* is highly probable; it does *not* follow from each of these arguments that it is highly probable that that hypothesis is true given that it appears to some living things that they possess the power to act freely and the power to lead in that way lives ... . Still, someone's degree of belief in that hypothesis should increase and his degree of belief in the other hypothesis should decrease in case he has a degree of belief in each hypothesis.

Some Cosmological arguments

Introduction

Cosmological arguments have referred to other properties - properties other than having an end or purpose *or* having order - of individual things in the physical universe *or* to the physical universe itself *or* both in order to establish that God exists. There is to begin with a consideration of some cosmological arguments in what follows. Each of these cosmological arguments includes *or* is a line of argument which is associated in particular with Aquinas *or* early Islamic rational theology *or* Samuel Clarke (1675 - 1729) and Gottfried Leibniz (1648 - 1716). Following the consideration of these arguments, another cosmological argument is set out.

A cosmological argument

Here is a statement of a cosmological argument. (This cosmological argument includes a line of argument which is associated with among others Aquinas.[24]) Its initial stage is as follows :

there is a series of things which have been brought about *or* which are being brought by some other thing(s) ;

this series of things is *not* infinite ;

so, there is something which has brought about the first thing in this series of things and which itself has not been brought about *or* which is not being brought about by some other thing.

Further, it seeks to establish in a second stage that the thing which is referred to in the conclusion is God *or* is probably God. (It is the First Cause.)

The conclusion of its initial stage follows from the first premise and the second premise. The series which is referred to is temporal *or* non-temporal. Here is the series which is *temporal*: there is something which is brought about by some other thing *and* that other thing is brought about by some other thing at an earlier time *and* that yet other thing is brought about by yet some other thing at an earlier time than that time and so on.

Here is the series which is *non-temporal*: there is something now *and* there is some other thing which is bringing it about *and* there is some other thing which is bringing about that other thing and so on. (These series consist of things which are caused causes.)

(i) Let us say to begin with that the argument refers to a *temporal* series. The conclusion follows from its first premise and its second premise. The first premise is true. The second premise is that this series of things is *not* infinite. (The second premise in other words is that this series of things is *finite*.)

Why? Well, let us to begin with *not* take into account the current scientific understanding about the origins of the physical universe. Here is a statement of an argument for the second premise :

it cannot be that other such things are added to such a series after a now (or now) in case it is infinite ;

it can be that other such things are added to this instance of such a series after a now ;

so, it cannot be that this instance of such a series is infinite.

The conclusion follows from the first premise and the second premise. The second premise is true. Is the first premise true? Well, here is a statement of an argument for the first premise :

it cannot be that things are added to *any* series of things unless it increase its size ;

it cannot be that any infinite series of things increases its size ;

so, it cannot be that things are added to *any* infinite series of things.

The conclusion follows from the first premise and the second premise. The first premise is untrue: for instance, it can be that things, *viz.* the infinite series of numbers ..... *+ 3, + 2, + 1,* are added to a series of things, *viz.* the infinite series of numbers *0, -1, -2, -3* .... and that series of things does not increase in size – it is still infinite in size. This argument does not establish the truth of the first premise of this argument for the second premise of this cosmological argument. So, it does not establish the truth of the second premise of this cosmological argument.

Here is a statement of another argument for the second premise of this cosmological argument:

some thing now in this series is the end (at least currently) in this series;

this series is not infinite unless there is an infinite number of things between it and some other thing which precedes it in this series;

there is *not* an infinite number of things between it and some other thing which precedes it in this series. (There is nothing *or* there is a *finite* number of such things between it and some other thing which precedes it in this series.);

so, this series is not infinite.

The conclusion follows from the first premise and the second premise and the third premise. The first premise is true and the third premise is true. The second premise is untrue. Let the number *0* represent the end in question and the number -*1* represent the thing which precedes it in this series and the number *-2* represent the thing which precedes that thing .... in the following (infinite) series: *0, -1, -2, ...* . This series has an end and it is infinite even though there is not an infinite number of numbers or things between the end in it and some other thing in it. So, this argument does not establish the truth of the second premise of this cosmological argument.

Further, the proponent of this cosmological argument (with a temporal series of things which have been brought about) seeks to establish that the thing which is referred to in its conclusion is (among other things) the cause of the physical universe. There is in that case (and in any case) an immediate difficulty. The argument does not establish that this thing is the cause of the physical universe *unless* the series which it refers to constitutes *or* includes the things of the physical universe. So, here is a re-statement of this cosmological argument:

there is a (temporal) series of things which have been brought about by some other thing(s) ;

this series constitutes *or* includes the things of the physical universe ;

this series of things is *not* infinite ;

so, there is something which has brought about the first thing in this series of things and which has not been brought about and which is the (ultimate) cause of the physical universe.

The conclusion follows from the first premise and the second premise and the third premise. The first premise is true. There are difficulties, as we have seen, with the third premise. Still, let us suppose, for the sake of argument, that it is true. (So, there is a series of things which have been brought about by some other thing(s) and this series of things is finite.) Is the second premise true? Does this series constitute *or* include the physical universe? Does the following series of things instead constitute the physical universe: a series of physical things which have been brought about by some other physical things *and* some first physical thing which has brought about the first of those things and which has not been brought about? What is to say that this is not so?[25]

Finally, there are questions about the claim that the thing which is referred to in the conclusion of this cosmological argument is God *or* is probably God. Here is an example of such a question. (Let us recall that it cannot be God does not exist eternally in time in case it can be that he exists.) Why is the thing which is referred to in the conclusion of this cosmological argument such that it cannot be that it does not exist eternally in time?

Let us recall that this consideration of the second premise of this cosmological argument, *viz.* the premise that the series of things (which have been brought about by some other thing(s)) is not infinite, does *not* take into account the current scientific understanding about the origins of the physical universe. Let us now take that understanding into account. The second premise *is* true according to that understanding.

The conclusion of this cosmological argument follows from its first premise and its second premise. Its first premise is true. (Its second premise is true according to the current scientific understanding about the origins of the physical universe.) So, its conclusion is true according to the current scientific understanding about the origins of the physical universe.

But, the thing which is referred to in its conclusion is the following according to this understanding: some physical things, *viz.* elementary particles, which have brought about the first thing(s) in the series of things which is referred to in the argument and which have not been brought about.

(ii) Let us say that this cosmological argument refers to a *non-temporal* series. The conclusion follows from its first premise and its second premise. The first premise is true. The second premise is that this series of things is *not* infinite. (The second premise in other words is that this series of things is *finite*.) There are difficulties, as we have seen, with the second premise. Still, here is a statement of a further argument for the second premise :

such a series is occurring ;

such a series is not occurring unless there is something which is bringing about a first thing in it and which itself is not being brought about ;

there is no such thing in case the series is infinite ;

so, such a series is not infinite.

The conclusion follows from the first premise and the second premise and the third premise. The first premise is true and the third premise is true. But, the second premise is untrue. The series of such things is occurring in case each thing bringing about some other (succeeding) thing in it is occurring. Each thing bringing about some other (succeeding) thing is occurring in case each thing bringing about some other thing is being brought about. Each thing bringing about some other thing is being brought about. So, the series of such things is occurring.

The proponent of the argument (with a non-temporal series of things which are being brought about) seeks to establish that the thing which is referred to in its conclusion is (among other things) the cause of the physical universe. There is in that case (and in any case) an immediate difficulty. It is just along the lines of the difficulty in case this cosmological argument refers to a temporal series.

Finally, there are questions about the claim that the thing which is referred to in the conclusion of this cosmological argument is God *or* is probably God. These are once more along the lines of the questions raised in case this cosmological argument refers to a temporal series.

Another cosmological argument

Here is a statement of another cosmological argument. (This cosmological argument includes a line of argument which is associated in particular with early Islamic rational theology.[26]) Its initial stage is as follows :

the physical universe began to exist ;

everything which begins to exist has a cause ;

so, the physical universe has a cause.

Further, it seeks to establish in a second stage that the thing which is referred to in the conclusion is God *or* is probably God.

The conclusion of the initial stage follows from the first premise and the second premise. Here is a statement of an argument for the first premise. It is in two stages. Here is the first stage :

there is a series of things: there is something which is brought about by some other such thing *and* that other thing is brought about by some other such thing at an earlier time *and* that yet other thing is brought about by yet some other such thing at an earlier time than that time and so on ;

this series of things is *not* infinite ;

so, there is something which has brought about the first thing in this series of things and which itself has not been brought about by some other such thing.

The conclusion follows from the first premise and the second premise. The first premise is true. Just as before, there are difficulties with the second premise in case the current scientific understanding about the origins of the physical universe is not taken into account. Still, it is true according to the current scientific understanding about the origins of the physical universe.

Here is the second stage :

the series of things and the thing which has brought about the first thing in this series of things and which itself has not been brought about by some other such thing constitute the physical universe ;

the thing which has brought about the first thing in this series of things and which itself has not been brought by some other such thing has not existed endlessly or infinitely in time ;

so, the physical universe has a beginning.

The conclusion follows from the first premise and the second premise. Let us take it that the first premise is true. Here is a statement of an argument for the second premise :

there is the following series: there is a present time, and there is a time prior to it, and there is a time prior to that time, and so on ;

this series is *not* infinite ;

so, the thing which has brought about the first thing in that series of things and which itself has not been brought by some other such thing has *not* existed endlessly or infinitely in time.

The conclusion follows from the first premise and the second premise. The first premise is true. Just as before, there are difficulties with the second premise in case the current scientific understanding about the origins of the physical universe is not taken into account. Still, it is true according to the current scientific understanding about the origins of the physical universe.

The conclusions of both stages of the argument for the first premise of this cosmological argument are true in case the current scientific understanding about the origins of the physical universe is true. What about the second premise of this cosmological argument? Well, it is untrue in case that understanding is true for the physical things which bring about the first thing in the series in question and which are not brought about by some other such thing and which begin to exist, *viz.* some elementary particles, do *not* in that case have a cause.

In passing, let us consider the following the question: is there an argument which establishes that the second premise is true in spite of the current scientific understanding about the origins of the physical universe? Well, there is such an argument in case there is an argument which establishes that it cannot be that something begins to exist without a cause. But, such an argument is not readily forthcoming. Here is a statement of an argument for the claim that it cannot be that something begins to exist without a cause :

an absurdity follows in case it can be that something begins without a cause *just as* an absurdity follows in case it can be that an effect precedes its cause ;

the latter is untrue for an absurdity follows in case it can be that that is so ;

so, the former is untrue.

The conclusion follows from its first premise and its second premise. The second premise, as we have seen in the course of the first chapter, is true. But, the first premise is highly questionable. So, it is highly questionable whether this argument establishes that it cannot be that something begins to exist without a cause.[27]

A further cosmological argument

Here is a statement of a further cosmological argument. (This cosmological argument is a line argument which is associated in particular with Clarke and Leibniz.[28]) It assumes the following principle: the existence of every individual thing has an explanation; the explanation is some other individual thing(s) which brings it about *or* it itself. Here is the initial stage of the argument:

some individual things have existed. (This refers to the individual things which have existed at any time(s) – any time includes now.) ;

every such thing is a thing which has existed because it is brought about by some other thing(s) *or* a thing which has existed because of it itself ;

some such things are the former ;

not all such things are the former ;

so, some such thing is a thing which has existed because of it itself.

Further, it seeks to establish that there is the fact God exists by way of this conclusion.

The conclusion of the initial argument follows from the first premise and the second premise and the third premise and the fourth premise. The first premise is true and the third premise is true. The second premise follows from the first premise and the assumed principle. Is the assumed principle true? Well, what is to say to begin with that there is not some individual thing which is without explanation – a brute fact?

Further, the assumed principle assumes it can be that an individual thing exists because of it itself - its existence is explained by it itself. But, can it be that this is so? Well, let us suppose that it can be that an individual thing exists because of it itself. It can be in that case that the explanation for its existence, *viz.* it itself, has an explanation, *viz.* it itself, ... But, this is a *vicious* infinite regress. So, it cannot be that this is so.

Is it the case instead that it can be that an individual thing exists because of it itself in that it exists because of its nature's or essence's (or that property's) instantiation - its existence is in that way explained by it itself? (A nature or essence of a particular or individual thing is a property which a particular thing has to have in order to be that particular thing. Here is an example of such a nature of essence: being Aeschylus. Aeschylus has to have this property in order to be Aeschylus.[29]) Well, this is not so for the existence of an individual thing is the explanation of its nature's or essence's (or that property's) instantiation and not *vice versa.*[30]

What about its fourth premise? Well, here there is a reference to a Principle of Sufficient Reason in order to establish that it is true. It states that any fact has an explanation in its unrestricted form. It states that any contingent fact has an explanation in its restricted form. A fact consists in this or that. Some other this or that which is a fact and which is such that it cannot be that it is so and that this or that is not so is an explanation of that fact.

Here is a statement of an argument for the fourth premise, *viz.* the premise that not every individual thing which has existed is a thing which has existed because it is brought about by some other thing(s). To begin with, let us consider the series – or conjunction - of these individual things. (These are the individual things which are referred to in the third premise. The third premise refers to the first and second premises.) :

there is an individual thing and there is some other individual thing which brings it about – brings it about such that it cannot be that it is so and that thing is not so - and there is some other individual thing which brings that other thing about – brings that other thing about such that it cannot be that it is so and that other thing is not so – and so on.

There is a series – or conjunction – of these facts :

there is a fact which consists in an individual thing and another fact which consists in some other individual thing which brings it about – brings it about such that it cannot be that it is so and that thing is not so - *and* another fact which consists in some other individual thing which brings that other thing about – brings that other thing about such that it cannot be that it is so and that other thing is not so – and so on.

A proponent of this argument considers these facts and the fact there is a series of such facts simply as facts and uses the un-restricted form of the Principle *or* a proponent of this argument considers these facts and the series of such facts as contingent facts and uses the restricted form of the Principle. The argument in *any* case proceeds along the following lines. Further, the argument proceeds along the following lines whether the series of such facts is finite *or* infinite.

Each of these individual facts consists at least in the existence of an individual thing. The existence of each individual thing is explained in that there is some other thing which brings it about – brings it about such that it cannot be that it is so and that thing is not so. It cannot be that the latter fact (which consists in that other thing) is so and the former fact is not so. There is accordingly an explanation for each of these facts *in so far as* each of these facts consists at least in the existence of an individual thing. So, there is an explanation of the fact there is a series (or conjunction) of such facts *in so far as* it consists in a series (or conjunction) of the existence of individual things.

But, what about the fact there is a series (or conjunction) of *such* individual things, *viz.* things which have existed because they are brought about by some other thing(s)? Well, there *is* an explanation of why there is the fact there is a series (or conjunction) of such individual things. The explanation is *not* a fact which consists in any such individual thing for any such fact still requires an explanation. (The fact consists in some other individual thing(s).) So, it is *not* the case that every individual thing which has existed is a thing which has existed because it is brought about by some other thing(s). Some individual thing which has existed is a thing which has existed because of it itself. (It has existed at any time(s) – any time includes now.)[31]

With regard to this conclusion, there is to begin with a difficulty whether a proponent of the argument for the fourth premise considers the facts which are identified to begin with and the fact there is a series of such facts simply as facts and uses the un-restricted form of the Principle *or* a proponent of the argument for the fourth premise considers the facts which are identified to begin with and the series of such facts as contingent facts and uses the restricted form of the Principle.

Here is the difficulty. The initial stage of this cosmological argument seeks to establish the individual things which are referred to in its third premise constitute the (physical) universe and (following the argument for its fourth premise) that there is an additional fact which consists in some individual thing which has not been brought about by some other thing and which has existed because of it itself and which explains why there is the series (or conjunction) of individual things which are referred to in its third premise and which constitute the physical universe. But, it does *not* establish that this is so. It does *not* among other things establish that this individual thing is not some individual thing in the (physical) universe.

Further, let us suppose that a proponent of this argument for the fourth premise considers the facts which are identified to begin with and the fact there is a series of such facts simply as facts and uses the un-restricted form of the Principle. (A proponent of this argument is a proponent of the cosmological argument which is being considered.) Let us also suppose that he establishes the conclusion of this cosmological argument, *viz.* there is the fact God exists. Why there is the fact God exists in that case has an explanation and that explanation is a fact; why there is *that* fact also has an explanation and that explanation is a fact; and so on. The fact God exists (even in case it is a fact) in that case is *not* an ultimate explanation. (Such a proponent seeks ultimately to establish that there is the fact God exists and the fact God exists is the ultimate explanation of the fact there is such a series of facts.)

Further, what does such a series of facts consist in? Well, this proponent has the difficulty of identifying what such a series of facts consists in. Finally, there is in any case *no* explanation (as we have seen in the course of the consideration of God's nature) of why there is the fact God exists in case it is a fact. So, a proponent of the argument for the fourth premise with all of this in mind should *not* consider the facts which are identified to begin with and the fact there is a series of such facts simply as facts and use the un-restricted form of the Principle.

Let us suppose on the other hand that a proponent of the argument for the fourth premise considers the facts which are identified to begin with and the fact there is a series of such facts as contingent facts and uses the restricted form of the Principle. (A proponent of this argument is a proponent of the cosmological argument which is being considered.) Such a proponent seeks ultimately to establish that there is the fact God exists and the fact God exists is the ultimate explanation of the fact there is such a series of such facts. But, any explanation of the fact there is a series of such facts is the beginning of an *endless* series of explanations in case this proponent uses the restricted form of the Principle. There is *no* ultimate explanation. Here is a statement of an argument for this claim. Let us take it to begin with that there is an explanation of the fact there is such a series of facts, *viz.* an additional fact which consists in some individual thing which has been brought about by it itself and which is such that that it cannot be that it is so and the fact there is such a series of facts is not so. The argument is in two stages. Here is the first stage. Its initial premises are as follows:

the fact there is a series of such facts is contingent;

the fact there is that individual thing is an explanation of that fact.

Let us suppose that the fact there is that individual thing is necessary.

It cannot be in that case that *there is that individual thing* is not a fact. (This initial conclusion follows from the supposition and the definition of a necessary fact.)

It cannot be that *there is that individual thing* is a fact and *there is a series of such facts* is not a fact. (This further conclusion follows from the first premise and the second premise.)

It cannot be in that case that *there is a series of such facts* is not a fact. (This still further conclusion follows from the initial conclusion and the further conclusion.)

The fact there is a series of such facts is contingent *and* necessary. (This follows from the first premise and the still further conclusion.) That's absurd!

So, it is untrue that the fact there is that individual thing is necessary.

Here is the second stage. Here are its initial premises :

facts are contingent facts *or* necessary facts ;

the fact there is that individual thing is a contingent fact ;

any contingent fact has an explanation ;

any explanation of a contingent fact (although it is a fact) is not a necessary fact.

The fact there is that individual thing in that case is a contingent fact and it has an explanation. (This initial conclusion follows from the second premise and the third premise.)

Its explanation (although it is a fact) in that case is not a necessary fact. (This further conclusion follows from the fourth premise and the initial conclusion.)

Its explanation in that case is a contingent fact and its explanation has an explanation. (This still further conclusion follows from the first premise and the third premise and the further conclusion.)

......

The first premise is true. The second premise follows from the first premise and the ultimate conclusion of the first stage. The third premise (it has been supposed) is true. The fourth premise is true. (Otherwise, there is a fact which is contingent and necessary as the first stage demonstrates. That's absurd! So, the fourth premise is true.) So, the series of explanations is endless : ..... There is *no* ultimate explanation.

Further, what once more does such a series of facts consist in? Well, this proponent has the difficulty of identifying what such a series of facts consists in. So, a proponent of the argument for the fourth premise with all of this in mind should *not* consider the facts which are identified to begin with and the fact there is a series of such facts as contingent facts and use the restricted form of the Principle. (A proponent of the argument for the fourth premise as we have seen should *not* consider the facts which are identified to begin with and the fact there is a series of such facts simply as facts and use the unrestricted form of the Principle.) Such a proponent in that case is unable to establish that the fourth premise of the initial stage of this cosmological argument is true. But, such a proponent is a proponent of this cosmological argument. So, a proponent of this cosmological argument is unable to establish the conclusion of the initial stage of the argument and accordingly its ultimate conclusion, *viz.* that there is the fact God exists.

A final cosmological argument

Here is another cosmological argument (A48). Here is its initial stage (A48.1). (The conclusion of the initial stage is that there is some non-physical individual thing *or* there are some non-physical individual things which is *or* are not brought about by some other (non-physical) individual thing(s) and it is *or* they are the ultimate explanation of why some individual things of the physical kind have existed and it is *or* they are concrete.) Its initial stage itself consists of four stages. Here is the first (A48.1.1) of these four stages :

individual things are of a physical kind *or* a non-physical kind ;

any explanation of why individual things of a particular kind have existed is some individual thing(s) of some *other* kind ;

some individual things of the former kind have existed *and* they have been brought about by some other individual thing(s) of that kind *or* they have not been brought about by some other individual thing(s) of that kind *and* they constitute the physical universe. (This refers to the individual things which have existed at any time(s).) ;

there *is* an explanation of why some individual things of the former kind have existed ;

the explanation of why some individual things of the former kind have existed in that case is some individual thing(s) of some *other* kind. (This initial conclusion follows from the first premise and the second premise and the third premise and the fourth premise.) ;

the explanation in that case is some individual thing(s) of the *latter* kind. (This further conclusion follows from the first premise and the initial conclusion.) ;

so, the explanation of why individual things of the physical kind have existed is some individual thing(s) of the non-physical kind.

The ultimate conclusion follows ultimately from the first premise and the second premise and the third premise and the fourth premise. The first premise is true. The second premise is true. (Any explanation of why individual things of a particular kind have existed is not some individual thing(s) of that kind for some individual thing of that kind still has an explanation.) The third premise is true. So, the ultimate conclusion is true in case the fourth premise is true. The explanation of why individual things of the physical kind have existed is some individual thing(s) of the non-physical kind in case there is an explanation of why some individual things of the physical kind have existed.

Here is the second stage (A48.1.2) of these four stages :

individual things of the non-physical kind are of the kind which are brought about by some other (non-physical) individual thing(s) *or* they are of the kind which are not brought about by some other (non-physical) individual thing(s) ;

any explanation of why individual things of a particular kind have existed is some individual thing(s) of some *other* kind ;

there *is* an explanation of why some non-physical thing(s) of the former kind have existed in case some individual thing(s) of that kind have existed ;

keeping in mind the first stage, any explanation of why non-physical things of the former kind have existed is some individual thing(s) of the latter kind.

Let us suppose that the non-physical individual thing *or* the non-physical individual things which is *or* are referred to in the ultimate conclusion of the first stage (A48.1.1) is *or* are of the former kind.

There is in that case an explanation of why this individual thing *or* these individual things of the former kind has *or* have existed. (This initial conclusion follows from the first premise and the third premise and the supposition.)

The explanation in that case is some individual thing(s) of the latter kind. (This further conclusion follows from the first premise and the second premise and the fourth premise and the initial conclusion.)

So, there is some non-physical individual thing *or* there are some non-physical individual things which is *or* are not brought about by some other (non-physical) individual thing(s) and which is *or* are an explanation of why this individual thing *or* these individual things of the former kind has *or* have existed.

The ultimate conclusion follows from the first premise and the second premise and the third premise and the fourth premise and the supposition. The first premise is true. The second premise is true. The fourth premise is true. (The fourth premise is true for any explanation of why some non-physical individual thing *or* things of the former kind has *or* have existed is some individual thing(s) of some *other* kind. But, there is no remaining kind other than the latter kind of non-physical thing keeping in mind the first stage. Any explanation of why some individual non-physical thing(s) of the former kind has *or* have existed in that case is some individual thing(s) of the latter kind.) So, the ultimate conclusion is true in case the third premise is true and the supposition is true. There is some non-physical individual thing *or* there are some non-physical individual things which is *or* are not brought about by some other (non-physical) individual thing(s) and which is *or* are an explanation of why this individual thing *or* these individual things of the former kind has *or* have existed in case the non-physical individual thing(s) which is *or* are referred to in the conclusion of the first stage (A48.1.1) is *or* are of the former kind and there is an explanation of why it has *or* they have existed.

Here is the third stage (A48.1.3) of these four stages :

individual things of the non-physical kind are of the kind which are brought about by some other (non-physical) individual things *or* they are of the kind which are not brought about by some other (non-physical) individual things ;

keeping in mind the first stage, there is no explanation of why non-physical things of the latter kind have existed in case some individual thing(s) of that kind have existed.

Let us suppose that the non-physical individual thing *or* the non-physical individual things which is *or* are referred to in the ultimate conclusion of the first stage (A48.1.1) is *or* are of the latter kind.

So, there is *no* explanation of this non-physical individual thing *or* these non-physical individual things.

The conclusion follows from the first premise and the second premise and the supposition. The first premise is true. The second premise is true. (Any explanation of some non-physical individual thing(s) of the latter kind is some individual thing(s) of some other remaining kind, *viz.* some individual thing(s) of the physical kind. But, any explanation is *not* some individual thing(s) of the physical kind keeping in mind the first stage. There is in that case *no* explanation of why non-physical things of the latter kind have existed in case some individual thing(s) of that kind have existed and keeping in mind the first stage.) So, the conclusion is true in case the supposition is true. There is *no* explanation of this non-physical individual thing *or* these non-physical individual things (which is *or* are not brought about by some other (non-physical) individual things) in case the non-physical individual thing *or* the non-physical individual things which is *or* are referred to in the ultimate conclusion of the first stage (A48.1.1) is *or* are of this kind.

Here is the fourth stage (A48.1.4) of these four stages :

things are abstract *or* concrete ;

there is some non-physical individual thing *or* there are some non-physical individual things which is *or* are not brought about by some other (non-physical) individual thing(s) *and* it is *or* they are the *ultimate* explanation of why some individual things of the physical kind have existed ;

it cannot be that that an abstract thing brings about – or is an explanation of - some other thing(s) ;

so, it is *or* they are concrete.

The conclusion follows from the first premise and the second premise and the third premise. The first premise is true. The second premise (following the first three stages) is true in case there is an explanation of why some individual things of the physical kind have existed and *whether* that explanation is some non-physical thing(s) of the kind which are brought about by some other (non-physical) individual thing(s) and there is an explanation of why some non-physical thing(s) of this kind have existed *or* that explanation is some non-physical thing(s) of the kind which are not brought about by some other (non-physical) individual thing(s). The third premise is true. So, the conclusion is true in case there is an explanation of why some individual things of the physical kind have existed and whether that explanation is some non-physical thing(s) of the kind which are brought about by some other (non-physical) individual thing(s) and there is an explanation of why some non-physical thing(s) of this kind have existed *or* that explanation is some non-physical thing(s) of the kind which are not brought about by some other (non-physical) individual thing(s).

There is in other words some non-physical individual thing *or* there are some non-physical individual things which is *or* are not brought about by some other (non-physical) individual thing(s) and it is *or* they are the ultimate explanation of why individual things of the physical kind have existed and it is *or* they are concrete in case that is so.

This is the initial stage of this cosmological argument. The final stage of this argument claims that this explanation is God.[32]

Some remarks on this final cosmological argument

Here are some questions in relation to this cosmological argument: is there is an explanation of why individual things of the physical kind have existed?; is there is an explanation of why some non-physical individual thing(s) of the kind which are brought about by some other (non-physical) individual thing(s) have existed in case it *or* they is *or* are the explanation of why some individual things of the physical kind have existed?; is the ultimate explanation which is referred to in the pen-ultimate paragraph God?

This argument does *not* establish that this ultimate explanation *is* God even in case there are the first and second explanations which are referred to in the preceding paragraph. Further, this argument does *not* establish *sufficient grounds* for the claim this ultimate explanation is God even in case there are the first and second explanations which are referred to in the preceding paragraph. Still, this argument does establish *some* grounds for the claim that this ultimate explanation is God in case there are these explanations.

An argument from the religious experience of God

Introduction

Are there (sufficient) grounds for someone to hold the belief that God exists other than any grounds provided by such arguments? Are there (sufficient) grounds for someone to hold the belief that God exists in case he has an experience of God?

Are there (sufficient) grounds for *someone else* to hold the belief that God exists in case that someone has an experience of God? Well, let us consider an argument for the claim that some human beings, *viz. some* human beings who have an experience of God, have sufficient grounds to hold the belief that God exists and some other human being(s) can have sufficient grounds to hold the belief that God exists.

An argument: an argument which consists of four premises and a conclusion

Let us consider the following argument (A49) :

some human beings have an experience of God ;

some human beings who have an experience of God have sufficient grounds to hold the belief that they *are* aware of God and accordingly the belief that God exists ;

some other human being has sufficient grounds to hold the belief that God exists in case he has sufficient grounds to hold the belief that such a human being has sufficient grounds to hold the belief that God exists ;

it can be that some other human being has sufficient grounds to hold the belief that such a human being has sufficient grounds to hold the belief that God exists ;

so, some human beings, *viz. some* human beings who have an experience of God, have sufficient grounds to hold the belief that God exists and some other human being(s) can have sufficient grounds to hold the belief that God exists.

The conclusion follows from the first premise and the second premise and the third premise and the fourth premise. The first premise is true. The second premise is plausible. The third premise is true. The fourth premise is plausible. So, the conclusion is plausible. It is plausible some human beings, *viz. some* human beings who have an experience of God, have sufficient grounds to hold the belief that God exists and other human being(s) can have sufficient grounds to hold the belief that God exists.

The first premise: some remarks

Let us consider a particular kind of experience of human beings. A human being experiences a thing which is just like something and in doing so he experiences (that) something *or* he does not experience (that) something. Here is an example: a human being hears a sound which is just like a ringing bell (or a ringing bell-like sound) and in doing so he hears a ringing bell *or* he does not hear a ringing bell.

A human being does not experience (that) something (in this particular kind of experience) unless his experience is in some (particular) way brought about by it. Here is an example: a human being does not hear a ringing bell unless his experience of hearing a sound which is just like a ringing bell is in some (particular) way brought about by a ringing bell.[33]

Human beings' religious experiences of God are experiences of this kind. A human being is aware of a relation which is just like a relation to God (or a relation to God-like relation)[34] and in doing so he is aware of a relation with God *or* he is not aware of a relation with God. (Here are some features of some of these experiences: he is aware *independently of his ordinary senses* of it; he is aware *immediately* of it; and, he is aware *only* of it.)

What is at issue is one of the following relations to God: being in some way in the presence of God as this or that; being in union with God. Here is an example: a human being being aware of hearing God and God as the only God. (This is not to say that he is aware of a relation to God.) He is not aware of a relation with God unless his experience of being aware of a relation which is just like a relation to God is in some (particular) way brought about by God.

Is such an experience of a human being sufficient grounds for him to hold the belief that he *is* aware of a relation to God (and accordingly the belief that God exists)? Well, let us make some further remarks prior to a consideration of this question.

Our initial example refers to a sound which is just like a ringing bell. It is taken in this example that there are sufficient grounds for us to hold the belief that the sound of ringing bell is just like ________. How is it that there are sufficient grounds for us to hold the belief that the sound of ringing bell is just like ________? Well, this is so because there are sufficient grounds for us to hold the belief that some experiences of ours *are* an experience of a ringing bell and it is ________ .

The consideration of human beings' religious experience of God refers to a relation which is just like a relation to *God*. It is taken in this consideration that there are sufficient grounds for us to hold the belief that a relation to God is just like ________ . How is it that there are sufficient grounds for us to hold the belief that a relation to God is just like ________? Well, it is so by way of a consideration of in particular the nature of God.[35] (It is not taken that this is so because there are sufficient grounds for us to hold the belief that some experiences of ours *are* an experience of God and they are ________ . It is *not* accordingly taken in these remarks that the second premise is true. Incidentally, some human beings claim that they have an experience of God *and* that experience is such that there is not in fact an awareness of a relation which is just like a relation to God. These experiences of human beings are *not* at issue.)

This experience is for example an experience of a relation to a thing which has *or* more or less has the following :

(i) a property *or* properties which is *or* are identified in the course of the consideration of God's nature in the first chapter and in the chapters which follow

or

(ii) a property *or* properties which is *or* are suitable given this consideration

or

(iii) (i) and (ii).

Here is an example of a property which is *more or less* a property which is identified in the course of this consideration: being everlasting. Here is an example of a property which is *suitable* given this consideration: being a "father".

The consideration of human beings' religious experience of God refers to a human being who experiences a relation which is just like a relation to God. What is at issue is a human being who experiences a relation which is just like a relation to God and who at least *recognises* it. (He recognises some property *or* properties of his experience and it is *or* they are such that it is *or* they are sufficient to identify it as a relation which is just like a relation to God.)

But, he does not recognise it unless he is *able* to do so. He is able to do so for example by way of means which he acquires in one of the great monotheistic religions of the Middle East. (The great monotheistic religions of the Middle East include references to God. They include references which are accurate and references which are more or less accurate and references which are suitable. Here is an example of a reference which is accurate: a reference to God as the *only* God. Here is an example of a reference which is more or less accurate: a reference to God as "everlasting". Here is an example of a reference which is suitable: a reference to God as "father".) Incidentally, this is *not* to say that he is able to recognise every property of his experience; and, it is *not* to say that each and every belief which he acquires about God as a result of his experience is true.

Finally, there are sufficient grounds for the following beliefs: that such an experience of a human being is not a common experience of human beings; that the procedures which we are able to use to determine whether there is a *sensible* something in some place and at some time in case someone experiences a thing which is just like (that) something in that place and at that time are not procedures which we are able to use to determine whether God exists at that time in case someone experiences a relation to God-like relation at that time; and, that such an experience of a human being who undertakes ________ is not such that any other human being would have it in case he were to undertake ________. (A human being's experience of being aware of being in some way in the presence of God as this or that-like relation after he thinks only about God in isolation for a few days for example is not such that any other human being would have just such an experience in case he were to think only about God in isolation for a few days.)

The second premise

Let us suppose that a human being has an experience of this particular kind. There are not sufficient grounds for him to hold the belief that he experiences (that) something *and* he has sufficient grounds to hold the belief that he does not experience (that) something *and* he holds the belief that he does not experience that something in case

1. He holds some other belief(s) that ________ (_) as a result of 2 and 3

and

2. He is aware of any sufficient grounds for someone to hold this other belief *or* these other beliefs and he understands these grounds

and

3. There are sufficient grounds for someone to hold this other belief *or* these other beliefs

and

4. These grounds are such that there are not sufficient grounds for him (or anyone) to hold the belief that he experiences (that) something

and

5. He understands additionally that this is so and accordingly he does not hold the belief that he experiences (that) something.

2 and 1 are the result of 3.

Here is an example. Let us suppose that a human being hears a sound which is just like a ringing bell in some place and at some time. There are not sufficient grounds for him to hold the belief that he hears a ringing bell in that place and at that time and he does not hold this belief in case

3* There are sufficient grounds for someone to hold the belief that he is injected with a drug which brings it about that he hears sounds which are just like a ringing bell although there is no ringing bell.

(2* and 1* are a result of 3* :

2* He is aware of the grounds referred to in 3* and he understands these grounds

1* He holds as a result the belief that he is injected with a drug which brings it about that he hears sounds which are just like a ringing bell although there is no ringing bell.)

and

4* These grounds are such that there are not sufficient grounds for him (or anyone) to hold the belief that he hears a ringing bell in that place and at that time

and

5* He understands additionally that this is so and accordingly he does not hold the belief that he hears a ringing bell.

It is taken that there are sufficient grounds for him to hold the belief that he experiences (that) something in case it is untrue that 3.[36] Why is this taken to be so? Well, this is taken to be so for it is taken that a human being's *powers* are such that there are sufficient grounds for him to hold the belief that he experiences (that) something in case it is untrue that 3.

It is taken that this is so by anyone other than an extreme sceptic. Let us take it that the extreme sceptic is mistaken in this matter. So, there are sufficient grounds for him to hold the belief that he experiences something in case it is untrue that 3. (These grounds are *not* infallible.) Otherwise, there are not sufficient grounds for him to do so.

Is a human being's religious experience of God sufficient grounds for him to hold the belief that he is aware of a relation with God and accordingly the belief that God exists? [37, 38] Well, there are not sufficient grounds for him to do so in case

3 a there are sufficient grounds for someone to hold these beliefs:

(i) that God cannot exist

and

(ii) that he (or anyone) does not have an experience of a relation to God unless God can exist.

(4 a: These grounds are such that there are not sufficient grounds for him (or anyone) to hold the belief that he is aware of a relation to God.[39])

But, are there sufficient grounds for the belief 3 a (i)? Well, sufficient grounds for the belief 3 a (i) are not readily forthcoming. (There is a consideration of the thing at issue in 3 a (i), *viz.* God, in the first chapter.)

There are not sufficient grounds for him to do so in case

3 b there are sufficient grounds for someone to hold these beliefs:

(i) it is untrue that it can be that God interacts with things in a physical universe (even) in case he exists and there is a physical universe

and

(ii) that he (or any human being) is a thing in a physical universe and he (or any human being) does not have an experience of a relation to God unless it is true that it can be that this is so.

But, are there sufficient grounds for the belief 3 b (i)? Well, sufficient grounds for the belief 3 b (i) are not readily forthcoming. (There is some consideration of whether a non-physical thing such as God can interact with physical things in the introduction to the first chapter.)

There are not sufficient grounds for him to do so in case

3 c there are sufficient grounds for someone to hold these beliefs :

(i) that it is untrue that it can be that a human being experiences a relation to God (even) in case he exists

and

(ii) that a human being who has an experience of a relation to God is not aware of a relation to God unless it can be that this is so.

But, are there sufficient grounds for the belief 3 c (i)? Well, sufficient grounds for the belief 3 c (i) are not readily forthcoming. (There is a consideration indirectly of whether it can be that a living thing which possesses the power to act freely and independently of God experiences a relation to him in case it can be that he exists and it can be that a living thing possesses the power to bring about in the very first instance other living things which possess the power to act freely in the second part of the second chapter.)

There are not sufficient grounds for him to do so in case

3 d there are sufficient grounds for someone to hold these beliefs :

(i) that it is untrue that God exists

and

(ii) that a human being who has an experience of God is not aware of a relation to God unless God exists.

But, are there sufficient grounds for the belief 3 d (i)? Well, sufficient grounds for the belief 3 d (i) are not readily forthcoming. (There is a consideration of the principal arguments for the claim that God does not exist in the third chapter.)

There are not sufficient grounds for him to do so in case

3 e there are sufficient grounds for someone to hold these beliefs:

(i) that such an experience of a human being is not a common experience of human beings

and

(ii) that there are not sufficient grounds for someone to hold the belief that he experiences something because he experiences a (that) something-like thing unless it is a common experience of human beings.

But, 3 e is untrue. 3 e is untrue because there are not sufficient grounds for someone to hold the belief 3 e (ii). (There are sometimes sufficient grounds for someone to hold the belief that he experiences something because he experiences a something-like thing although such an experience is not a common experience of human beings. There are sufficient grounds for example for Captain Scott to hold the belief that he sees the Antarctic ice cap because he experiences an Antarctic ice cap-like appearance although such an experience is not a common experience of human beings. This is so in case there are no other matters to consider.)

There are not sufficient grounds for him to do so in case

3 f there are sufficient grounds for someone to hold these beliefs :

(i) that the procedures which we are able to use to determine whether there is a sensible something in some place and at some time in case someone experiences a thing which is just like (that) something in that place and at that time are not procedures which we are able to use to determine whether God exists at a time in case someone experiences a relation to God-like relation at that time

and

(ii) that there are not sufficient grounds for someone to hold the belief that he experiences a relation to God in case he experiences a relation to God-like relation unless we are able to use these procedures.

But, 3 f is untrue. 3 f is untrue because there are not sufficient grounds for someone to hold the belief 3 f (ii).

There are not sufficient grounds for someone who has undertaken ________ to do so in case

3 g there are sufficient grounds for someone to hold these beliefs :

(i) that such an experience of a human being is not such that any other human being would have it in case he were to undertake ________

and

(ii) that there are not sufficient grounds for a human being who has undertaken ________ to hold the belief that he is aware of a relation to God because he is aware of a relation to God-like relation unless such an awareness is such that any other human being would have it in case he were to undertake ________.

But, are there sufficient grounds for someone to hold 3 g (ii)? Well, sufficient grounds for someone to hold the belief 3 g (ii) are not readily forthcoming. (It is taken that there are in contrast sufficient grounds for someone to hold the following belief : there are not sufficient grounds for a human being to hold the belief that he experiences some sensible thing in some place and at some time because he has an experience of a (that) something-like thing in that place and at that time *unless* any other human being would have such an experience in that place and at that time in case he were to undertake ________. Here is an example : there are not sufficient grounds for a human being to hold the belief that he experiences a ringing bell in some place and at some time because he has an experience of a ringing bell-like sound in that place and at that time unless any other human being would have an experience of a ringing bell-like sound in that place and at that time in case he were there at that time. This is so in case there are no other matters to consider. Why? Well, this is so because there are sufficient grounds for someone to hold the belief that any other human being would experience a ringing bell-like sound in that place and at that time in case he were in that place and at that time in case there is a ringing bell ringing in that place and at that time. This is so in case there are no other matters to consider.)

There are not sufficient grounds for someone to hold the belief 3 g (ii) unless there are sufficient grounds for someone to hold the belief that any other human being would have such an experience in case he were to undertake ________ in case God exists. There are not sufficient grounds for someone to hold this belief unless there are sufficient grounds for someone to hold the belief that such an experience would be *appropriate* for any other human being in case he were to undertake ________ in case God exists. But, sufficient grounds for this belief are not readily forthcoming. So, sufficient grounds for someone to hold the belief 3 g (ii) are not readily forthcoming.

Here is an example to illustrate that this is so. Let us suppose someone experiences being aware of being in some way in the presence of God as this or that-like relation after thinking solely about God in isolation for a few days. Is it the case that there are sufficient grounds for him to hold the following belief: that there are not sufficient grounds for him to hold the belief that he *is* aware of a relation to God because he is aware of this unless this is such that any other human being would be aware of it in case he were to think about God in isolation for a few days?

Well, there are not sufficient grounds for him to hold this belief unless there are sufficient grounds for someone to hold the belief that any other human being would be aware of this in case he were to think about God in isolation for a few days in case God exists. There are not sufficient grounds for him to hold this belief unless there are sufficient grounds for someone to hold the belief that this would be appropriate for any other human being in case he were to think about God in isolation for a few days in case God exists. But, sufficient grounds for this belief are not readily forthcoming. So, sufficient grounds for him to hold the belief that there are not sufficient grounds for him to hold the belief that he is aware of a relation to God because he is aware of this unless this is such that any other human being would be aware of it in case he were to think about God in isolation for a few days are not readily forthcoming.

There are not sufficient grounds for him to do so in case

3 h there are sufficient grounds for someone to hold these beliefs :

(i) that he is aware of a relation to God-like relation independently of his ordinary senses

and

(ii) that there are not sufficient grounds for someone to hold the belief that he experiences something because he experiences a (that) something-like thing unless it is by way of ordinary senses.

But, 3 h is untrue. 3 h is untrue because there are not sufficient grounds for someone to hold the belief 3 h (ii).

There are not sufficient grounds for him to do so in case

3 i there are sufficient grounds for someone to hold these beliefs :

(i) that there are particular neurone occurrences in the case of religious experiences of human beings of God

and

(ii) that religious experiences of human beings of God in that case are just because of these occurrences.

But, 3 i is untrue. 3 i is untrue because there are not sufficient grounds for someone to hold the belief 3 i (ii).

There are not sufficient grounds for him to do so in case

3 j there are sufficient grounds for someone to hold these beliefs :

(i) that he does not know *how* his experience is brought about by God

and

(ii) that there are not sufficient grounds for someone to hold the belief that he experiences something in case he experiences a (that) something-like thing unless he knows how his experience is brought about by it.

But, 3 j is untrue. 3 j is untrue because there are not sufficient grounds for someone to hold the belief 3 j (ii). (There are for example sufficient grounds for someone to hold the belief that he sees something because he experiences a (that) something-like appearance although he does not how his experience is brought about by it. Consider for example someone prior to the time when the physical sciences determined how someone's experience of seeing something is brought about it. This is so in case there are no other matters to consider.)

There are not sufficient grounds for him to do so in case

3 k there are sufficient grounds for someone to hold these beliefs :

(i) that his experience is just the result of his psychological state of being *or* just the result of his physical state of being

and

(ii) that he is not aware of a relation to God unless his experience is *not* just the result of his psychological state of being *or* just the result of his physical state of being.

Here is an instance of 3 k :

there are sufficient grounds for someone to hold these beliefs :

(i) that his experience is just the result of a conscious wish to experience God

and

(ii) that he is not aware of a relation to God unless this is not so.

Here is another instance of 3 k :

there are sufficient grounds for someone to hold these beliefs :

(i) that he has this experience just because of a drug which someone has injected into him

and

(ii) that he is not aware of a relation to God unless this is not so.

There are sufficient grounds for someone to hold the belief 3 k (ii). So, there are not sufficient grounds for him to do so in case there are sufficient grounds for someone to hold in short the belief 3 k (i).

There are not sufficient grounds for him to do so in case

3 l there are sufficient grounds for someone to hold these beliefs :

(i) that he is not in some radically altered and particular state *or* states – such as the state of being at peace – immediately following *or* shortly after such an experience

and

(ii) that any experience of a human being of God would be such that he is in some such radically altered and particular state *or* states.

There are sufficient grounds for someone to hold the belief 3 l (ii). So, there are not in short sufficient grounds for him to do so in case there are sufficient grounds for someone to hold the belief 3 l (i).

Some human beings have an experience of a relation to God and that experience is such that sufficient grounds are not readily forthcoming *or* there are not sufficient grounds for someone to hold the belief 3 k (i) *or* 3 l (i). Are there sufficient grounds for such a human being to hold the belief that he is aware of a relation to God and accordingly the belief that God exists?

Well, there are sufficient grounds for him to hold the belief that he is aware of something which is greater in value than anything else and which is transcendent of ordinary experience and which is such that the ultimate end or purpose of a human being's life is related to it *or* him in case there are sufficient grounds for him to hold the belief that that he is aware of a relation to God and accordingly the belief that God exists.

But, there are not sufficient grounds for such a human being to hold the belief that he is aware of a relation to God and accordingly the belief that God exists in case there are not sufficient grounds for him to hold the belief that he is aware of something which is greater in value than anything else and which is transcendent of ordinary experience and which is such that the ultimate end or purpose of a human being's life is related to it *or* him.

Are there sufficient grounds for him to hold the belief that he is aware of something which is greater in value than anything else and which is transcendent of ordinary experience and which is such that the ultimate end or purpose of a human being's life is related to it *or* him even though (in Hinduism and Buddhism) there are other human beings who have an experience of a thing which is just like Brahman *or* nirvāṇa *and* they hold the belief that it is greater in value than anything else and it is transcendent of ordinary experience and it is such that the ultimate end or purpose of a human being's life is related to it *and* it is not sufficiently like God *and* they do not recognise it as God?

Each of these other human beings has an experience of a thing which is just like Brahman *or* nirvāṇa. He has an experience of a thing which has particular properties which are such that that thing is just like Brahman *or* nirvāṇa. He recognises it as Brahman *or* nirvāṇa.

But, he does not have sufficient grounds to hold the belief that he experiences Brahman *or* nirvāṇa in case there are sufficient grounds for someone to hold (with the substitution of "Brahman" *or* "nirvāṇa" for "God") 3 k (i) *or* 3 l (i). Each of these other human beings in question is a human being who has an experience of a thing which is just like Brahman *or* nirvāṇa and that experience is such that sufficient grounds are not readily forthcoming *or* there are not sufficient grounds for someone to hold (with the substitution of "Brahman" *or* "nirvāṇa" for "God") 3 k (i) *or* 3 l (i).

Let us consider again a human being who has an experience of a relation to God and that experience is such that sufficient grounds are not readily forthcoming *or* that there are not sufficient grounds for someone to hold the belief 3 k (i) *or* 3 l (i).

He does not have sufficient grounds to hold the belief that he is aware of a relation to God in case

3 m there are sufficient grounds for someone to hold these beliefs :

(i) that there are other such human beings who have an experience of a thing which is just like Brahman *or* nirvāṇa *and* they hold the belief that it is greater in value than anything else and it is transcendent of ordinary experience and it is such that the ultimate end or purpose of a human being's life is related to it *and* it is not sufficiently like God *and* they do not recognise it as God

and

(ii) that there are not sufficient grounds for him to hold the belief that he is aware of God unless this is *not* so.

But, there are not sufficient grounds for someone to hold the belief 3 m (ii) *in case* there are *not* sufficient grounds for someone to hold the following belief :

that it cannot be that God is experienced by a human being in line with the experience of such human beings, *viz.* those human beings referred to in 3 m (i), in case he exists.

Are there sufficient grounds for someone to hold this belief? Well, let us consider for example a human being who experiences a thing which is just like Brahman. What are the properties of Brahman? Well, the Upaniṣads are the final part of Hindu sacred scripture, *viz.* the Veda. (Some Upaniṣads are non-theistic and some Upaniṣads are theistic.[40] Upaniṣads which are non-theistic are at issue in what follows.) The Upaniṣads include references which are about Brahman. These references are appropriate.[41]

Brahman is in particular something with the properties of being eternal and being imperceptible and being impersonal and being such that it possesses power and being such that it brings about the physical universe and being such that it maintains the regularity of the physical universe and being such that an experience of it by a human being brings about peace and joy. These properties are not such that it is sufficiently like God.

But, there are not sufficient grounds *or* at least sufficient grounds are not readily forthcoming for someone to hold the belief that it cannot be that God is experienced by a human being in line with the experience of such human beings, *viz.* those human beings referred to in 3 m (i), in case he exists. (There are not sufficient grounds *or* at least sufficient grounds are not readily forthcoming for someone to hold the belief that it cannot be that an experience of God by a human being is just in terms of his being something which has the properties - or which has some of the properties - of being eternal and being imperceptible and being such that it possesses power and being such that it brings about the physical universe and being such that it maintains the regularity of the physical universe and being such that an experience of this something by a human being brings about peace and joy and accordingly of something which is impersonal in case he exists.)

What about nirvāṇa? Well, let us consider for example a human being who experiences a thing which has particular properties which are such that that thing is just like nirvāṇa. What is nirvāṇa ? What are the properties of nirvāṇa?

Well, the principal early Buddhist sources such as the Pali Canon include references which are about nirvāṇa. These references are appropriate. (There is nirvāṇa with "substrate" and nirvāṇa without "substrate". Nirvāṇa with "substrate" is a human being who realises a particular state of being and he has psycho-physical constituents. Nirvāṇa without "substrate" is this state of being without psycho-physical constituents after the death of a human being. It is nirvāṇa with "substrate" which is at issue in what follows.)

Nirvāṇa is a human being's realisation of a particular state of being. It is the realisation of a state of being which is such that the "basic impurities" of a human being[42] – *viz.* a desire for the sensual and a desire for continued existence or "manifestation" and ignorance of the nature of reality - have been (gradually) eliminated[43] and accordingly being among other things without "attachment" to things and being in a state of peace. The properties of this thing are not such that it is sufficiently like God.

But, there are not sufficient grounds *or* at least sufficient grounds are not readily forthcoming for someone to hold the belief that it cannot be that God is experienced by a human being as he is experienced by such human beings, *viz.* those human beings referred to in 3 m (i), in case he exists. (There are not sufficient grounds *or* at least sufficient grounds are not readily forthcoming for someone to hold the belief that it cannot be that an experience of God by a human being is just in terms of that human being realising a state of being which is such that the "basic impurities" of a human being have been gradually eliminated and being without "attachment" to things and being in a state of peace in case God exists.) There are not in that case sufficient grounds for someone to hold the belief 3 m (ii). So, there are not sufficient grounds for someone to hold that 3 m.

Let us recall the second premise: some human beings who have an experience of God have sufficient grounds to hold the belief that they *are* aware of God and accordingly the belief that God exists. (The experience is the experience which is identified in the course of the remarks on the first premise.) It is plausible that the second premise is true. Why? Well, there are some human beings who have an experience of God and that experience is such that sufficient grounds are not readily forthcoming *or* there are not sufficient grounds for someone to hold the belief 3 k (i) *or* 3 l (i). It is plausible that these human beings have sufficient grounds to hold the belief that they *are* aware of a relation to God and accordingly the belief that God exists. (It is plausible that a human being who has an experience of God and who is aware that his experience is such that sufficient grounds are not readily forthcoming *or* there are not sufficient grounds to hold the belief 3 k (i) *or* 3 l (i) has sufficient grounds to hold the belief that he is aware of a relation to God and accordingly the belief that God exists.)

The third and fourth premises

Here is the third premise: some other human being has sufficient grounds to hold the belief that God exists in case he has sufficient grounds to hold the belief that such a human being has sufficient grounds to hold the belief that God exists.

The third premise is an instance of a general principle in relation to someone who has an experience of a thing which is just like something (which is mind independent) and who has sufficient grounds to hold the belief that he *is* aware of (that) something and accordingly that belief that that something exists. Here is the principle: some other human being has sufficient grounds to hold the belief that that something exists in case he has sufficient grounds to hold the belief that such a human being has sufficient grounds to hold the belief that that something exists.

Here is an example to illustrate that this is so. Let us consider someone who has an experience of a sound which is just like a bell ringing in some place and at some time and who has sufficient grounds to hold the belief that he is aware of a bell ringing in that place and at that time and accordingly the belief that there is a bell ringing at that place and at that time. Some other human being (who is not there at that time) has sufficient grounds to hold the belief that there is a bell ringing at that place and at that time in case he has sufficient grounds to hold the belief that such a human being has sufficient grounds to hold that belief. The third premise is true.

Here is the fourth premise: it can be that some *other* human being has sufficient grounds to hold the belief that such a human being has sufficient grounds to hold the belief that God exists. (It is plausible that he has sufficient grounds to hold this belief in case he has sufficient grounds to hold the belief that such a human being has had such an experience *and* the belief that sufficient grounds are not readily forthcoming *or* there are not sufficient grounds for someone to hold the belief 3 k (i) *or* 3 l (i).) The fourth premise is plausible.

Some remarks following the consideration of this argument

Following the consideration of this argument, it is plausible that some human beings who have an experience of God have sufficient grounds to hold the belief that God exists and some other human being(s) can have sufficient grounds to hold the belief that God exists. (The experience is the experience which is identified in the course of the remarks on the first premise.)

Notes

1. M. Charlesworth, *St. Anselm's Proslogion* (Oxford, 1965).

Incidentally, Anselm's *Proslogion* was written in 1077 - 1078.

2. Here is an objection to this re-statement in the first instance of Anselm's statement: the appropriate re-statement of Anselm's statement is instead that it cannot be that a living thing thinks about a thing which is greater than that thing.

See the two paragraphs which follow the paragraph which includes this re-statement for a reply to this objection.

See in particular the third note for a reply to this objection.

3. Here is an objection to this re-statement in the third instance of Anselm's statement: the appropriate re-statement of Anselm's statement is instead that it cannot be that a living thing thinks about a thing which is greater than that thing and that thing can exist and that thing is good. Let us consider the following argument in order to address this objection:

it *can* be that a living thing thinks about *anything* which *can* exist;

it cannot be that a living thing thinks about a thing which is greater than that thing *and* that thing can exist *and* that thing is good;

so, it cannot be that there is a thing which is greater than it and that thing can exist and that thing is good.

The conclusion follows from the first premise and the second premise. The first premise is presumably true. The second premise is the re-statement in the objection. So, the conclusion – the conclusion is in other words the re-statement in the third instance of Anselm's statement - follows in any event.

Incidentally, Anselm states in the fifteenth chapter that that thing, *viz.* God, is greater than can be conceived. God is presumably greater than can be conceived by living things *other than* God.

With this in mind, here is an objection *to* the objection: the appropriate re-statement of Anselm's statement is instead that it cannot be that a living thing *other than* that thing, *viz.* God, thinks about a thing which is greater than *or* equal to that thing and that thing can exist and that thing is good.

Let us consider the following argument :

it can be that a living thing other than that thing, *viz.* God, thinks about anything other than that thing, *viz.* God, which can exist ;

it cannot be that a living thing other than that thing, *viz.* God, thinks about a thing which is greater than *or* equal to that thing and that thing can exist and that thing is good ;

so, it cannot be that there is a thing which is greater than *or* equal to it and that thing can exist and that thing is good.

The conclusion follows from the first premise and the second premise. The first premise is presumably true. The second premise is the re-statement in the objection to the objection. The conclusion follows and the re-statement in the third instance of Anselm's statement follows from the conclusion. So, the re-statement in the third instance of Anselm's statement follows in any event.

4. The re-statement in the third instance of Anselm's statement is the following: there is a thing, *viz.* God, which can exist (in reality) and which is good and which is such that it cannot be that there is a thing which is greater than it.

But, Anselm states the following in the fifteenth chapter: that thing, *viz.* God, is [a thing which is] *greater* than [a thing which] can be conceived. There is in that case a thing, *viz.* God, which can exist (in reality) and which is good and which is such that it cannot be that there is a thing which is greater than it *and* it is greater than a thing which can exist. That's absurd!

Let us take it that there is no such absurdity in the *Proslogion.* Here is an appropriate re-statement of this statement in the fifteenth chapter in order to avoid such an absurdity: that thing, *viz.* God, (is a thing which can exist and which is good and which) is such that it cannot be that a living thing other than it wholly understands its greatness.

5. In the fourth chapter, Anselm states that *that* thing is a thing than which no greater can be conceived.

6. The Fool of *Psalms* 14 and 53.

7. Here is this premise once more: that thing, *viz.* God, is greater in case it exists in reality and in the understanding than in case it exists only in the understanding.

It is just that God is greater in the first case than he is in the second case for Anselm. It is *not* that "existence in reality" is a predicate. Immanuel Kant (1724 - 1804) is incorrect in his claim that "existence in reality" is a predicate in Anselm's argument. Norman Kemp Smith, *Immanuel Kant's Critique of Pure Reason* (London 1929), p.505.

8. See the Introduction.

9. Strictly speaking, states of affairs do not have a value.

But, there is a thing which can exist and which is good and which is at issue in both cases, *viz.* God.

It is the same in value in both cases.

So, it is not greater in the first case than in the second case.

*

10. For example, *Dialogues concerning Natural Religion*, N. Kemp Smith (ed.), (Edinburgh,1947), p.143.

11. They have been brought about as well by the "thought" and "wisdom" of human beings. *Ibid.*, p.143.

12. *Ibid.*, p.143.

13. For example, *Enquiry concerning Human Understanding*, L.A. Selby-Bigge (ed.), 3rd edition (Oxford, 1975), p.135.

14. For example, *Dialogues concerning Natural Religion*, p.146.

15. For example, *ibid.*, p.144.

This is the criticism which he makes in more places than any other criticism of this argument.

16. For example, *ibid.*, p.149 and p.150.

17. For example, *Enquiry concerning Human Understanding*, Selby-Bigge (ed.), p.135.

18. *Dialogues concerning Natural Religion*, pp.193-213.

19. *Ibid.*, p.167.

20. *Ibid.*, pp.160-164.

21. This is the *prior* probability of the hypothesis.

22. This probability is the *posterior* probability of the hypothesis.

23. Here are some remarks with the introduction in mind :

these design arguments are *not* arguments by analogy ;

each of these design arguments provides sufficient *or* plausible grounds for the claim that it is likelier that God is the ultimate *cause* of what is observed than that a uniform chance process *or* a process which includes a uniform chance process is the ultimate cause of it in the absence of our "experience of the origins of worlds" ;

it is *God* who is at issue in each of these arguments ;

what is at is issue – in line with the discussion of God's nature in the first chapter - is not itself in need of explanation.

*

24. The Second Way, *Summa Theologiae,* 1, 2, and 3.

25. The argument begs the issue in case it simply assumes that this is not so.

26. It is referred to by the Arabic word كلام or *kalām*. It means "word" or "discourse": the rational discourse of early Islamic theologians.

See, for example, William Lane Craig, *The Kalām Cosmological Argument* (London, 1979).

27. Incidentally, here is a statement of an argument which does *not* establish that the second premise is *not* readily acceptable. It is in two stages. Here is the first stage **:**

the conclusion of this cosmological argument is true in case its first premise and its second premise are true ;

its first premise is true ;

the conclusion in that case is true in case its second premise is true. (This initial conclusion follows from the first premise and the second premise.) ;

the conclusion is not readily acceptable. (This is an additional premise.) ;

so, the second premise is not readily acceptable.

The ultimate conclusion follows from the initial conclusion and the additional premise. Is the initial conclusion true? Well, the initial conclusion follows from the first premise and the second premise. The first premise is true. The second premise is true in case the current scientific view about the origins of the physical universe is true. So, the initial conclusion is true in case the current scientific view about the physical universe is true.

The ultimate conclusion follows from the initial conclusion and the additional premise. The initial conclusion is true in case the current scientific view about the physical universe is true. Is the additional premise true? Well, here is the second stage of this argument: it is a statement of the argument for the additional premise. Its initial premises are as follows :

any claim which is contrary to our experience of each thing of a particular kind is not *readily* acceptable ;

our experience of each thing which is of a physical kind and which begins to exist is that it is brought about from some other pre-existing physical thing ;

at least some thing(s) which is of a physical kind and which begins to exist is not brought about from some other pre-existing physical thing in case the physical universe *itself* is brought about by something.

Let us suppose that the claim that the physical universe itself is brought about by something is true.

At least some thing(s) which is of a physical kind and which begins to exist in that case is not brought about from some other pre-existing physical thing. (This initial conclusion follows from the third premise and the supposition.)

This is contrary to our experience of each thing which is of a physical kind and which begins to exist. (This further conclusion follows from the second premise and the initial conclusion.)

So, the claim of the supposition is not readily acceptable.

The ultimate conclusion follows ultimately from the first premise and the second premise and the third premise and the supposition. The first premise is true and the third premise is true. The second premise is untrue in case "our experience" includes our experience of the physical universe and the current (generally accepted) theory about it for in that case the following is true: the particles which are physical and which exist at the beginning of the physical universe are not themselves brought about from some other pre-existing physical thing. Grounds for the claim that it should not do so are not readily forthcoming. Let us take it in that case that the second premise is untrue. So, this stage does not establish that its ultimate conclusion is true. It does not establish that the claim that the physical universe itself is brought about by something is true is not readily acceptable. (It does not establish that the additional premise is true.) So, the ultimate conclusion of the first stage is not established.

28. *The Leibniz-Clarke Correspondence,* H. G. Alexander (ed.), (Manchester, 1956).

29. A nature or essence of things of a particular kind is a property which a particular thing has to have in order to be a thing of that kind.

Here is an example of such a nature of essence: *being alive.* It is the nature or essence of things of the following kind: *living thing.* A thing has to have this property in order to be a thing of that kind.

30. In any case, let us suppose, for the sake of argument, that an individual thing exists because of it itself in that it exists because of its nature's or essence's instantiation - its existence is in that way explained by it itself. The explanation of the existence of that individual thing, *viz.* its nature or essence, is *its* nature's or essence's instantiation. Its nature or essence is *being that nature or essence.* The explanation of *its* existence is *its* nature or essence's instantiation...... This is a *vicious* infinite regress.

31. The argument for the fourth premise proceeds in this way whether the series of such facts which it refers to is finite *or* infinite. How is an *infinite* series of such facts due to the individual thing which it refers to in its conclusion?

Incidentally, the series of such facts which it refers to is identified with the physical universe. Few theists in that case would maintain that that series is infinite. The (Hebrew) Bible and the Qur'an in that case suggest that it is finite – it has a beginning.

32. This cosmological argument does not use a restricted Principle of Sufficient Reason and it does not use an un-restricted Principle of Sufficient Reason.

*

33. Here is *another* kind of experience of human beings: a human being experiences a thing which is just like something and in doing so he experiences (that) something.

Here is an example: a human being experiences a feeling which is just like a pain (or a pain-like feeling) and in doing so he experiences a pain.

34. He believes that this is so at the time of the experience *or* after it *or* at that time and after it.

35. It need hardly be added that this is *not* to say that a consideration of the nature of God such as the consideration in the first chapter identifies the whole of the nature of God.

36. This claim is along the lines of a claim made by (among others) Richard Swinburne. Richard Swinburne, *The Existence of God* (Oxford, 1979), p.254.

37. Here is an argument for the claim that a human being who experiences a relation which is just like a relation to God does not have sufficient grounds to hold the belief that he experiences a relation to God :

a human being who experiences a thing which is just like some sensible thing has (in case there are no other matters to consider) sufficient grounds to hold the belief that he experiences that sensible thing for there are further and independent grounds to hold that belief. (These further and independent grounds are that human beings have acquired a means to control to some degree and to predict to some degree natural events on the basis of such experience.) ;

in the case of a human being who experiences a relation which is just like a relation to God, there are *no* further and independent grounds for him to hold the belief that he experiences a relation to God ;

so, a human being who experiences a relation which is just like a relation to God does not have sufficient grounds to hold the belief that he experiences a relation to God.

In relation to the first premise, here is an observation in passing: the claim that human beings have acquired a means to control to some degree and to predict to some degree natural events on the basis of sensory experience is itself established by way of sensory experience!

The second premise in any case is untrue. Some human beings who have an experience of a relation which is just like a relation to God are such that their states of being are radically altered and they have particular states of being such as the state of being at peace. These *are* further and independent grounds to hold the belief that he experiences God. (This matter is considered further in what follows.) So, this argument does not establish its conclusion. It does not establish that a human being who experiences a relation which is just like a relation to God does not have sufficient grounds to hold the belief that he experiences a relation to God.

38. Let us consider the following: it is not someone's experience that God exists at some time. Is this sufficient grounds for him to hold the belief that God does not exist at that time?

Well, let us consider some sensible physical thing. There are sufficient grounds for someone to hold the belief that it does not exist in some place and at some time in case it is not his experience that there is a thing which is just like it in that place and at that time. This is so because there are sufficient grounds for him to hold the belief that a human being would experience a thing which is just like it in that place and at that time (and it brings it about in some particular way) in case it were to exist in that place and at that time. This is so in case there are no other matters to consider.

The fact it is not someone's experience that God exists at some time is not sufficient grounds for him to hold the belief that God does not exist at that time unless there are sufficient grounds for him to hold the belief that he would experience a thing which is just like God at that time (and God brings it about in some particular way) in case God were to exist at that time.

Are there sufficient grounds to hold this belief? Well, there are not sufficient grounds for him to hold this belief in case he possesses the power to act freely and independently of God at that time. (This is because he would *not* possess the power to act freely and independently of God at that time in case he were to have an experience a thing which is just like God at that time and God brings it about in some particular way.) So, the fact it is not someone's experience that God exists at some time is not sufficient grounds in this case for him to hold the belief that God does not exist at that time.

More generally, it is not the case that he would experience a thing which is just like God at that time (and God brings it about in some particular way) in case God were to exist at that time unless it would be *appropriate* to do so.

39. Here is 5a :

5a He understands additionally that this is so and accordingly he does not hold the belief that he experiences a relation to God in these circumstances.

2 a and 1a are a result of 3 a :

2a He is aware of any sufficient grounds for someone to hold these beliefs (*viz.* 3 a (i) and 3 a (ii)) and he understands these grounds.

1a He holds as a result the belief that God cannot exist and the belief that he (or anyone) does not have an experience of a relation to God unless God can exist.

40. The Chāndogya Upaniṣad is an example of a non-theistic Upaniṣad. The Īśa Upaniṣad is an example of a theistic Upaniṣad.

41. The Ṛg Veda is an initial part of the Veda. The Ṛg Veda also refers to Brahman. In the Ṛg Veda, Brahman principally refers to the things which are uttered in (sacred) rituals by priests and which are such that they have a sacred power.

Brahman also refers to the Veda itself for it is such that it has a sacred power.

42. Sanskrit: *āśrava* or "defilements".

43. The word "nirvāṇa" includes a Sanskrit root which is *vā or vṛ*. *Vṛ* means "to cover": to cover a flame and to deprive it gradually of fuel and to extinguish it. For the early Buddhist sources, it is this root which is included in the word "nirvāṇa". Hence, the word "gradually" is used in this sentence.

Main Conclusions

First chapter

Traditionally, God is good and God is better (or greater) than any other thing ; God is (in that case) all-knowing and all-powerful. Is God all-knowing and all-powerful? Well, God is in time. (The claim that God is not in time is considered in the course of the first chapter.) God cannot be all-knowing at some time in case it can be that he exists and it can be that a living thing possesses the power to bring about (in the very first instance) other living things which possess the power to do this or that freely. God cannot be all-powerful at some time in case it can be that he exists and it can be that a living thing possesses the power to bring about (in the very first instance) other living things which possess the power to do this or that freely.

Theists maintain that it can be that God exists. Most theists maintain that it can be that a living thing, *viz.* God himself, possesses the power to bring about (in the very first instance) other living things which possess the power to do this or that freely.

Ought a theist who maintains that it can be that a thing possesses this power to be concerned that God cannot be all-powerful at some time and he cannot be all-knowing at some time in case it can be that this is so? Well, he ought not to be concerned that this is so for this is in accord with God being worthy of worship.

In the Judaeo-Christian tradition, there is a significant tradition which claims that God is simple and he is immutable. God cannot be simple in case it can be that he exists and it can be that a living thing possesses the power to bring about (in the very first instance) other living things which possess the power to do this or that freely. God cannot be immutable in case it can be that that is so.

Ought a theist who maintains that it can be that a thing possesses this power to be concerned that God cannot be simple and he cannot be immutable in case it can be that that is so? Well, he ought not to be concerned that this is so for this is in accord with God being worthy of worship.

Incidentally, can it be that God exists? Well, there are no grounds which are identified in the course of this work for the claim that it is untrue that it can be that God exists. Still, it does not follow that it can be that God exists.

Can it be that a living thing possesses the power to bring about (in the very first instance) other living things which possess the power to do this or that freely? (It cannot be that a living thing possesses the power to do this or that *freely* unless it is not brought to exercise it by something else and unless it possesses the power to not do that this or that.) Well, this is a question which is not considered in this work for it is beyond its scope. Still, see one of the main conclusions of the fourth chapter (as a result of the consideration of some design arguments) below.

Finally, it cannot be that God has always known a living thing, X, exercises a power to do this or that freely at a particular time in case it can be that it, X, exercises it freely at that time. Theists in the main strongly maintain that human beings are free. They maintain, for example, the following: there is a Day of Judgement – God on this Day judges what a human being has done during his life on earth and God rewards *or* punishes him accordingly; God does not possess the power to do so unless a human being possesses the power to act freely during his time on earth; a human being in that case possesses the power to act freely during his time on earth. They maintain that there are passages in the Bible and the Qur'an which state that this is so: *eg*, Deuteronomy 30:19; Qur'an 2:158.

Given this, these theists should maintain that it cannot be that God has always known this or that human being exercises a power to do this or that freely at a particular time. God knows what a human being does freely at a particular time when he does it.

Second chapter

It cannot be that God (does not possess at any time and) does not exercise the power to bring about (in the very first instance) some other living things which possess the power to act freely and independently of him and which possess the power to lead in that way a life and which possess powers such as the power to know in that way about what is the case and its value and its relations to what else is the case and the power to reason in that way at a time in case it can be that he exists and it can be that a living thing possesses the power to bring about (in the very first instance) other living things which possess the power to act freely.

It cannot be that some other living thing possesses the power to act freely and *independently* of God unless it is *not* immediately aware of God. So, it cannot be that such a living thing is immediately aware of God. (A living thing which is *not* immediately aware of God is at least in this way *separated* from him.) It is plausible that it cannot be that these other living things are not liable to experience any evil due to the conditions which prevail in a whole or universe which includes them.

Let us suppose that it cannot be that these other living things are not liable to experience any evil due to the conditions which prevail in a whole which includes them. It cannot be that these other such living things (in the very first instance) do not possess powers such as the power to be considerate of other such living things and their powers and their lives. It cannot be that they are not such that they hold the belief that it is better that a state of affairs which they know is (morally) good obtains rather than it does not obtain and they possess as a result the desire (to some degree) to bring it about.

There is a whole state of affairs which is good: there are living things other than God *and* they possess the power to lead lives *and* they possess other powers such as the power to know about what is the case and its value and its relations to what else is the case and the power to *not* do so and the power to reason and the power to *not* do so *and* they are not immediately aware of God (and they are liable to experience evil due to their conditions) *and* they possess powers such as the power to be considerate of other such living things and their lives and their powers and the power to *not* be so *and* they are such that they hold the belief that it is better that a state of affairs which they know is (morally) good obtains rather than it does not obtain and they possess as a result the desire (to some degree) to bring it about. It is a state of affairs of other livings things (which are not debased and) which possess the power to lead (rationally) lives (which are morally significant and) which are free and independent of God.

It includes an evil state of affairs, *viz.* that living things possess powers such as the power to *not* know about what is the case and its value and its relations to what else is the case and the power to *not* reason *and* they are *not* immediately aware of God (and they are liable to experience evil due to their conditions) *and* they possess powers such as the power to *not* be considerate of other such living things and their powers and their lives. This evil state of affairs is *overridden* in the whole good state of affairs.

Third chapter

The principal arguments for the claim that God does not exist refer to the evil which exists. They refer in particular to the evil which exists and which is related to human beings. These arguments do not establish that this claim is true *or* do not provide sufficient grounds for this claim in case it can be that God exists and it can be that a living thing possesses the power to bring about (in the very first instance) other living things which possess the power to act freely.

Fourth chapter

Anselm considers the existence of God in his *Proslogion*. The second chapter of his *Proslogion* includes an ontological argument for the claim that God exists in reality. It does not establish that God exists in reality.

The third chapter of his *Proslogion* includes an ontological argument for the claim that it is untrue that it can be that God does not exist in reality. This argument also does not establish that it is untrue that it can be that God does not exist in reality.

There are some design arguments which refer to observations of the physical universe and human beings *and* which establish the following. (These design arguments refer to a principle of likelihood.):

someone's degree of belief in the hypothesis that it can be that God exists and it can be that a living thing possesses the power to bring about (in the very first instance) other living things which possess the power to act freely should increase and his degree of belief in the hypothesis that there is a uniform chance process in operation *or* there is a process which includes a uniform chance process in operation should decrease in case he has a degree of belief in each hypothesis.

There is a cosmological argument which establishes *some* grounds for the claim that the ultimate explanation of why some individual things of the physical kind have existed is God in case the following is the case:

(i) there is an explanation of why some individual things of the physical kind have existed

and

(ii) there is an explanation of why some non-physical individual thing(s) of the kind which are brought about by some other (non-physical) individual thing(s) have existed in case it *or* they is *or* are the explanation of why some individual things of the physical kind have existed.

Finally, it is plausible that *some* human beings who have an experience of God have sufficient grounds to hold the belief that God exists and some other human being(s) can have sufficient grounds to hold the belief that God exists.

Appendix 1

God's sovereignty

The Introduction refers to some of the fundamental kinds of things there are (and some of their features) according to this work. These things include abstract things. Abstract things include properties and states of affairs. (Properties include properties (or natures) such as the property of being triangular *or* the property of being alive.) States of affairs have a value.

It cannot be that abstract things do not exist. (It cannot be in that case that properties such as the property of being triangular *or* the property of being alive do not exist.) It cannot be that states of affairs do not have a value.

Indeed, it cannot be that there *are* abstract things due to God's will even in case it can be that he exists. (It cannot be in that case that there *are* properties (including properties such as the property being triangular *or* the property of being alive) and states of affairs due to God's will even in case it can be that he exists.) It cannot be that states of affairs *have* their value due to his will even in case it can be that he exists. It cannot be that these things are affected (intrinsically) due to his will even in case it can be that he exists.

It cannot be in that case that these things are in these ways not *independent of* God's will even in case it can be that he exists. But, it cannot be that God is sovereign over these things in these ways unless this is not so. So, it cannot be that God is sovereign over these things in these ways even in case it can be that he exists.

Let us consider another view of this matter. To begin with, it can be that there *are* properties (or natures) such as the property of being triangular *or* being alive due to God's will although there are no abstract things in case it can be that he exists.[1] How? Well, here is an argument (Ap1. A1) for this claim. Here are its initial premises :

it can be that God exists just in case he exists ;

it is untrue that it can be that there are abstract things in case it can be that God exists ;

it can be that God wills there are things such as *particular* triangular things *or particular* living things in case it can be that exists ;

it can be that there *are* properties (or natures) such as the property of being triangular *or* being alive in case it can be that God wills there are things such as particular triangular things *or* particular living things.

Let us suppose (God exists and in that case - from the first premise -) that it can be that God exists.

It is untrue in that case that it can be that there are abstract things. (This initial conclusion follows from the second premise and the supposition.)

Still, it can be in that case that God wills there are things such as *particular* triangular things *or particular* living things. (This further conclusion follows from the third premise and the supposition.)

So, it can be that there *are* properties (or natures) such as the property of being triangular *or* being alive due to God's will although there are no abstract things. (This ultimate conclusion follows from the fourth premise and the initial conclusion and the further conclusion.)

The ultimate conclusion follows ultimately from the initial premises and the supposition. The initial premises (for an advocate of this other view) are true. So, the ultimate conclusion is true in case the supposition is true. It can be that there *are* properties (or natures) such as the property of being triangular *or* being alive due to God's will although there are no abstract things in case it can be that he exists. *It is in this way that an advocate of this other view maintains that God is in this way sovereign over these things.*

(Incidentally, the fourth premise is *not* stated as follows: it can be that there are properties such as the property of being triangular *or* being alive *just in case* it can be that God wills there are things such as particular triangular things *or* particular living things. Why? Well, there is a conclusion, *viz. God exists*, in case it is stated in this way. Here is an argument (Ap1. A2) for the claim that there is this conclusion, *viz.* God exists, in case it is stated in this way. It is in two stages. Here is the first stage (Ap1. A2.1) :

it can be that there is the property of being triangular for there *is* this or that particular triangle ;

it can be that there are properties such as the property of being triangular *or* being alive *just in case* it can be that God wills there are things such as particular triangular things *or* particular living things ;

so, it can be that God wills there are particular triangular things.

The conclusion follows from the first premise and the second premise. The first premise is true. For our present purposes, the second premise is true for an advocate of Ap1. A1. (It is the fourth premise of Ap1. A1 re-stated.) So, the conclusion is true. It can be that God wills there are particular triangular things.

Here is the second stage (Ap1. A2.2) :

it can be that God wills there are particular triangular things ;

but, it is untrue that it can be that God wills there are particular triangular things unless it can be that he exists ;

it can be that God exists just in case he exists ;

so, God exists.

The conclusion follows from the first premise and the second premise and the third premise. The first premise – the first premise is the conclusion of the first stage – is true. The second premise is true. The third premise (for an advocate of Ap1. A1) is true. So, the conclusion is true. God exists. But, this conclusion is presumably unintended for an advocate of

Ap1. A1. So, the fourth premise of Ap1. A1 is not stated in this way.)

In passing, let us observe that it is untrue that it can be that God does not exist in case it can be that he exists for an advocate of this other view. Here is an argument (Ap1. A3) for this claim. Its initial premises are as follows :

it can be that God exists just in case God exists ;

(can it be that God is other than that?) it is untrue that it can be that God is other than that.

Let us suppose that it can be that God exists.

God in that case exists. (This initial conclusion follows from the first premise and the supposition.)

It is untrue that it can be that God is other than that. (This further conclusion follows from the second premise and the initial conclusion.)

So, it is untrue that it can be that God does not exist.

The ultimate conclusion follows ultimately from the first premise and the second premise and the supposition. The first premise (for an advocate of this other view as we have seen) is true. The second premise is true for an advocate of this other view. So, the conclusion (for an advocate of this other view) is true in case the supposition is true. It is untrue that it can be that God does not exist in case it can be that he exists. (This work concludes in the course of its first chapter that it is untrue that it can be that God does not exist in case it can be that he exists. But, its grounds for this conclusion are different: *eg*, its grounds do not include the first premise of Ap1. A3. Indeed, the first premise is untrue according to it.)

That done, let us suppose, for the sake of argument, that the initial premises and the supposition of Ap1. A1 are true. It can be in that case that God wills there are things such as particular triangular things and it can be that there are properties such as the property of being triangular. Can it be that, for example, triangles are other than that? Well, no. It cannot be (according to this other view) that triangles are other than that. (What can be in relation to this or that is what God wills alone.)

Finally, there is an argument for the claim that it can be that there are particular states of affairs (in terms of this other view *or* particular facts in terms of this work) and these particular states of affairs (or particular facts) have a (or their) value due to God's will although there are no abstract things in case it can be that he exists along the lines of Ap1. A1.[2] *It is in this way that an advocate of this other view maintains that God is in this way sovereign over these things.*

Is this other view correct? Well, let us take it, for the sake of argument, that the initial premises and the supposition of Ap1. A1 are true. Here, in that case, is an implication: a triangle, for example, is *whatever* God wills. (The abstract property of being triangular does not circumscribe God's will for there are no abstract things.)

Further, God cannot be sovereign in relation to, for example, how triangles are. Why? Well, it can be to begin with that God wills there are things such as particular triangular things and there are properties such as the property of being triangular. (Can it be that triangles are other than that? Well, no.) What *can* be the case (according to this other view) in relation to how triangles are is nothing other than that. (It is untrue that it can be that triangles are other than that. It is untrue that it can be that triangles are otherwise.) God cannot, in that case, possess the power to bring about triangles in some other way. God cannot do otherwise. But, God cannot be sovereign in relation to how triangles are unless he possesses the power to do otherwise. So, God cannot be sovereign in relation to how triangles are.

*

It cannot be that God does not instantiate properties such as the property of being worthy of worship and the property of being morally perfect. (It cannot be that God is otherwise.) It cannot be that God does not instantiate properties such as the property of being worthy of worship and the property of being morally perfect for it cannot be that he does not instantiate his *nature.*

The nature (or essence) of this or that is a property. (The nature of God includes being worthy of worship and being morally perfect.) The first chapter refers to God's nature.

It can be that there is an instance of that property – that nature (or essence) - in case it can be that God exists. (It cannot be that there is an instance of this or that property without that property.) But, it is untrue that it can be that properties do not exist. So, it is untrue that it can be that that property does not exist in case it can be that God exists.

It cannot be that there *are* properties (including that property) due to God's will even in case it can be that he exists. It cannot be in that case that that property is in this way not *independent of* his will even in case it can be that he exists. But, it cannot be that God is sovereign over his nature unless this is not so. So, it cannot be that God is sovereign over his nature even in case it can be that he exists.

Incidentally, it cannot be (as we have seen in the first chapter) that God does not exercise the power to bring about (in the very first instance) other living things which possess the power to do this or that freely at a time in case it can be that he exists and it can be that a living thing possesses the power to bring about (in the very first instance) other living things which possess the power to do this or that freely. It cannot be that God does not exercise the power to bring about other such living things in case it can be that that is so for this is in accord with God being worthy of worship. It cannot be that God possesses the power to do otherwise. But, it cannot be that God is sovereign in relation to the matter of whether there are other such living things in case it can be that that is so unless it can be that he possesses the power to do otherwise. So, it cannot be that God is sovereign in relation to the matter of whether there are other such living things in case it can be that that is so.

Let us consider another view of this matter. It is that it can be that God's nature *is* due to his will although abstract things do not exist in case it can be that he exists.[3] How? Well, here is an argument (Ap1. A4) for this claim. Here are its initial premises :

it can be that God exists just in case he exists ;

it is untrue that it can be that there are abstract things in case it can be that God exists ;

it can be that God wills (timelessly) there is a universe and sustains it and governs it in case it can be that he exists ;

it can be that God wills (timelessly) there is a universe and sustains it and governs it in a way that is among other things worthy of worship and morally perfect in case it can be that he exists ;

God *is* as he wills ;

(it can be that there are properties such as the property of being worthy of worship and the property of being morally perfect just in case God wills (timelessly) there is a universe and sustains it and governs it.)

Let us suppose (God exists and in that case - from the first premise -) that it can be that God exists.

It is untrue in that case that it can be that there are abstract things. (This initial conclusion follows from the second premise and the supposition.)

Still, it can be in that case that God wills (timelessly) there is a universe and sustains it and governs it and in a way that is among other things worthy of worship and morally perfect. (This further conclusion follows from the third premise and the fourth premise and the supposition.)

So, it can be that God *is* among other things worthy of worship and morally perfect and this is due to his will although there are no abstract things. (Indeed, it is untrue that it can be that there are these properties otherwise.) (This ultimate conclusion follows from the fifth premise (and the sixth premise) and the initial conclusion and the further conclusion.)

The ultimate conclusion follows ultimately from the initial premises and the supposition. The initial premises are true according to an advocate of this argument. So, the ultimate conclusion is true in case the supposition is true. It can be that God is among other things worthy of worship and morally perfect due to his will although there are no abstract things in case it can be that he exists.

But, is it not the case that God is nonetheless without a nature for he is ontologically prior to this exercise of his will just as a human being is ontologically prior to an exercise of his will? Well, this is not so (according to this other view) for God is simple. So, God is *indistinguishable* from (among other things) his will. *It is in this way that an advocate of this other view maintains that God is sovereign in this way over his nature.*

(Incidentally, let us consider an argument (Ap1. A5) for the claim that God is not sovereign in relation to the universe which he wills in case it can be that he exists :

it is untrue that it can be that God does not will the best of all possible worlds *or* he does not will one of the best of all possible worlds *or* he does not will some other particular possible world (is actualised) in case it can be that he exists ;

but, it is untrue that it can be that God is sovereign in relation to a universe which he wills unless this is not so ;

so, it is untrue that it can be that God is sovereign in relation to a universe which he wills in case it can be that he exists.

The conclusion follows from the first premise and the second premise.

An advocate of this other view maintains that it can be that God is sovereign in relation to a universe which he wills in case it can be that he exists.[4] How? Well, such an advocate to begin with maintains that the first premise of Ap1. A5 is untrue :

it is untrue that it can be that there are possible worlds in case it can be that he exists. (It is untrue for possible words are abstract things.) ;

so, it is untrue that it can be that God wills the best of all possible worlds *or* a best of all possible worlds *or* some other possible world (is actualised) in case it can be that he exists.

The conclusion follows from the premise. The premise follows from the second premise of Ap1. A4 (and the premise (which is true) that abstract things include possible worlds.) So, it can be in other words that God does not will the best of all possible worlds *or* he does not will one of the best of all possible worlds *or* he does not will some other particular possible world (is actualised) in case it can be that he exists for an advocate of this other view.

Further, God wills this or that universe *without* "a plan" for an advocate of this other view. God wills it "spontaneously" and yet with "perfect mastery" as a "perfect artist".[5] *It is in this way that an advocate of this other view maintains that God is sovereign in relation to the universe he wills.*

But, there are a number of difficulties in case this analogy is used. Here is one of these difficulties: we find an artist produces a particular piece of art "spontaneously" and yet with "perfect mastery" because he *or* she has acquired "mastery" through (among other things) practice; God in that case wills this or that universe "spontaneously" and yet with "perfect mastery" as a "perfect artist" because he has acquired "mastery" through (among other things) practice - that's absurd!)

Is this other view of God's nature correct? Well, let us take it, for the sake of argument, that the initial premises and the supposition of Ap1. A4 are true. Here in that case is an implication: the property, for example, of being worthy of worship is *whatever* God wills. (The abstract property of being worthy of worship does not circumscribe God's will for there are no abstract things.)

Further, God cannot be sovereign in relation to a universe which he wills. It can be to begin with that God wills timelessly there is a universe and sustains it and governs it. (Can it be that it is other than that? Well, no.) What *can* be the case (according to this other view) in relation to it is nothing other than that. (It is untrue that it can be other than that. It is untrue that it can be otherwise.) God cannot in that case possess the power to bring it about in some other way. God cannot do otherwise. But, God cannot be sovereign in relation to it unless he possesses the power to do otherwise. So, God cannot be sovereign in relation it.

Finally, it is untrue that it can be that God is sovereign over his nature. Here is *an* argument (Ap1. A6) for this claim. Here are its initial premises :

it cannot be that God is sovereign over his nature unless his nature is due to his will.

(that is to say, it cannot be that God is sovereign over his nature unless among other things *being worthy of worship* and *being morally perfect* is due to his will.) ;

it cannot be that God's will itself is distinguishable.

Let us suppose that it can be that God is sovereign over his nature.

It can be in that case that God's nature is due to his will although that will itself is not distinguishable. (This initial conclusion follows from the first premise and the second premise and the supposition.) That's absurd!

So, it is untrue that it can be that God is sovereign over his nature.

The first premise is true. The second premise (according to an advocate of this other view) is true for God is simple. The supposition is such that an absurdity follows from its addition. So, the conclusion – the conclusion is the denial of the supposition – is true. It is untrue that it can be that God is sovereign over his nature.

*

It can be (as we have seen) that some other living thing wills this or that (and acts in line with what it wills) freely in case it can be that God exists and it can be that a living thing possesses the power to bring about (in the very first instance) other living things which possess the power to do this or that freely.

But, it cannot be that some other such living thing wills this or that (and acts in line with what it wills) *freely* unless *it* (ultimately) wills (that) this or that. It cannot be in that case that some other such living thing's will is in this way not *independent of* God's will. But, it cannot be that God is sovereign over its will unless this is not so. So, it cannot be that God is sovereign over its will.

Let us consider another view of this matter. It is that it can be that some other living thing wills this or that (and acts in line with what it wills) freely (although it is) due to God's will in case it can be that he exists.[6] How? Well, here is an argument (Ap1. A7) for this claim. Here are its initial premises:

it can be that God exists just in case he exists;

it can be that God wills (timelessly and directly) some other living thing wills this or that (and acts in line with what it wills) in case it can be that he exists.

(it can be that this, *viz.* some (or that) other living thing wills (that) this or that (and acts in line with what it wills), manifests God's will.);

it can be that some other thing does not bring it about (even proximately) that some (or that) other living thing wills (that) this or that (and acts in line with what it wills) in case it can be that God wills (timelessly and directly) some (or that) other living thing wills (that) this or that (and acts in line with what it wills);

it can be that that other living thing other wills (that) this or that (and acts in line with what it wills) *freely* due to God's will in case some other thing does not bring it about (even proximately) that it wills (that) this or that (and acts in line with what it wills).

Let us suppose (God exists and in that case - from the first premise -) that it can be that God exists.

It can be in that case that God wills (timelessly and directly) some other living thing wills this or that (and acts in line with what it wills). (This initial conclusion follows from the first premise and the supposition.)

It can be in that case that some other thing does *not* bring it about (even proximately) that some (or that) other living thing wills (that) this or that (and acts in line with what it wills). (This further conclusion follows from the second premise and the initial conclusion.)

So, it can be that that other living thing other wills (that) this or that (and acts in line with what it wills) freely due to God's will.

The ultimate conclusion follows ultimately from the initial premises and the supposition. The initial premises are true according to an advocate of this argument. So, the ultimate conclusion follows in case the supposition is true. It can be that that other living thing other wills (that) this or that (and acts in line with what it wills) freely due to God's will it can be that he exists. *It is in this way that an advocate of this other view maintains that God is sovereign over some other such living thing's will.*

Is this so? Well, it is not so as (apart from anything else) the fourth premise is untrue : it cannot be that some other living thing wills this or that (and acts in line with what it wills) *freely* unless it is *not* due to some other thing's will that it wills (that) this or that (and acts in line with what it wills) ; some (or that) other living thing in this case wills this or that (and acts in line with what it wills) due to God's will ; so, it is untrue that it wills (that) this or that (and acts in line with what it wills) *freely*.

Notes

1. This is in effect the view of, for instance, a contemporary analytic philosopher, Hugh McCann.

See, for example, his article, "Divine Power and Action", in William E. Mann (ed.), *The Blackwell Guide to the Philosophy of Religion* (Blackwell, 2005), pp.40-42.

2. *Ibid.*, pp.37-42.

3. *Ibid.*, pp.42-46.

4. *Ibid.*, pp.34-37.

5. *Ibid.*, p.36.

6. *Ibid.*, pp.30-34.

Appendix 2

Evil being overridden and some discussions of God and evil

The second chapter refers to an evil state of affairs being *overridden*. It consists of the following :

there is an evil state of affairs; it is a (temporally immediate) part of a good state of affairs; the degree of value of the good state of affairs is *greater than* the degree value of the evil state of affairs; the degree of value of the good state of affairs is *greater than* the value of any good state of affairs which is a (temporally immediate) part of it; it is *not* the case that the value of the good state of affairs is determined by its parts and it is *not* the case the relation of its degree of value to the degree of value of a part is determined by its parts.

It is identifiable in a number of discussions of God and evil. There is a consideration of two of these discussions in what follows. First of all, there is a consideration of Richard Swinburne's discussion of this matter in an article entitled "Knowledge from Experience and the Problem of Evil".[1] Secondly, there is a consideration of John Mackie's discussion of this matter in his work *The Miracle of Theism.*[2]

*

In "Knowledge from Experience and the Problem of Evil" (and elsewhere), Swinburne claims that it is plausible that a morally perfect being would eliminate any evil which he is able to so long as in doing so it would not eliminate a greater good. He writes: " ... [it is a] plausible premise [that] ... 'A perfectly good being will eliminate evil in so far as he can do so without eliminating any greater good'...".[3]

He continues: "... it may well be that there are greater goods for the occurrence of which allowing some lesser evil to occur is a logically necessary condition ... Some well-known defences of theism argue that this is in fact so. The existence of evil, or at any rate the existence of a natural possibility of evil, is logically necessary if certain goods are to be possible. Argument along these lines is characteristic of the best-known theistic defence, the 'free will defence'."[4]

He continues: "The free will defence is sometimes stated ... [in this way] ... that it is good that men should have free will in the sense that the man who chooses is the ultimate source of his choosing this rather than that; that choice is not necessitated by prior choices ... [but] free will in this sense would exist if men had free choices between equally good states of affairs ... . So, what the defence must state is that it is good that men have [on occasion] free and responsible choice, ... [i.e.] ... they are [in addition] aware of ... morally good and evil alternatives ... and ... they are aware of them as morally good and evil alternatives. It is good ... that [thereby] agents other than God have a ... deep responsibility ... [but] if men have a free and responsible choice, they may well choose to do evil ... [this] is a logical consequence of the good of their having free and responsible choice."[5]

Swinburne refers to a whole good state of affairs, *viz.* a "free and responsible choice" of human beings, in the last passage:

that on occasion human beings possess the power to will ________ *freely* and the power to will *not* ________ *freely*

and

they are aware that

(i) they possess the power to will ________ - ________ is morally good

and

(ii) they possess the power to will *not* ________ - *not* ________ is morally evil

and

they are aware that ________ *is* morally good and *not* ________ *is* morally evil.

There is an evil state of affairs:

that they possess the power to will *not* ________ - *not* ________ is morally evil.

It is a (temporally immediate) part of the whole good state of affairs. (It is the "existence of evil, or at any rate, the existence of a natural possibility of evil, [which] is logically necessary if ... [this good is] to be possible".)

The degree of value of the whole good state of affairs is *greater than* the degree of it. (The whole good state of affairs is *a* "[greater good] for the occurrence of which allowing some lesser evil to occur is a logically necessary condition".)

There is a good state of affairs:

that on occasion human beings possess the power to will ________ *freely* and the power to will *not* ________ *freely*

and

they possess the power to will ________ - ________ is morally good

and

they are *aware* that they possess the power to will ________ and the power to will *not* ________

and

they are *aware* that ________ *is* morally good and *not* ________ *is* morally evil.

It is a (temporally immediate) part of the whole good state of affairs. (We are able to add the following about the second conjunct in line with Swinburne's statement about "the existence of evil ...": it is the "existence of good, or at any rate, the existence of a natural possibility of good, [which] is logically necessary if ... [this good is] to be possible".)

The degree of value of the whole good state of affairs is *greater than* the degree of it. (The whole good state of affairs is an instance of "agents [*viz.* human beings] other than God [who] have a ... deep responsibility". It is a great good. The good state of affairs which is a part of it is *not* an instance of "agents [*viz.* human beings] ... [who] have a ... deep responsibility". So, it is a lesser good.)

It is *not* the case that this relation between the whole good state of affairs and its evil part and its good part is determined by its parts. Let us consider the good part in order to illustrate that this is so. Let us suppose that this relation *is* determined by its parts. The part which is evil in that case is *good.* (The whole good state of affairs is not greater than its good part otherwise.) That's absurd! So, the supposition is untrue. It is *not* the case that this relation is determined by its parts.

Finally, the value – the degree of value - of the whole good state of affairs is not determined by its parts. Let us suppose that its value – its degree of value - *is* determined by its parts. The degree of value of its good part in that case is greater than the degree of value of its evil part. (It is not good otherwise.) Further, its degree of value is the degree of value of its good part *minus* the degree of value of its evil part. Its degree is *less than* the degree of value of its good part. It is greater than the degree of value of its good part *and* it is less than the degree of value of its good part. That's absurd! So, the supposition is untrue. Its value – its degree of value – is *not* determined by its parts.

So, the evil state of affairs which is a (temporally immediate) part of the whole good state of affairs is *overridden* in it.

*

In *The Miracle of Theism* (and elsewhere), Mackie considers a number of solutions of the problem of the co-existence of God and evil. He writes: "... [a solution is] ... that things that are evil in themselves may contribute to the goodness of an 'organic whole' in which they are found, so that the world is better as it is ... ".[6]

He continues: "To understand this solution, let us call pain, suffering ...'first-order evil' ... Distinct from this will be 'second-order good'... the second-order good is greater in magnitude...than the first-order evil which is logically necessary for it ... For example ... miseries or injustices that are ... overcome by a struggle whose nobility is a higher good ...".[7]

He continues: "[This solution] denies that a wholly good being would eliminate evil as far as it could, but explains this denial by pointing to a reason why a being who is wholly good, in a sense that is thoroughly intelligible to us and coherent with the ordinary concept of goodness, might not eliminate evils ... ".[8]

Mackie refers to a whole good state of affairs, *viz.* nobility, in the pen-ultimate passage:

that someone "struggles" to overcome something, *viz.* that he is subject to "injustices", and that something is "overcome".

It is an instance of "nobility".

There is an evil state of affairs:

that he is subject to injustices.

It is a (temporally immediate) part of the whole good state of affairs. (It is "the first-order evil which is logically necessary for it [*viz.* the whole good state of affairs that he "struggles" to overcome something, *viz.* that he is subject to "injustices", and that something is "overcome" or the "second order good"]".)

The degree of value of the whole good state of affairs is *greater than* the degree of it. (" ... the second-order good [*viz.* the whole good state of affairs that he "struggles" to overcome something, *viz.* that he is subject to "injustices", and that something is "overcome"] is greater in magnitude ... than the first-order evil [*viz.* the evil state of affairs that he is subject to injustices] which is logically necessary for it ... " ; " ... injustices that are ... overcome by a struggle whose nobility is a higher good ...".)

There is a good state of affairs:

that someone struggles to overcome something *and* that something is overcome.

It is a (temporally immediate) part of the whole good state of affairs.

The degree of value of the whole good state of affairs is *greater than* the degree of it. (The evil state of affairs that he is subject to injustices is an instance of an evil which "contribute[s] to the goodness of an 'organic whole' [*viz.* the whole good state of affairs] in which ... [it is] found". So, the whole good state of affairs is *greater than* the good state of affairs which is a part of it.)

It is *not* the case that this relation between the whole good state of affairs and its evil part and its good part is determined by its parts. Let us consider the good part in order to illustrate that this is so. Let us suppose that this relation *is* determined by its parts. The part which is evil in that case is *good.* (The whole good state of affairs is not greater than its good part otherwise). That's absurd! So, the supposition is untrue. It is *not* the case that this relation is determined by its parts.

Finally, the value – the degree of value - of the whole good state of affairs is not determined by its parts. Let us suppose that its value – its degree of value - *is* determined by its parts. The degree of value of its good part in that case is greater than the degree of value of its evil part. (It is not good otherwise.) Further, its degree of value is the degree of value of its good part *minus* the degree of value of its evil part. Its degree is *less than* the degree of value of its good part. It is greater than the degree of value of its good part *and* it is less than the degree of value of its good part. That's absurd! So, the supposition is untrue. Its value – its degree of value – is *not* determined by its parts.

So, the evil state of affairs which is a (temporally immediate) part of the whole good state of affairs is *overridden* it.

Notes

1. "Knowledge from Experience, and the Problem of Evil", in William J. Abraham and Stephen W. Holtzer (eds.), *The Rationality of Religious Belief: Essays in Honour of Basil Mitchell* (Oxford, 1987), pp.141-167.

See also, for example, *The Existence of God* (Oxford, 1979), pp.152-224.

2. *The Miracle of Theism* (Oxford, 1982), pp.150-176.

See also, for example, "Evil and Omnipotence", *Mind*, 64, 1955, pp.200-212. "Evil and Omnipotence" is reprinted in M. M. Adams and R. M. Adams (eds.), *The Problem of Evil* (Oxford, 1990), pp.25-37.

3. William J. Abraham and Stephen W Holtzer (eds.), *op. cit.*, p.142.

4. *Ibid.*, pp.142-143.

5. *Ibid.*, p.143.

6. *The Miracle of Theism*, p.153.

7. *Ibid.*, pp.153-154.

8. *Ibid.*, p.154.

Appendix 3

Some of the moral and other features of God bringing about a particular kind of universe and God being morally perfect

It cannot be that God does not exercise the power to bring about a particular kind of universe, *viz.* a universe which includes other living things which possess the power to act freely and independently of him ... , at a time in case it can be that he exists and it can be that a living thing possesses the power to bring about (in the very first instance) other living things which possess the power to act freely. (This is so as we have seen in the course of the first chapter and the second chapter.)

Let us consider the following claim. (It refers to universes which are good.):

in case a universe is greater (or better) than some other universe, God bringing it about is (morally) better than God bringing about the other universe.

But, this claim is *false* in the case that he exists and it can be that a living thing possesses the power to bring about (in the very first instance) some other living things which possess the power to act freely.

We have seen the following in the course of the second chapter. (The universes at issue are good):

it can be that God brings about a universe (which includes other living things which possess the power to act freely and independently ...) at a time

and

he possesses the power to bring about (such) a universe which is greater in value at that time

and

it is *not* morally inappropriate to do so in case it can be that that is so.[1]

God bringing it about is *not* morally worse than God bringing about (such) a universe which is greater in value at that time in case it can be that that is so.

God being morally perfect does *not* entail that he brings about a particular universe in case it is greater (or better) than some other universe in case it can be that that is so.

*

Can it be that God has *a duty* to bring about a universe which includes other living things which possess the power to act freely and independently ... at a time in case it can be that that is so?

Well, God cannot have a duty to do so unless he possesses the power to *not* bring about such a universe at a time according to the standard duty theory of morality. He cannot (as we have seen) possess this power in case it can be that that is so. So, he cannot have a duty to do so in case it can be that that is so according to the standard duty theory of morality.

God being morally perfect in that case does *not* entail that he fulfils a duty to do so in case it can be that that is so.

*

God's exercise of his power to bring about other living things which possess the power to act freely and independently of him ... at a time is a moral good.[2] God does not possess the power to not do so. God's exercise of this power to bring about other living things which possess the power to act freely and independently of him ... at a time is a moral good even though he does not possess the power to not do so.

So, the following claim is *false* in case it can be that that is so:

it cannot be a living thing exercises a power such as the power to keep a promise at a time and its exercise is a *moral* good unless

it possesses the power to do so at that time

and

it possesses the power to *not* do so at that time

and

it exercises its power to do so at that time.

*

God's exercise of this power to bring about other living things which possess the power to act freely and independently of him ... in a universe at a time is in line with his will to do so. Why does he will to do so?

Well, he wills do so (at least in part) in order that *they* are afforded the opportunity to act freely and independently of him. (His will in that case has *the virtue of* a will which wills _________ in order that *other* living things are able to benefit.)

It is a *moral* good that this is so.

God being morally perfect *entails* that there is such a moral good.

He wills to do so in the absence of something which takes away from its value such as envy of these other living things.

God being morally perfect *entails* that he wills to do so in the absence of something which takes away from its value such as envy of these other living things.

*

It cannot be that God does not will to do so at a time. (It cannot be that God does not will to do so at a time in case it can be that he exists and it can be that a living thing possesses the power to bring about in the very first instance other living things which possess the power to act freely.[3])

It cannot be that God wills to do so is *not* in order that they are afforded the opportunity to act freely and independently of him.

God wills to do so is in line with what he knows.

God knows he has to will to bring about these other living things which possess the power to act freely and independently of him ... in a universe at a time.[4]

God knows he wills to bring about these other living things which possess the power to act freely and independently of him ... in a universe at a time in order that they are afforded the opportunity to act freely and independently of him.[5]

God knows his exercise of his power to bring about these other living things which possess the power to act freely and independently of him ... in a universe at a time is a moral good.[6]

*

God cares for these other living things at that time. (This is a temporally immediate part of the state of affairs that he brings about other living things which possess the power to act freely and independently of him ... in a universe at a time.) It is a *moral* good that he does so.

He does so in the absence of something which takes away from its value such as envy of these other living things.

God being moral perfect *entails* that he cares for these other living things at that time and that there is the absence of something which takes away from its value such as envy of these other living things.

God cares for these other living things thereafter. (This is a temporally non-immediate part of the state of affairs that he brings about other living things which possess the power to act freely and independently of him ... in a universe at a time.) It is a *moral* good that he does so.

He does so in the absence of something which takes away from its value such as envy of these other living things.

God being moral perfect *entails* that he cares for these other living things thereafter and that there is the absence of something which takes away from its value such as envy of these other living things.

*

It cannot be that these other living things do not possess powers which include the following: the power to know about their conditions; the power to reason; the power to relieve any evil which they are experiencing and which is due to their conditions; the power to be considerate of other such living things and their powers and their lives; the power to diminish their power to not be considerate of other such living things and their powers and their lives.[7] (It cannot be that these other living things do not possess powers which include these powers as we seen in the course of the second chapter.)

God instructions and commands to these other living things would be to use these (and other) powers. These instructions and commands would be in line with his will. His will would be so in order that there is a benefit to them and their lives. (His will in that case would have *the virtue of* a will which wills ________ in order that there is a benefit to *other* living things.)

It would be a *moral* good that this is so.

God being morally perfect *entails* that there would be such a moral good.

He would will to do so in the absence of something which takes away from its value such as envy of these other living things.

God being morally perfect *entails* that he would will to do so in the absence of something which takes away from its value such as envy of these other living things.

Notes

1. It can be that God exercises a power to bring about *a* universe which includes other living things which possess the power to act freely and independently ... at a time in case it can be that that is so.

It can be that he possesses the power to bring about such a universe which is better at that time in case it can be that that is so.

God exercises the power to bring it about at a time in the absence of sufficient grounds to bring it about rather than some other such universe which is better at that time.

So, the following principle is *false* in case it can be that that is so:

it cannot be that God exercises a power to bring about this or that at a time in the absence of sufficient grounds to exercise it rather than any other power at that time.

See also the 9th note of the first chapter.

2. The denial of this statement is absurd! This statement is true.

3. This is in line with what we have seen in the course of the consideration of God's power in the first chapter. Here is the argument for this claim in line with what we have seen:

it cannot be that he does not possess the power to will to do so at a time in case it can be that that is so ;

it cannot be that he does not exercise a power in case it is unworthy of him to not exercise it ;

it is unworthy of him to not exercise this power and thereby to not afford such an opportunity to other living things ;

so, it cannot be that God does not will to do so at a time in case it can be that that is so.

The conclusion follows from the first premise and the second premise and the third premise. The first premise is true. The second premise is true. The third premise is true. So, the conclusion is true. It cannot be that God does not will to do so at a time in case it can be that that is so.

4. God knows the state of affairs that he wills to bring about these other living things which possess the power to act freely and independently of him ... in a universe at a time *is entailed by* the state of affairs that he exists and he possesses the power to will to bring about these other living things and he does not possess the power to not exercise this power at a time (for that power, *viz.* the power to not exercise this power at a time, is unworthy of him.)

5. God knows the state of affairs that he wills to bring about these other living things which possess the power to act freely and independently of him ... in a universe at a time *in order that* they are afforded the opportunity to act freely and independently of him *is entailed by* the state of affairs that he exists and he possesses the power to will to bring about these other living things and he does not possess the power to not exercise this power at a time and he possesses this power in part in order that other living things are afforded the opportunity to act freely and independently of him.

6. God knows the state of affairs that he exercises his power to bring about these other living things which possess the power to act freely and independently of him ... in a universe at a time is a moral good.

7. They become more God-like as they begin to diminish powers such as the power to not be considerate of other such living things and their powers and their lives.

Their exercise of the power to diminish such a power is a moral good.

It cannot be that God possesses *such* a power. It cannot be in that case that he possesses the power to diminish such a power.

So, the following claim is false in case it can be that God exists: it cannot be that living thing is morally perfect unless it possesses the power to diminish such a power.

Appendix 4

Are there sufficient grounds for the claim that, very probably, God does not exist?

The third chapter considers the principal arguments for the claim that God does not exist. These arguments do not establish that this claim is true *or* sufficient grounds are not readily forthcoming for this claim in case it can be that God exists and it can be that a living thing possesses the power to bring about (in the very first instance) other living things which possess the power to act freely.

What about arguments for the claim that, very probably, God does not exist? Well, let us consider *some* arguments for this claim. Here is an argument (Ap4. A1) for this claim. It is in two stages. Here is the first stage (Ap4. A1.1). Here are its initial premises :

some living things, *viz.* human beings, observe there is the following evil: *a few* living things which possess the power to lead a life and which possess other powers such as the power to know about their conditions and the power to reason and the power to be considerate *or* not of some other such living thing(s) and its life and its powers [*viz.* human beings] exercise *on occasion* a power to *not* be considerate *at all* of some other such living thing(s) and its life and its powers ;

the probability that there is this evil in case the hypothesis that God exists is true is *low* ;

the probability that there is this evil in case the hypothesis that there is a uniform chance process in operation *or* there is a process which includes a uniform chance process in operation is true is *much* higher ;

with regard to something which is observed and two hypotheses about it, what is observed supports one of these hypotheses much more than it supports the other hypothesis just in case its probability in case one of these hypotheses is true is much greater than its probability in case the other hypothesis is true.

Let us suppose that there are the following two hypotheses about the observation there is this evil: God exists; there is a uniform chance process in operation *or* there is a process which includes a uniform chance process in operation.

So, the observation there is this evil supports the second of these hypotheses much more than it supports the first of these hypotheses.

The conclusion follows from the initial premises and the supposition.

Here is the second stage (Ap4. A1.2) :

the observation there is this evil supports the hypothesis that there is a uniform chance process in operation *or* there is a process which includes a uniform chance process in operation much more than it supports the hypothesis that God exists ;

the hypothesis that there is a uniform chance process in operation *or* there is a process which includes a uniform chance process in operation is at least as plausible as the hypothesis that God exists (in case no other observations are considered) ;

so, it is very probable that God does not exist (in case no other observations are considered).

The conclusion follows from the first premise and the second premise. The first premise – the first premise is the conclusion of the first stage – is true according to an advocate of this argument. The second premise is true according to an advocate of this argument. So, the conclusion is true. It is very probable that God does not exist (in case no other observations are considered).

Is this so? Well, let us consider the first stage of this argument. Its first premise is true. Is its second premise true? (Here is its second premise once more: the probability that there is this evil in case the hypothesis that God exists is true is *low*.)

Well, it is *untrue* to begin with that the probability that there is this evil in case the hypothesis that God exists *and* he possesses the power to bring about (in the very first instance) other living things which possess the power to do this or that freely is true is *low*. Here is an argument (Ap4. A2) for this claim. It is in two stages. Here is the first stage (Ap4. A2.1). Its initial premises are as follows :

it can be that God exists and it can be that a living thing possesses this power in case this hypothesis is true ;

it cannot be that God does not exercise the power to bring about other living things which possess the power to lead a life and which possess other powers such as the power to know about their conditions and the power to reason and the power to be considerate *or* not of some other such living thing(s) and its life and its powers *and* which possess other powers such as the power to diminish (*or* not) the power to be considerate of some other such living thing(s) and its life and its powers in case it can be that that is so.

Let us suppose that this hypothesis is true.

So, there are other living things which possess the power to lead a life and which possess other powers such as the power to know about their conditions and the power to reason and the power to be considerate *or* not of some other such living thing(s) and its life and its powers *and* which possess other powers such as the power to diminish (*or* not) the power to be considerate of some other such living thing(s) and its life and its powers.

The conclusion follows from the first premise and the second premise and the supposition. The first premise is true. The second premise (as we have seen in the course of the second chapter) is true. So, the conclusion is true in the supposition is true.

Here is the second stage (Ap4. A2.2). Its initial premises are as follows :

there are other living things which possess the power to lead a life and which possess other powers such as the power to know about their conditions and the power to reason and the power to be considerate *or* not of some other such living thing(s) and its life and its powers and which possess other powers such as the power to diminish (*or* not) the power to be considerate of some other such living thing(s) and its life and its powers in case this hypothesis is true ;

it is *untrue* that the probability that *a few* of these living things (which possess the power to lead a life ... and which possess the power to be considerate *or* not of some other such living thing(s) and its life and its powers and which possess other powers such as the power to diminish (*or* not) the power to be considerate of some other such living thing(s) and its life and its powers) exercise *on occasion* the power to not be considerate at all of some other such living thing(s) and its life and its powers in case there are these other living things is *low*.

Let us suppose that this hypothesis is true.

There are in that case other living things which possess the power to lead a life and which possess other powers such as the power to know about their conditions and the power to reason and the power to be considerate *or* not of some other such living thing(s) and its life and its powers and which possess other powers such as the power to diminish (*or* not) the power to be considerate of some other such living thing(s) and its life and its powers. (This initial conclusion follows from the first premise and the supposition.)

So, it is *untrue* that the probability that *a few* of these living things (which possess the power to lead a life ... and which possess the power to be considerate *or* not of some other such living thing(s) and its life and its powers and which possess other powers such as the power to diminish (*or* not) the power to be considerate of some other such living thing(s) and its life and its powers) exercise *on occasion* the power to not be considerate at all of some other such living thing(s) and its life and its powers is *low.*

The ultimate conclusion follows ultimately from the first premise and the second premise and the supposition. The first premise – the first premise is the conclusion of the first stage – is true. The second premise is true. So, the conclusion is true in case the supposition is true. It is untrue in other words that the probability that there is this evil in case the hypothesis that God exists and he possesses the power to bring about (in the very first instance) other living things which possess the power to do this or that freely is true is low.

Now, are there sufficient grounds finally for the claim that God does not possess the power to bring about (in the very first instance) other living things which possess the power to act freely in case he exists? (God possesses it in case it can be that a living thing possesses it.)

Well, there are not sufficient grounds for this claim unless there are sufficient grounds for the claim that it is untrue that it can be that a living thing possesses this power. There are not in that case sufficient grounds for the claim the second premise of Ap4. A1.1 is true in the absence of these grounds. So, there are not sufficient grounds for the claim that Ap4. A1 establishes its conclusion in the absence of these grounds.

*

Here is another argument (Ap4. A3) for the claim that, very probably, God does not exist. It is in two stages. Here is the first stage (Ap4. A3.1). Here are its initial premises :

some living things, *viz.* human beings, observe there is evil of this kind and degree: *some* living things which possess the power to lead a life and which possess other powers such as the power to know about their conditions and the power to reason and which possess the power to do so independently of God [*viz.* human beings] experience *on occasion* pain and suffering such as the pain and suffering brought about by a major earthquake due to their conditions ;

the probability that there is evil of this kind and degree in case the hypothesis that God exists is true is *low* ;

the probability that there is evil of this kind and degree in case the hypothesis that there is a uniform chance process in operation *or* there is a process which includes a uniform chance process in operation is true is *much* higher ;

with regard to something which is observed and two hypotheses about it, what is observed supports one of these hypotheses much more than it supports the other hypothesis just in case its probability in case one of these hypotheses is true is much greater than its probability in case the other hypothesis is true.

Let us suppose that there are the following two hypotheses about the observation there is evil of this kind and this degree: God exists; there is a uniform chance process in operation *or* there is a process which includes a uniform chance process in operation.

So, the observation there is evil of this kind and this degree supports the second of these hypotheses much more than it supports the first of these hypotheses.

The conclusion follows from the initial premises and the supposition.

Here is the second stage (Ap4. A3.2) :

the observation there is evil of this kind and this degree supports the hypothesis that there is a uniform chance process in operation *or* there is a process which includes a uniform chance process in operation much more than it supports the hypothesis that God exists ;

the hypothesis that there is a uniform chance process in operation *or* there is a process which includes a uniform chance process in operation is at least as plausible as the hypothesis that God exists (in case no other observations are considered) ;

so, it is very probable that God does not exist (in case no other observations are considered).

The conclusion follows from the first premise and the second premise. The first premise – the first premise is the conclusion of the first stage – is true according to an advocate of this argument. The second premise is true according to an advocate of this argument. So, the conclusion is true. It is very probable that God does not exist (in case no other observations are considered).

Is this so? Well, let us consider the first stage of this argument. Its first premise is true. Is its second premise true? (Here is its second premise once more: the probability that there is evil of this kind and degree in case the hypothesis that God exists is true is *low*.)

Well, sufficient grounds are not readily forthcoming to begin with for the claim that the probability that there is evil of this kind and this degree in case the hypothesis that God exists *and* he possesses the power to bring about (in the very first instance) other living things which possess the power to act freely is true is *low*. Let us begin by considering the following argument (Ap4. A4). Here are its initial premises :

it can be that God exists and it can be that a living possesses this power in case this hypothesis is true ;

it cannot be that God does not exercise the power to bring about some other living things which possess the power to lead a life and which possess other powers such as the power to know about their conditions and the power to reason and which possess the power to do so *independently* of him in case it can be that he exists and it can be that a living possesses this power ;

it cannot be that these other living things which possess the power to lead a life.... and which possess the power to do so *independently* of him are not liable to experience any evil due to the conditions which prevail in a whole which includes them.

Let us suppose that this hypothesis is true.

So, there are living things which possess the power to lead a life and which possess other powers such as the power to know about their conditions and the power to reason and which possess the power to do so independently of him and which are liable to experience evil due to their conditions.

The conclusion follows from the first premise and the second premise and the third premise and the supposition. The first premise is true. The second premise (as we have seen in the course of the second chapter) is true. The third premise (as we have seen in the second chapter is plausible and it is supposed) is true. So, the conclusion is true in case the supposition is true. There are living things which possess the power to lead a life and which possess other powers such as the power to know about their conditions and the power to reason and which possess the power to do so independently of God and which are liable to experience evil due to their conditions in case this hypothesis is true. (Any liability to experience evil and any evil which they experience due to their conditions is a matter of degree. The degree is to the degree that they are independent of God.)

It can be (as we have also seen in the course of the second chapter) that these living things possess the power to interact with some physical thing(s).

Sufficient grounds are *not* readily forthcoming for the claim that the probability that some of these living things experience on occasion evil of this kind and this degree is low.

Now, are there sufficient grounds finally for the claim that God does not possess the power to bring about (in the very first instance) other living things which possess the power to act freely in case he exists? (God possesses it in case it can be that a living thing possesses it.)

Well, there are not sufficient grounds for this claim unless there are sufficient grounds for the claim that it is untrue that it can be that a living thing possesses this power. Sufficient grounds in that case for the claim the second premise of Ap4. A3.1 is true are not readily forthcoming in the absence of these grounds. So, sufficient grounds for the claim that Ap4. A3 establishes its conclusion are not readily forthcoming in the absence of these grounds.

*

Let us consider another argument (Ap4. A5) for the claim that, very probably, God does not exist. It is in two stages. Here is the first stage (Ap4. A5.1). Its initial premises are as follows :

some living things, *viz.* human beings, observe there is evil (*or* good) of this kind: *some* living things which possess the power to lead a life and which possess other powers such as the power to know about their conditions and the power to reason and which possess the power to do so independently of God [*viz.* human beings] experience *on occasion* evil, *viz.* pain (*or* good, *viz.* pleasure) which is due to their conditions *and* which enables them to survive ;

the probability that there is evil (*or* good) of this kind in case the hypothesis that God exists is true is *low* ;

the probability that there is evil (*or* good) of this kind in case the hypothesis that there is a uniform chance process in operation *or* there is a process which includes a uniform chance process in operation is true is *much* higher ;

with regard to something which is observed and two hypotheses about it, what is observed supports one of these hypotheses much more than it supports the other hypothesis just in case its probability in case one of these hypotheses is true is much greater than its probability in case the other hypothesis is true.

Let us suppose that there are the following two hypotheses about the observation there is evil (*or* good) of this kind: God exists; there is a uniform chance process in operation *or* there is a process which includes a uniform chance process in operation.

So, the observation there is evil (*or* good) of this kind supports the second of these hypotheses much more than it supports the first of these hypotheses.

The conclusion follows from the first premise and the second premise and the third premise and the fourth premise and the supposition. Here are some remarks on the first premise and the second premise and the third premise.

According to the first premise, human beings observe evil, *viz.* pain (*or* good, *viz.* pleasure) which is experienced on occasion by some living things which possess the power to lead a life ... *and* which is due to their conditions and which enables them to survive. (This argument refers to some evil *and* some good unlike the other two principal arguments considered in this Appendix.) Here is an example of such an evil: such a living thing [*viz.* a human being] who experiences a burning pain due to his proximity to a raging natural fire and who as a result leaves the scene. This is one kind of evil (*or* good) among others kinds which they observe. (The evil, *viz.* pain (*or* good, *viz.* pleasure) which is experienced by sentient living things *and* which enables them to survive on earth is the key kind of evil (*or* good) in the observation (or "evidence") which is at issue in a premise of an argument of a contemporary analytic philosopher, Paul Draper.[1] Draper refers to the evil, *viz.* pain (*or* good, *viz.* pleasure) which is "biologically useful" rather than to the evil, *viz.* pain (*or* good, *viz.* pleasure) "which enables them to survive". The argument is for the same claim, *viz.* very probably, God does not exist; the argument is along similar lines.)

The second premise, according to an advocate of this line of argument, is true because God can bring about such living things which are able to survive *without* this kind of evil and in that case would do so. (Draper believes that God can bring about sentient living things which are able to survive without this kind of evil and in that case would do so.[2])

The third premise includes the hypothesis that there is a uniform chance process in operation *or* there is a process which includes a uniform chance process in operation in relation to the universe. (That is to say there is a uniform chance process in operation *or* there is a process which includes a uniform chance process in operation *alone* in relation to the universe.) This hypothesis in case it is true entails among other things that the universe is *not* due to some good *or* bad acts on the part of some non-human persons. (Draper's hypothesis instead is that the nature and conditions of sentient living things on earth is *not* due to some good *or* bad acts on the part of some non-human persons.[3] So, this hypothesis entails Draper's hypothesis.)

Here is the second stage (Ap4. A5.2) :

the observation there is evil and good of this kind supports the hypothesis that there is a uniform chance process in operation *or* there is a process which includes a uniform chance process in operation much more than it supports the hypothesis that God exists ;

the hypothesis that there is a uniform chance process in operation *or* there is a process which includes a uniform chance process in operation is at least as plausible as the hypothesis that God exists (in case no other observations are considered) ;

so, it is very probable that God does not exist (in case no other observations are considered).

The conclusion follows from the first premise and the second premise. The first premise – the first premise is the conclusion of the first stage – is true according to an advocate of this argument. The second premise is true according to an advocate of this argument. So, the conclusion is true. It is very probable that God does not exist (in case no other observations are considered).

Is this so? Well, let us consider the first stage of this argument. Its first premise is true. Is its second premise true? (Here is its second premise once more: the probability that there is evil (*or* good) of this kind in case the hypothesis that God exists is true is *low.*)

Well, sufficient grounds are not readily forthcoming to begin with for the claim that the probability that there is evil (or good) of this kind in case the hypothesis that God exists *and* he possesses the power to bring about (in the very first instance) other living things which possess the power to act freely is true is *low.*

Let us begin by keeping in mind the conclusion of Ap4. A4: there are living things which possess the power to lead a life and which possess other powers such as the power to know about their conditions and the power to reason and which possess the power to do so independently of God and which are liable to experience evil due to their conditions in case this hypothesis is true. (Any liability to experience evil and any evil which they experience due to their conditions is a matter of degree. The degree is to the degree that they are independent of God.)

It cannot be (as we have seen in the course of the second chapter) that the degree of the liability of these living things to experience evil due to their conditions is such they are *only* liable to experience such evil. (God is not worthy of worship otherwise.) It cannot be that these living things are not liable to experience good, too. Here is an argument (Ap4. A6) for this claim. Its initial premises are as follows :

it cannot be that their conditions are such that they are *only* liable to experience evil due to them ;

it cannot be that God does not possess the power to bring it about that their conditions are such that they are liable to experience something else, *viz.* good, *in case* it cannot be that their conditions are such that they are only liable to experience evil due to them ;

it can be that God does not act in a way which is worthy of him in case it can be that he does not exercise this power even though he possesses it.

Let us suppose that it can be that he does not exercise this power.

But, it cannot be that God does not possess it. (This initial conclusion follows from the first premise and the second premise.)

It can be in that case that he does not exercise this power even though he possesses it. (This further conclusion follows from the supposition and the initial conclusion.)

It can be in that case that God acts in a way which is not worthy of him. (This still further conclusion follows from the third premise and the further conclusion.) That's absurd!

So, it is untrue that it can be that he does not exercise this power.

The first premise is true. The second premise is true. The third premise is true. The supposition is such that an absurdity follows with its addition. So the ultimate conclusion – the ultimate conclusion is the denial of the supposition - is true. It is untrue that it can be that he does not exercise this power. It is untrue in other words that it can be that these living things are not liable to experience good, too.[4]

It can be (as we have also seen in the course of the second chapter) that these living things possess the power to interact with some physical thing(s).

It is *untrue* that the probability that some of these living things (which can possess the power to interact with some physical thing(s)) experience on occasion evil, *viz.* pain (*or* good, *viz.* pleasure) which is due to their conditions and which enables them to survive is low *in case* the degree of their liability to experience evil due their conditions and the degree of this evil is such that the survival of some of them is on occasion at risk.

Sufficient grounds are *not* readily forthcoming for the claim the degree of their liability to experience evil due to their conditions and the degree of this evil is not such that this is so.

So, sufficient grounds are not readily forthcoming for the claim that the probability that some of these living things (which possess the power to interact with some physical thing(s)) experience on occasion evil, *viz.* pain (*or* good, *viz.* pleasure) which is due to their conditions and which enables them to survive in case this hypothesis is true is low.

Now, are there sufficient grounds finally for the claim that God does not possess the power to bring about (in the very first instance) other living things which possess the power to act freely in case he exists? (God possesses it in case it can be that a living thing possesses it.)

Well, there are not sufficient grounds for this claim unless there are sufficient grounds for the claim that it is untrue that it can be that a living thing possesses this power. Sufficient grounds in that case for the claim the second premise of Ap4. A5.1 is true are not readily forthcoming in the absence of these grounds. So, sufficient grounds for the claim that Ap4. A5 establishes its conclusion are not readily forthcoming in the absence of these grounds.

Notes

1. Paul Draper, " Pain and Pleasure: An Evidential Problem for Theists", *Nous* 23, pp.331-350.

Re-printed in Daniel Howard-Snyder (ed.), *The Evidential Argument from Evil* (Indiana University Press, 1996), pp.12-29.

Also, see, for example, "Evil and the Proper Basicality of Belief in God", *Faith and Philosophy* 8, pp.135-147.

"The Argument from Evil", in Paul Copan and Chad Meister (eds.), *Philosophy of Religion: Classic and Contemporary Issues* (Oxford, 2007).

2. Daniel Howard-Snyder (ed.), *The Evidential Argument from Evil*, p.17.

3. *Ibid.*, p.13.

4. It cannot be that the universe (or "whole") which includes these living things (and which is brought about by God) does not include the following, too: that these other living things are liable to experience good due to the conditions which prevail in it.

Appendix 5

Theodicy and some theodicies

There is evil. There is evil of the following kinds:

evil which apparently is due to the power of human beings to act freely ;

evil which apparently is due to __________ which is independent of this power.

Here is an instance of the first kind: a human being who is suffering due to some other human being who is wilfully persecuting him.

Here is an instance of the second kind: a human being who is suffering due to cholera.

The evil which exists has a degree. Further, there is an amount of the evil which exists.

Why is there (the kind and degree and amount of) evil assuming that God exists? Well, a "theodicy"[1] in the main is an explanation of why there is (the kind and degree and amount of) evil *or* some of it in relation to human beings assuming (among other things) that God exists.[2]

An advocate of a theodicy in the main claims (explicitly *or* implicitly) at least the following :

(i) the (kind and degree and amount of) evil in relation to human beings *is* due to _________ *or* in some part *is* due to _________ and _________ is *a part of* a greater good ;

(ii) this good is *good enough* for God to bring about ;

(iii) this good is *identified* in the theodicy ;

(iv) this good *in part appears* to be so *or* this good *as a whole appears* to be so.[3]

Here are *some* remarks about (i) – (iv) :

(i) does *not* imply that we are able to *know* this good *is* so ;

(ii) implies it is *not* (morally) better in case this good *or* evil is not so. (This is so for otherwise there is a moral failing on the part of God and that's absurd!) ;

(iii) implies that we are able to know this good. (We are able to know this good even in case we are unable to know all goods.) ;

(iv) implies that this good is *not* one which in part appears (only) at a later time *or* one which as a whole appears (only) at a later time.

An advocate of a theodicy ought not to state *or* imply *or* even suggest that an evil is other than it is. Apart from anything else, this is so because an explanation of it does not affect its value.

An advocate of a theodicy ought not to state *or* imply *or* even suggest something which turns our attention away from an evil. This is so because we ought to attend to an evil.

An advocate of a theodicy ought not to state *or* imply *or* even suggest something which undermines our resolve to deal with an evil. This is so because we ought to be resolved to deal with an evil. (This is so in case there are no other matters to consider.)

There are ways to assess a theodicy. Here are *some* of these ways. To begin with, does it explain evil as a whole *or* evil only in part?

Does the greater good which it identifies appear as a whole to be so *or* appear only in part to be so?

How plausible is the explanation which it provides?

Is an explanation of the evil *or* some of the evil which is experienced by other animals readily identifiable given it in case it only provides an explanation of the evil which is experienced by human beings?

*

Saint Irenaeus (c.130 – 202) sets out one of the principal theodicies of the Christian tradition in a work entitled *Against Heresies*.[4] A contemporary theologian and philosopher, John Hick, has re-stated this theodicy.[5] Here is a brief statement of this re-statement.

God created a universe which includes human beings. To begin with human beings are innocent and immature. Human beings are self-centred and live in competition with each other. This is so because God's existence is not evident to them. (It is this which explains why they are self-centred and live in competition with each other rather than a tradition which explains that they are so as a result of Adam's original disobedience in the Garden of Eden[6] and the subsequent break in the harmonious relationship with God and the subsequent entry into a material world - the Fall.)

But, each human being is made in the "image of God".[7] Each human being in that case possesses (among other things) the power to will freely (and the power to do what he *or* she wills freely). [He *or* she in effect possesses the power to act freely.] Each human being possesses the power to exercise his *or* her will in relation to himself *or* herself and in relation to others in a morally responsible way. Each human being possesses the power to become a being who is morally and spiritually mature. Indeed, each human being possesses the power to be in the "likeness" of God.

A human being almost certainly has to experience disappointments in his *or* her relations with others, pain and suffering, ... in order to become morally and spiritually mature. (Even in case a human being does not have to do so, it is better that a human being is morally and spiritually mature in this way than not.)

Well, God has brought it about that their powers and conditions are sufficient to facilitate them to become morally and spiritually mature in this way. They are sufficient to facilitate their *soul-making*. (These powers and conditions are an instrument to that end.)

They possess the power to interact with others and the power to enter into relationships with others and the power to act morally well *or* not. They possess the power to interact with their conditions and these conditions are such that they are liable to experience pain and suffering and they possess the power to overcome their experiences *or* not.

Some of their experiences facilitate moral and spiritual growth; but, some of their experiences appear not to facilitate moral and spiritual growth. They are able to reflect on the latter - a mystery. This itself facilitates moral and spiritual growth.

Further, they possess the power to believe in God and the power to not believe in God for God's existence is not evident to them. (They possess the power to have faith in God and the power to not have faith in God.)

God's aim is that each human being becomes morally and spiritually mature for it is in this that their salvation lies; but, each human being does not become morally and spiritually mature by the end of their life. So, there are conditions to facilitate even more this growth after death for these human beings.

This theodicy explains why there is (the kind and the degree and amount of) evil in relation to human beings assuming (most notably) that God exists and he possesses the power to bring about other living things with the power to will freely and the power to do what they will freely.

The (kind and degree and amount of) evil in relation to human beings is due to the power of human beings to will freely and the power to do what they will freely and the power to interact with others and the power to exercise these powers in a morally responsible way and the power to become morally and spiritually mature and it is due to the conditions which prevail and which are independent of their will and these powers and these conditions are a part of a greater good, *viz.* to facilitate (in the first instance) human beings to become morally and spiritually mature – to facilitate their "soul-making" into a "likeness" of God.[8] (This does not imply that human beings are able to know this good is so.)

This good is good enough for God to bring about. (It is not morally better in case this good *or* evil is not so. This is so for otherwise there is a moral failing on the part of God and that's absurd!)

This good is identified in this theodicy. (We are able to know this good even in case we are unable to know all goods.)

This good in part appears to be so. (This good is not one which in part appears only at a later time.)

*

Saint Augustine of Hippo (354 - 430) sets out one of the other principal theodicies of the Christian tradition. His work entitled *On the Free Choice of the Will*[9] is important in this regard. (Book 3 of this work is the key book.) Here is a brief statement of the theodicy in this work.

God created a universe which includes human beings (or human "souls") who each possesses the power to will freely (and the power to do what he *or* she wills freely). [He *or* she in effect possesses the power to act freely.] Each human being possesses the power to will evil *or* not. Human beings are of a kind of living thing which is "corruptible" and they in that case are liable to will evil. (A "perfect" universe requires the existence of "souls" - such as human "souls".)

There is evil or "sin" which is due to the free will of (some) human beings. It is due solely to a human being's will. (It is not due to his nature; it is not due to his will being inclined to evil by God; and, it is not due to this: he wills that he wills this or that evil.) God knew some human beings would sin and some human beings would not sin.[10]

Still, he brings it about immediately that a human being who sins is punished and he "suffers" and he is unhappy and that a human being who does not sin is happy.[11] So, there is evil which is not due to the free will of human beings and which is a human being who "suffers" and is unhappy, too. This evil is in large part a *just punishment* for the sins of a human being.[12] The universe is (more) just as a result. (It is not as just without it.)

Indeed, the universe is "perfect" so long as a human being who sins is unhappy and a human being who does not sin is happy. A "perfect" universe can include sin. (A "perfect" universe can include sin although a "perfect" universe does not require it and the punishment which follows it.)

Finally, there are some human beings who have not sinned and who "suffer" – for example, an infant. God brings about some good by way of his *or* her suffering and his *or* her life in the long term is as good as his *or* her life is without it.

This theodicy explains why there is some of the evil, *viz.* (the kind and the degree and amount of) evil which apparently is due to __________ which is independent of the power of human beings to act freely, in relation to human beings assuming (most notably) that God exists and he possesses the power to bring about other living things with the power to will freely (and the power to do what they will freely). (It is in large part a just punishment for the sins of human beings. The universe is more just as a result. Indeed, it is "perfect" with this evil.)

Is there an identifiable explanation of the other evil, *viz.* (the kind and the degree and amount of) evil which apparently is due to the power of human beings to act freely, in relation to human beings? (Well, the explanation is not that it is a part of *any* “perfect” universe for it can be that a universe is “perfect” although it does not include this evil or “sin” according to Augustine.) It is a part of *this* “perfect” universe.

The (kind and degree and amount of) evil in relation to human beings is due to the power of human beings to will freely (and the power to do what they will freely and the power to do evil or “sin”) and it is due to God who is independent of this power and who brings it about that human beings who “sin” suffer and are unhappy and the power of human beings to will freely (and the power to do what they will freely and the power to do evil or “sin”) and God bringing it about that human beings who “sin” suffer and are unhappy is a part of a greater good, *viz. this* perfect universe.[13] (This does not imply that human beings are able to know this good is so.)

This good is good enough for God to bring about. (It is not morally better in case this good *or* evil is not so. This is so for otherwise there is a moral failing on the part of God and that’s absurd!)

This good is identified in this theodicy. (We are able to know this good even in case we are unable to know all goods.)

This good in part appears to be so. (This good is not one which in part appears only at a later time.)

*

There is a theodicy which is identifiable in this work. (A theodicy is identifiable as a result in particular of the second chapter.) Here is a brief statement of this theodicy.

God brought about a universe which includes other living things which possess the power to act freely[14] and independently of him, *viz.* human beings. Human beings' powers include the power to lead in that way a life and the power to know in that way what is the case and its value and its relations to what else is the case and the power to reason in that way.

Since they possess the power to act independently of him, they are separated from him. Hence, they are liable to experience evil due to the conditions which prevail in the universe. (The degree of this liability and the degree of this evil is due to the degree of their independence from him.)

But, they possess the power to relieve this evil and the power to not to relieve this evil. They possess these powers in relation to themselves and in relation to other human beings for they are not brought about in complete isolation. (They are not brought about in complete isolation in order that this universe - among other things - is such that they possess the power to be considerate of other human beings and their lives and their powers.)

They possess powers in relation to their conditions and in relation to other human beings. Their powers include powers which are morally significant. Here is an example: the power to be considerate of some other human being and his *or* her life and his *or* her powers and the power to not be considerate (at all) of some other human being and his *or* her life and his *or* her powers.

They are such that they hold the belief that it is better that that which they know is (morally) good obtains rather than it does not obtain and they possess as a result the desire (to some degree) to bring it about.

In this universe, God affords other living things the opportunity to act freely and independently. (There is the good of other livings things which are not debased and which possess the power to lead rational lives which are morally significant and which are free and independent of him.)

This theodicy explains at least in very large part why there is (the kind and the degree and amount of) evil in relation to human beings assuming (most notably) that God exists and he possesses the power to bring about (in the very first instance) other living things which possess the power to act freely. (Why does the preceding sentence include the words "at least in very large part"? Well, see the next paragraph which sets out a claim of this theodicy.)

The (kind and degree and amount of) evil in relation to human beings is at least in very large part due to the power of human beings to act freely and independently and the power to interact with others and the power to act in a morally significant way and it is due to the conditions which prevail and which are independent of their powers to act freely and independently and the power of human beings to act freely and independently and the power to interact with others and the power to act in a morally significant way and their conditions are a part of a greater good, *viz.* there being other living things, human beings, (who are not debased and) who possess the power to lead (rationally) lives (which are morally significant and) who are free and independent of God.[15, 16, 17, 18] (This does not imply that human beings are able to know this good is so.)

This good is good enough for God to bring about. (It is not morally better in case this good *or* evil is not so. This is so for otherwise there is a moral failing on the part of God and that's absurd!)

This good is identified in this theodicy. (We are able to know this good even in case we are unable to know all goods.)

This good as a whole appears to be so. (This good is not one which in part *or* as a whole appears only at a later time.)

Here are some further features of this theodicy. The greater good which it identifies is not the (greater) good of the theodicy of Irenaeus and Hick, *viz.* to facilitate (in the first instance) human beings to become morally and spiritually mature. Still, its greater good includes the power of human beings to become more and more morally and spiritually mature as *a* (good) *part of* it.[19] Here is an instance of this power: the power of human beings to *diminish* the power to not be considerate of other such living things and their powers and their lives.

The greater good which it identifies is not the greater good of the theodicy of Augustine, *viz. this* perfect universe which is such that it includes evil or "sin" due to the free will of (some) human beings and a just punishment (for this "sin") due to God. Still, its greater good is such that it can be that God interacts with human beings on occasion and a human being experiences this or that as a punishment – a punishment due to God. Here is an example of such a punishment: a human being who brings about an evil and who experiences some mental distress as a punishment due to God for the sake of his *or* her *rehabilitation.*

This theodicy explains at least in very large part evil in relation to human beings. (It is in that case unlike a theodicy which explains evil in relation to human beings in a smaller part in terms of how much evil in relation to human beings it explains.)

This theodicy identifies a greater good which appears as a whole to be so. It is in that case unlike the theodicy of Irenaeus and Hick and the theodicy of Augustine in terms of how much the greater good at issue appears to be so.

This theodicy is plausible. Is it more plausible than the theodicy of Irenaeus and Hick and the theodicy of Augustine? Well, a full consideration of this question is beyond the scope of this Appendix. But, here is a question (among others) in relation to the theodicy of Irenaeus and Hick: how plausible is it that God's aim is that each human being becomes morally and spiritually mature given that each human being possesses the power to will freely - and in that case the power to *not* become morally and spiritually mature – throughout the process of their soul-making?

Here is a question (among others) in relation to the theodicy of Augustine: how plausible is it that this "perfect" universe which includes human beings who suffer and are unhappy is (morally) good enough for God to bring about given that he possesses the power to bring about a "perfect" universe with human beings who do not suffer and are unhappy?

Finally, this theodicy is such that an explanation of some of the evil which is experienced by other animals is readily identifiable given it. In relation to other animals, there is evil which apparently is due to the power of human beings to act freely. There is also evil which apparently is due to ________ which is independent of the power of human beings to act freely.

Some of the evil which other animals experience *is* due to the conditions which prevail and which are independent of the power of human beings to act freely according to this theodicy. What is the explanation of this evil? Well, the explanation is as follows: since they possess the power to do this or that independently of God, they are *separated* from him; hence, they are liable to experience evil due to their conditions.

This theodicy is unlike the theodicy of Irenaeus and Hick and the theodicy of Augustine in terms of whether an explanation of the evil *or* some of the evil which is experienced by other animals is readily identifiable given it.

Notes

1. The first use of this word is by Leibniz.

It is used in a letter to Bartholomew Des Bosses (6.1.1712).

It is also the title of one of his works.

2. In the third chapter, an argument of Plantinga in *The Nature of Necessity* is considered.

His argument deals with whether it *can* be that God exists and there is the evil there is.

3. It need hardly be added that a theodicy does *not* imply that an advocate of it is arrogant *or* has pride.

4. Anti-Nicene Library.

5. See especially his work *Evil and the God of Love* (Macmillan, 1977).

6. Genesis 2: 4b – 3: 24.

7. Genesis 1: 26-27 9:6.

8. These powers, *viz.* the power to will freely and the power to do what is willed freely and the power to interact with others and the power to exercise these powers in a morally responsible way and the power to become morally and spiritually mature, and these conditions (or the equivalent) are a part of *any instance* of the greater good to facilitate (in the first instance) other living things to become morally and spiritually mature – to facilitate their "soul-making" into a "likeness" of God. (The greater good to facilitate in the first instance other living things to become morally and spiritually mature – to facilitate their "soul-making" into a "likeness" of God – is morally good enough for God to bring about.)

9. *On the Free Choice of the Will*, trans. A Benjamin (Indianapolis, 1964).

10. Augustine claims that God has always known how a human being exercises his will to do this or that freely at a particular time.

This claim is untrue. (The claim that it is untrue is in line with the conclusion of the consideration of whether it can be that God has always known how a living thing exercises a power to do this or that freely at a particular time in the first chapter.)

11. It need hardly be added that it does *not* appear that this is so.

12. But, Augustine writes here and elsewhere that human beings *lost* the power to lead good lives due to the Fall. (See, for example, *On the Free Choice of the Will*, 3.18.)

Some human beings thereafter possess the power to lead good lives due to the grace of God. A human being thereafter possesses the power to lead a good life only through God's grace. (See, for example, *On the Predestination of Saints*, 23 and 24.)

But, is it just to punish a human being who lost the power to lead a good life due to the Fall (and who is not a recipient of God's grace) and who sins? (The Fall, after all, is due to *Adam's* disobedience.)

Well, it is just to punish a human being in case his *or* her loss of the power to lead a good life is due to a previous misuse of his *or* her free will according to Augustine.

Perhaps a human being's (or a human soul's) loss of the power to lead a good life is due to the following according to Augustine: his *or* her soul is from that soul (or souls) which committed the original disobedience. So, perhaps it is just to punish a human being who sins.

13. This power, *viz.* the power of (some) human beings to will freely (and the power to do what they will freely and the power to do evil or "sin"), and God who brings it about that the human beings who "sin" suffer and are unhappy are not a part of *any instance* of the greater good of a "perfect" universe. (The greater good of a "perfect" universe is morally good enough for God to bring about.)

They are a part of the greater good of *this* perfect universe.

14. The power to act freely *includes* the power to will freely.

It also includes the power to do what is willed freely and the power to do what is willed freely also has a value which is good.

This theodicy recognises (implicitly) its value unlike a theodicy which only refers to the value of the power to will freely.

Some theodicies, *viz. free will* theodicies, *prima facie* only refer to the value of the power to will freely.

An advocate of a free will theodicy claims (explicitly *or* implicitly) at least the following:

the evil in relation to human beings in some part is due to the power of human beings to will ________ and ________ is morally inappropriate and this power is a part of a greater good, *viz.* that there are living things who possess (ordinarily) the power to lead a life and who possess (ordinarily) the power to will freely during it and this power includes the power to do so in a morally appropriate and morally inappropriate way in relation to others in a universe. (That a human being *wills* ________ and ________ is morally inappropriate is *itself* an evil.)

Such an advocate at least in the main claims (explicitly *or* implicitly) that human beings also possess the power *to do* what they will freely.

This good is good enough for God to bring about. (It is not morally better in case this good *or* evil is not so. This is so for otherwise there is a moral failing on the part of God and that's absurd!)

This good is identified in this theodicy. (We are able to know this good even in case we are unable to know all goods.)

This good as a whole appears to be so. (This good is not one which even in part only appears at a later time.)

Let us consider a human being who wills ________ and ________ is morally inappropriate on a number of occasions during a period of time which is prolonged and which is not the period at the end of his *or* her life.

There is in what follows a line of discussion which considers this human being and which identifies sufficient grounds for the following claim: it cannot be other than that on all of these occasions he *or* she possesses (ordinarily) the power to will freely ________ *and* the power *to do* ________ . (It cannot be other than that on these occasions he *or* she possesses ordinarily the power to will freely ________ and the power to do ________ in case God exists.)

To begin with, let us consider the following claim: he or she does *not* possess (ordinarily) the power to will freely ________ *after it* in case it appears on all of these occasions that to will ________ is ineffective (to bring about ________). (This claim assumes that there are no grounds other than to bring about ________ for him *or* her to will ________.)

Here is an argument for this claim. Here are its initial premises. (Its second premise assumes that there are no grounds other than to bring about ________ for him *or* her to will ________.) :

he *or* she believes (ordinarily) that to will ________ is *ineffective* (to bring about ________) at the end of it in case it appears on all of these occasions that to will ________ is ineffective (to bring about ________) ;

he *or* she does not possess (ordinarily) the power *to will* ________ after it in case he *or* she believes that to will ________ is *ineffective* (to bring about ________) at the end of it ;

he *or* she does not possess the power to will freely ________ after it unless he *or* she possesses the power *to will* ________ after this period.

Let us suppose that it appears on all of these occasions that to will ________ is ineffective (to bring about ________).

He *or* she in that case believes (ordinarily) that to will ________ is *ineffective* (to bring about ________) at the end of it. (This initial conclusion follows from the first premise and the supposition.)

He *or* she in that case does not possess (ordinarily) the power *to will* ________ after it. (This further conclusion follows from the second premise and the initial conclusion.)

So, he *or* she does not possess (ordinarily) the power to will freely ________ after it.

The ultimate conclusion follows ultimately from the first premise and the second premise and the third premise and the supposition. The first premise is true. The second premise is true. (The second premise is true given its assumption.) The third premise is true. So, the ultimate conclusion is true in case the supposition is true. He *or* she does not possess (ordinarily) the power to will freely ________ after it in case it appears on all of these occasions that to will ________ is ineffective (to bring about ________).

But, he *or* she possesses (ordinarily) the power *to will* ________ after it - and the power (ordinarily) to will freely ________ after it - in case it at least appears *on some of these occasions* that to will ________ is *effective* (to bring about ________).

Can it be on these occasions that he *or* she wills freely ________ and it *merely appears* that to will ________ is effective (to bring about ________)?

Well, it cannot be that this is so as in that case the good that there are living things, *viz.* human beings, ... who possess (ordinarily) the power to will freely .... is *not good enough* for God to bring about.

So, it cannot be other than that on these occasions he *or* she wills freely ________ and it is *not* the case that it *merely appears* that to will ________ is effective (to bring about ________).

In other words, it cannot be other than that on these occasions he *or* she wills freely ________ and to will ________ *is* effective (to bring about ________).

It cannot be other than that on these occasions he *or* she possesses the power to will freely ________ *and* the power *to do* ________ .

Can it be that on the *other* occasions it appears that to will ________ is ineffective (to bring about ________)?

Well, the good at issue, *viz.* that there are living things, human beings, ... who possess (ordinarily) the power to will freely .... , in that case is (again) *not* good enough for God to bring about.

So, it cannot be other than that on all of these occasions he *or* she possesses (ordinarily) the power to will freely ________ *and* the power *to do* ________ .

The theodicy which is identifiable in this work recognises (implicitly) that the good at issue, *viz.* that there are living things, *viz.* human beings, ... who possess (ordinarily) the power to will freely .... , is not good enough for God to bring about.

This theodicy explains at least in very large part evil - evil in relation to human beings - which apparently is due to the power of human beings to ________ freely *and* evil which apparently is due to ________ which is independent of this power. A free will theodicy does *not* explain evil which apparently is due to ________ which is independent of this power.

It identifies a greater good which appears as a whole to be so as we shall see. A free will theodicy also identifies a greater good which appears as a whole to be so.

It is plausible. It is more plausible than a free will theodicy which only refers to the value of human beings ... who possess (ordinarily) the power to will freely .... for the value of this is not good enough for God to bring about.

It is such that an explanation of some of the evil which is experienced by other animals is readily identifiable given it as we shall see. A free will theodicy is not such that an explanation of some of the evil which is experienced by other animals is readily identifiable given it.

15. Human beings know of good states of affairs which include this good state of affairs. Let us consider in passing the following argument. (Its premise is in line with the view of some contemporary analytic philosophers who are referred to as "sceptical theists".) **:**

there are not sufficient grounds for the claim that these good states of affairs represent good states of affairs as a whole in relation to being an explanation of any evil in a universe brought about by God **;**

so, there are not sufficient grounds for the claim that it is probable that this good state of affairs is an explanation of any evil which exists in a universe, *viz.* this universe, in case it has been brought about by God**.**

Is this so? Well, it is not so in case a universe – say, this universe - has been brought about by God and he possesses the power to bring about (in the very first instance) other living things which possess the power to act freely. Why? Well, human beings know of good states of affairs which include this good state of affairs *and* this state of affairs obtains as we have seen *by way of argument* (in the course of the second chapter) and it overrides and it is an explanation of any evil which exists in it in case that is so. So, the premise of the argument is *untrue* in case that is so.

16. The power of human beings to interact with others and the power to act in a morally significant way is a part of this greater good.

It is a part of the power to interact with others and the power to act in a morally significant way that there *are* others.

It is also a part of these powers that others and their lives and their powers *are* liable to be the subject of, for example, a lack of consideration altogether.

But, it is *not* a part of this greater good that, for example, someone's experience of being the subject of a lack of consideration altogether is *itself* a part of a greater good (for him *or* her) brought about by God. (*Cf.*, for example, Eleonore Stump, "The Problem of Evil", *Faith and Philosophy*, 2, 1985.)

17. These powers, *viz.* the power to act freely and independently and the power to interact with others and the power to act in a morally significant way, and these conditions (or the equivalent) are a part of *any instance* of the greater good of other livings things (which are not debased and) which possess the power to lead (rationally) lives (which are morally significant and) which are free and independent of God. (The greater good of other livings things which are not debased and which possess the power to lead rational lives which are morally significant and which are free and independent of God is morally good enough for God to bring about.)

18. These powers, *viz.* the power to act freely and independently and the power to interact with others and the power to act in a morally significant way, and these conditions (or the equivalent) are a part of *any instance* of the greater good of other livings things (which are not debased and) which possess the power to lead (rationally) lives (which are morally significant and) which are free and independent of God.

It is *not* a part of any instance of this greater good that there is as much evil due to the exercise of these powers (over the course of time) as it is due to the exercise of these powers of human beings (over the course of time).

Can it be in that case that God brings about this greater good with less evil due to the exercise of these powers (over the course of time) than the evil due to the exercise of these powers of human beings (over the course of time) *and* he knows this is so when he brings it about?

Well, God cannot bring about this greater good with less evil due to the exercise of these powers (over the course of time) than that evil (over the course of time) *and* he knows this is so when he brings it about unless he knows the amount of that evil when he brings it about.

But, he cannot know the amount of that evil when he brings it about for he cannot know (as we have seen in the course of the second chapter) about the exercise of any such powers of human beings (over the course of time) prior to the time of the exercise of these powers.

So, God cannot bring about this greater good with less evil due to the exercise of these powers (over the course of time) than the evil due to the exercise of these powers of human beings (over the course of time) *and* he knows this is so when he brings it about.

So, it is not a moral failing on his part in case he brings about this greater good and it does not include less evil (over the course of time) than that evil.

Still, it is a moral failing on his part in case powers to this degree and conditions to this degree are not a part of any instance of this greater good. Powers to this degree and conditions to this degree *are* a part of any instance of this greater good.

Some theists, *viz.* Open Theists, claim the following: God cannot bring about a greater good which includes the power to will freely of other living things as a part of it with less evil (over the course of time) than the evil (over the course of time) which there is in any other instance of this greater good *and* he knows this is so when he brings it about. (A greater good which let us add includes the power to will freely *and* the power to do what is willed freely *and* the power to do so in a morally significant way.)

God cannot bring about such a greater good with less evil (over the course of time) than that evil (over the course of time) *and* he knows this is so when he brings it about unless he knows the amount of that evil (over the course of time).

But, Open Theists claim (on some grounds or other) that he cannot know the amount of that evil when he brings it about for he cannot know about the exercise of such a power of other living things (over the course of time) prior to the time of the exercise of it.

So, God cannot bring about such a greater good with less evil (over the course of time) than that evil *and* he knows this is so when he brings it about.

So, they claim that is not a moral failing on his part in case he brings about such a greater good and it does not include less evil (over the course of time) than that evil. (William Hasker is an example of an Open Theist. See, for example, his work *Providence, Evil, and the Openness of God* (Routledge, 2004).)

What are we to say about their view? Well, a full consideration of this question is beyond the scope of this Appendix. But, here is a comment: it is nonetheless a moral failing on his part in case a power to will freely to the degree which is identified is not a part of any instance of such a greater good; is it the case that a power to will freely to the degree which is identified is a part of any instance of the greater good which is identified?

19. But, it is not the *aim* of God that each human being becomes morally and spiritually mature when he brings about its (greater) good.

Appendix 6

Some further remarks on God and time

There is a consideration of God and time in the first chapter. There is a consideration of some arguments in relation to this matter in the first chapter: *eg*, an argument for the claim that it can be that God is not in time in case it can be that he exists.

Here is an argument (Ap6. A1) for the claim that it cannot be that God is in time. (It takes it that it cannot be that God is not alive.) It is in two stages. Here is the first stage (Ap6. A1.1). (Its initial premise takes it that it cannot be that God is not alive for an eternal period of time in case he is in time.):

it cannot be that God is alive and time does not pass in case he is in time ;

it cannot be in that case that God is alive and he does not ... co-exist with a time, t, and co-exist with a later time, t1, ... in case he is in time. (It cannot be in that case God is alive and he does not undergo extrinsic relational change in case he is in time: *eg*, he co-exists with a time, t, at t and he does not co-exist with it at a later time, t1.) (This initial conclusion follows from the initial premise.) ;

it cannot be in that case that God is alive and his life does not have a part up to ... t, and another part up to t1, ... in case he is time.[1] (This further conclusion follows from the initial conclusion.) ;

so, it cannot be that God is alive and he (including his life) is simple in case he is in time. (This ultimate conclusion follows from the further conclusion and the traditional doctrine of God being simple. The traditional doctrine of God being simple states *or* entails among other things that his life does *not* have parts.)

The ultimate conclusion follows ultimately from the initial premise (and the traditional doctrine of God being simple.) The initial premise is true. So, the ultimate conclusion is true. (It is true given the traditional doctrine of God being simple.)

Here is the second stage (Ap6. A1.2) :

it cannot be that God is alive and he (including his life) is simple in case he is in time ;

it cannot be that God's life is (in this way, *viz.* in terms of temporal parts) not simple ;

so, it cannot be that God is in time.

The conclusion follows from the first premise and the second premise. The first premise - the first premise is the conclusion of the first stage - is true. (It is true given the traditional doctrine of God being simple.) Is the second premise true? Well, here is an argument (Ap6. A1.2: A1 - P2) for the claim that the second premise is true. Its initial premises are as follows :

it is untrue that it can be that God's life is (in some way) not complete ;

it can be that God's life is not complete at some (or any) time in case it can be that it has a part ... up to a time, t, and another part up to a later time, t1, ... - in case it can be that his life is (in this way, *viz.* in terms of temporal parts) not simple.

Let us suppose that it can be that his life is (in this way, *viz.* in terms of temporal parts) not simple.

It can be in that case that his life is not complete at some (or any) time *and* it is untrue that it can be that his life is (in some way) not complete. (This initial conclusion follows from the first premise and the second premise and the supposition.) That's absurd!

So, it is untrue that it can be that his life is (in this way, *viz.* in terms of temporal parts) not simple.

The ultimate conclusion follows ultimately from the first premise and the second premise and the supposition.

Is the first premise true? Well, it is not true. It can be that God's life is in a way not complete in that there is just a part of it at some (or any) time. He *himself* is fully realised even in case his life is in this way not complete at some (or any) time. So, he is a being worthy of worship even in case his life is in this way not complete at some (or any) time. This argument does not establish that the second premise of Ap6. A1.2 is true.

Here is another argument (Ap6. A1.2: A2 - P2) for the claim that the second premise of Ap6. A1.2 is true. Its initial premises are as follows :

it is untrue that it can be that God is alive and he is dependent on some other thing in order to lead his life ;

it can be that God is alive and he is dependent on some other thing, *viz.* time, in order to lead his life in case it can be that God's life is (in this way, *viz.* in terms of temporal parts) not simple.

Let us suppose that it can be that God's life is (in this way, *viz.* in terms of temporal parts) not simple.

It can be in that case that he is alive and he is dependent on some other thing, *viz.* time, in order to lead his life, and it is untrue that it can be God is alive and he is dependent on some other thing in order to lead his life. (This initial conclusion follows from the first premise and the second premise and the supposition.) That's absurd!

So, it cannot be that God's life is (in this way, *viz.* in terms of temporal parts) not simple.

The ultimate conclusion follows ultimately from the first premise and the second premise and the supposition.

Is apart from anything else the first premise true? Well, it is not true. It can be that God is alive and he is dependent on some other thing, *viz.* time, in order to lead his life.[2] He *himself* is fully realised even in case he is dependent on some other thing, *viz.* time, to lead his life. So, he is a being worthy of worship even in case he is dependent on some other thing, *viz.* time, in order to lead his life. This argument does not establish that the second premise of Ap6. A1.2 is true.

*

Here is an argument (Ap6. A2) for the claim that, presumably, it cannot be that God knows this or that other living thing does this or that freely at a particular time *and* he is not in time :

it cannot be that he knows this or that other living thing does this or that freely at a particular time unless he believes that (that) this or that other living thing does (that) this or that freely at a particular time ;

it cannot be that he believes that (that) this or that other living thing does (that) this or that freely at a particular time unless he holds this belief *directly* or *immediately* ;

it cannot be that he holds this belief directly or immediately unless he is in time ;

so, it cannot be that he knows this or that other living thing does this or that freely at a particular time *and* he is not in time.

The conclusion follows from the first premise and the second premise and the third premise. The first premise is true. The second premise presumably is true. (It is taken in the course of the consideration of God's power in the first chapter that he presumably is such that he holds this or that belief directly or immediately.) The third premise is true. So, the conclusion presumably is true. It cannot be presumably that God knows this or that other living thing does this or that freely at a particular time *and* he is not in time.

*

It cannot be in any case that God is not in time in case it can be that he exists and it can be that a living thing possesses the power to bring about (in the very first instance) other living things which possess the power to act freely.

Here is an argument (Ap6. A3) for the claim that it cannot be that God is not in time in case it can be that that is so. (It assumes that it can be that God possesses and exercises the power to bring about in the very first instance other living things which possess the power to act freely at a time in case it can be that he is not in time. Otherwise, the third conjunct of its supposition, *viz.* it can be that he is not in time, is *false* given its first premise and the first conjunct and the second conjunct of its supposition.) Its initial premises are as follows:

it is untrue that it can be that God (does not possess and) does not exercise the power to bring about (in the very first instance) other living things which possess the power to act freely at a time in case it can be that he exists and it can be that a living thing possesses the power to bring about (in the very first instance) other living things which possess the power to act freely;

it is untrue that it can be that God does not exist at that time (even) in case he is not in time;

it is untrue that it can be that God does not (already) know this or that such living thing exercises its power to do this or that freely (at a particular time) at that time in case he is not in time;

it is untrue that it can be that God (already) knows - or has always known - this or that such living thing exercises its power to do this or that freely (at a particular time) at that time.

Let us suppose that it can be that he exists *and* it can be that a living thing possesses the power to bring about (in the very first instance) other living things which possess the power to act freely *and* it can be that he is not in time.

It is untrue in that case that it can be that he (does not possess and) does not exercise the power to bring about (in the very first instance) other living things which possess the power to act freely at a time. (This initial conclusion follows from the first premise and the first conjunct and the second conjunct of the supposition.)

It can be in that case that he is not in time and he (possesses and) exercises the power to bring about (in the very first instance) other living things which possess the power to act freely at a time and he (exists[3] and already) knows this or that such living thing exercises its power to do this or that freely (at a particular time) at that time *and* it is untrue that it can be that he (already) knows - or has always known - this or that such living thing exercises its power to do this or that freely (at a particular time) at that time. (This further conclusion follows from the second premise and the third premise and the supposition and the initial conclusion.) That's absurd!

So, it is untrue that it can be that he exists and it can be that a living thing possesses the power to bring about (in the very first instance) other living things which possess the power to act freely and it can be that he is not in time.

The first premise (as we have seen in the course of the first chapter) is true. The second premise is true. The third premise is true. The fourth premise (as we have seen in the course of the first chapter) is true. An absurdity follows with the addition of the supposition. So, the ultimate conclusion - the ultimate conclusion is the denial of the supposition - is true. It cannot be, in other words, that God is not in time in case it can be that he exists and it can be that a living thing possesses the power to bring about (in the very first instance) other living things which possess the power to act freely.[4]

*

Finally, let us consider the following argument (Ap6. A4) for the claim that it cannot be that God is not in time :

it cannot be that God is not a person ;

it cannot be that God is a person unless he possesses at least some such powers: the power to remember, the power to will, ... ;

it cannot be that God possesses (even some) such powers unless he is in time ;

so, it cannot be that God is not in time.

The conclusion follows from the first premise and the second premise and the third premise.

Does this argument establish that it cannot be that God is not in time? Well, questions at the very least should be raised about its third premise.

It is true, for example, that it cannot be that God possesses the power to remember unless he is time.

But, can't it be, for example, that God possesses the power to will although he is not time? Can't it be, for example, that God wills to bring about (in the very first instance) other living things which possess the power to act freely at a time although he is not in time? (This question takes it that it can be that a living thing possesses the power to bring in the very first instance other living things which possess the power to act freely.)

Notes

1. Something happens in God's life at ... t, and at t1, ... : God grows older.

2. There is a brief consideration of the following question in the course of the first chapter: can it be that God exists *and* there is an explanation of his existence?

This explanation is such that it is something and God does not exist without it and it is enough for him to exist.

Following the consideration of this question, it is taken that it cannot be that God exists and there is an explanation of his existence. So, it cannot be that God exists *and* he is dependent on something for his existence.

*

There is a consideration of God's powers to know this or that in the course of the first chapter, too. Can it be that God is dependent on these powers in that their exercise takes time in case it can be that he exists? Can it be that he is dependent for example on his power to reason in that he deduces a conclusion from premises and this takes time in case it can be that he exists? (Can it be that he is dependent, for example, on his power to reason in that he deduces a conclusion from premises and this takes time, and he does not possess other powers such as the power to will this or that until their exercise is complete in case it can be that he exists?) Well, it cannot be that this is so in case it can be that he exists.

Here first of all is an argument for the claim that it cannot be that their exercise takes time in case it can be that he exists. Its initial premises are as follows :

it can be that their exercise does not take time in case it can be that he exists ;

God is better (or greater) in case their exercise does not take time than in case their exercise does take time.

Let us suppose that it can be that he exists and it can be that their exercise takes time.

It can be in that case that he is better (or greater) than he can be by supposition. (This initial conclusion follows from the first premise and the second premise and the supposition.) That's absurd!

So, it is untrue that it can be that he exists *and* it can be that their exercise takes time.

The first premise is true. The second premise is true. The supposition is such that an absurdity follows with its addition. So, the ultimate conclusion - the ultimate conclusion is the denial of the supposition - is true. It cannot be in other words that their exercise takes time in case it can be that he exists.

So, it cannot be that God is dependent on these powers in that their exercise takes time in case it can be that he exists.

*

Can it be that God is dependent in some way on something(s)? Well, it can be that God is dependent in some way on something(s) in case it can be that he exists and it can be that a living thing possesses the power to bring about (in the very first instance) other living things which possess the power to act freely. Here is *an* argument for this claim :

it cannot be that a thing is not dependent in some way on something(s), *viz.* some other thing(s), in case it cannot be that that thing exists at all times *without* that other thing *or* those other things ;

it cannot be that God exists at all times *without* some other living things which possess the power to act freely in case it can be that he exists and it can be that a living thing possesses the power to bring about (in the very first instance) other living things which possess the power to act freely ;

so, it cannot be that he is not dependent in some way on something(s), *viz.* those other living things, in case it can be that that is so.

The conclusion follows from the first premise and the second premise. The first premise is true. The second premise (as we have seen effectively in the course of the first chapter) is true. So, the conclusion is true. It cannot be that he is not dependent in some way on something(s), *viz.* those other living things, in case it can be that that is so.

How is he dependent on those other things in case it can be that that is so more precisely? Well, he is dependent on those other things in order, for example, to have the property of *being a being which has exercised the power to bring about other such living things* in case it can be that that is so. It cannot be after all that he does not have this property at all times in case it can be that that is so *and* it cannot be that he has this property unless there are other such living things.

How can it be that God is dependent in some way on those other living things in case it can be that that is so? Well, this is so, at least to begin with, for it is *not* the case that this relation is such that it cannot be that he exists without them. It cannot be after all (as we have seen in the course of the first chapter) that there are not any times when he exists without them.

3. This time is the first moment of time.

God co-exists with it. (He co-exists with later times, too.)

But, nothing happens in God's life.

He has an extrinsic relation, *viz. co-exists with it.*

But, he does *not* undergo an extrinsic relational change. (He does not undergo an extrinsic relational change for he is not in time.)

4. It cannot be in that case that God is not dependent on some other thing, *viz.* time, (assuming time is a "thing" other than God) in case it can be that that is so.

Appendix 7

Some further remarks on a living thing which possesses the power to do this or that *freely*

The chapters of this work refer to a living thing which possesses the power to do this or that *freely.*[1]

Here is an analysis in part of the concept of being a living thing which possesses the power to do this or that *freely.* (This analysis adds to the analysis in very small part of this concept in the first chapter and the second chapter.)

The power at issue is such that its exercise takes a period of time. Let us say t - t3. (A living thing begins its exercise at t; it continues: ... t1 ... t2 ... ; it ends its exercise at t3.)

A living thing which possesses this power is *a self*[2] :

(i) a living thing does not possess the power to do this or that freely unless it possesses the power *to attend to grounds for it to will ... to do that this or that and to understand* in let us say the period t - t1 *that these grounds are enough for it to begin to exercise a (or its) power to will ... to do that this or that.*[3]

The exercise of its power to attend to grounds for it to will ... to do that this or that and to understand that these grounds are enough for it to begin to exercise a (or its) power will ... to do that this or that begins at t; it continues: t + i + i + i + i - i is a small fraction of time in the period t - t3; it ends at more or less t1.

The exercise of its power to attend to grounds for it to will ... to do that this or that and to understand in the period t - t1 that these grounds are enough for it to begin to exercise a (or its) power to will ... to do that this or that is enough to bring about the exercise of a (or its) power to will ... to do that this or that ;

(ii) a living thing does not possess the power to attend to grounds for it to will ... to do that this or that and to understand in the period t - t1 that these grounds are enough for it to begin to exercise a (or its) power to will ... to do that this or that unless it is *not* the case that the exercise of a (or its) power to attend to grounds for it to will ... to *not* do that this or that and to understand in let us say the period t - t1 that these grounds are enough for it to begin to exercise a (or its) power to will ... to not do that this or that is caused deterministically[4] ;

(iii) a living thing does not possess the power to do this or that freely unless it *in a way* possesses the power to attend to grounds for it to will ... to do that this or that and to understand *freely* in the period t - t1 that these grounds are enough for it to begin to exercise a (or its) power to will ... to do that this or that.

In what way? Well, in (at least) this way: the exercise of its power to attend to grounds for it to will ... to do that this or that and to understand in the period t - t1 that these grounds are enough for it to begin to exercise a (or its) power to will ... to do that this or that is *not* caused deterministically *or* indeterministically.[5]

This is so for otherwise it does not possess[6] the power to attend to grounds for it to will ... to do that this or that and to understand *independently* in the period t - t1 that these grounds are enough for it to begin to exercise a (or its) power to will ... to do that this or that.[7]

But, the exercise of its power to attend to grounds for it to will ... to do that this or that and to understand in the period t - t1 that these grounds are enough for it to begin to exercise a (or its) power to will ... to do that this or that is *not* by chance. (It is not by chance due to the following among other things: it believes that it attends to a particular situation;[8] it possesses this power; it believes that an exercise of such a power is enough to bring about the exercise of a (or its) power to will ... to do that this or that - see, in particular, (ix); it believes that an exercise of a (or its) power to will ... to do that this or that is enough to bring about the exercise of a (or its) power to bring about that this or that - see, in particular, (x).[9, 10]

There are two cases which are considered in the next section of this Appendix. These cases illustrate some way(s) that the exercise of this power by a living thing is not by chance. See the illustration in (iv), too.) ;

(iv) a living thing does not possess the power to do this or that freely unless it *in a (or another) way* possesses the power to attend to grounds for it to will ... to do that this or that and to understand *freely* in the period t - t1 that these grounds are enough for it to begin to exercise a (or its) power to will ... to do that this or that.

In what way? Well, in this (other) way: it possesses the power to attend to grounds for it to will ... to *not* do that this or that and to understand in the period t - t1 that these grounds are enough for it to begin to exercise a (or its) power to will ... to not do that this or that.

This is so for otherwise it has *no other option.* (See (xi), too.)

Here is an illustration of a living which does not possess the power to attend to grounds for it to will ... to *not* do this or that and to understand in the period t - t1 that these grounds are enough for it to begin to exercise a (or its) power to will ... to not do that this or that.

Let us suppose the following:

(i) that it possesses a power to attend to grounds for it to will ... to do that this or that and to understand in the period which begins at t that these grounds are enough for it to begin to exercise a (or its) power to will ... to do that this or that ;

(ii) that it understands from some other living thing just prior to t that it (*viz.* that other living thing) would bring about a state of affairs which is contrary to what it (very strongly) prefers in case it were not to will ... to do that this or that and it understands that these are grounds for it to will ... to do that this or that and enough for it to will ... to do that this or that ;

(iii) that it is in a (or this) way rational: to exercise its power to attend to grounds for it to will ... to do that this or that and to understand in the period which begins at t that these grounds are enough for it to begin to exercise a (or its) power to will ... to do that this or that is in a (or this) way rational. (See (ix) and (x), too.); it is such that then it possesses - and exercises - this power and it does not possess its alternative.

It does not possess the power to attend to grounds for it to will ... to not do that this or that and to understand in the period t - t1 that these grounds are enough for it to begin to exercise a (or its) power to will ... to not do that this or that.

So, it in this (other) way does not possess the power to attend to grounds for it to will ... to do that this or that and to understand *freely* in the period t - t1 that these grounds are enough for it to begin to exercise a (or its) power to will ... to do that this or that and it in that case does not possess the power to do that this or that freely. (See (xi), too.)

Further, the subject of this particular illustration does *not* possess the power to attend to grounds for it to will ... to do that this or that ... *independently* in the period t - t1 ... .

-

(v) a living thing does not possess the power to do this or that freely unless it possesses the power *to will ... to do that this or that* earlier than t3 - let us say in the period t1 - t2.

The exercise of its power to will ... to do that this or that begins at t1; it continues: t1 + i; it ends at more or less t2.[11]

The exercise of its power to will ... to do that this or that in the period t1 - t2 is enough to bring about the exercise of a (or its) power to bring about that this or that - that this or that is at issue in its will ... to do that this or that - in the period t2 - t3 ;

(vi) a living thing does not possess the power to do this or that freely unless it *in a way* possesses the power to will ... to do that this or that *freely*.

In what way? Well, in (at least) this way: it possesses the power to will ... to *not* do that this or that freely in let us say the period t1 - t2.

This is so because otherwise it has *no other option.*[12] (See (xi), too.) ;

(vii) a living thing does not possess the power to do this or that freely unless it *in a way* does *not* possess the power to will ... to do that this or that *freely*.

In what way? Well, in this way: the exercise of its power to will ... to do that this or that is brought about by the exercise of a (or its) power to attend to grounds for it to will ... to do that this or that and to understand in the period t - t1 that these grounds are enough for it to begin to exercise a (or its) power to will ... to do that this or that ;

-

(viii) a living thing does not possess the power to do that this or that freely unless it possesses the power *to bring about* that this or that - that this or that is at issue in its will ... to do that this or that - in the period t2 - t3.[13]

Its exercise of its power to bring about that this or that begins at t2; it continues: t + i ... ; it ends at t3. (For example, a human being does not possess the power to keep a promise to meet someone unless he *or* she possesses the power - the cells, the neurones, the muscles, ... - to meet that person.) ;

-

(ix) the exercise of its power to attend to grounds for it to will ... to do that this or that and to understand in the period which begins at t that these grounds are enough for it to begin to exercise a (or its) power to will ... to do that this or that is enough to bring about the exercise of a (or its) power to will ... to do that this or that.

A living thing does not possess the power to do this or that freely unless, prior to any exercise of its power to attend to grounds for it to will ... to do that this or that and to understand in the period which begins at t that these grounds are enough for it to begin to exercise a (or its) power to will ... to do that this or that, it possesses the power to believe that an exercise of such a power is enough to bring about the exercise of a (or its) power to will ... to do that this or that *and* this power is exercised ;

(x) the exercise of its power to will ... to do that this or that is enough to bring about the exercise of a (or its) power to bring about that this or that - that this or that is at issue in its will ... to do that this or that.

A living thing does not possess the power to do that this or that freely unless, prior to any exercise of its power to attend to grounds for it to will ... to do that this or that and to understand in the period which begins at t that these grounds are enough for it to begin to exercise a (or its) power to will ... to do that this or that, it possesses the power to (also) believe that an exercise of a (or its) power to will ... to do that this or that is enough to bring about the exercise of a (or its) power to bring about that this or that *and* this power is exercised[14];

-

(xi) a living thing does not possess the power to do this or that freely unless it possesses the power to *not* do that this or that freely.[15, 16] (In relation to the power to not do that this or that freely, (i) - (x) - with the appropriate substitutions - hold true.)

This is so because otherwise it has *no other option.*

(xii) a living thing which possesses the power referred to in (i) and which is rational in the way identified in the illustration in (iv) does not possess the power to not do that this or that freely unless it is *not* the case that it understands from some other living thing just prior to t that it (*viz.* that other living thing) would bring about a state of affairs which is contrary to what it (very strongly) prefers in case it were not to will ... to do that this or that and it understands that there is nothing further to attend to in regard to this matter.

Otherwise, it possesses the power to attend to grounds for it to will ... to do that this or that and to understand in the period t - t1 that these grounds are enough for it to begin to exercise a (or its) power to will ... to do that this or that only.

It does not possess the power to attend to grounds for it to will ... to not do that this or that and to understand in the period t - t1 that these grounds are enough for it to begin to exercise a (or its) power to will ... to not do that this or that.

So, it does not possess the power to not do that this or that freely.

In relation to its power to do that this or that freely, (xii) - with the appropriate substitutions - holds true.[17]

There is a change in such a living thing *itself* in the period t - t1 in case its power to attend to grounds for it to will ... to do that this or that and to understand in the period t - t1 that these grounds are enough for it to begin to exercise a (or its) power to will ... to do that this or that is exercised. Something occurs in it in this period.

There is a further change in such a living thing *itself* in the period t1 - t2 in case this is so: its power to will ... to do that this or that is exercised. Something occurs in it in this period.

These powers are powers of the living thing *itself*.

Such a living thing *itself* exercises the first of these powers. Such a living thing *itself* exercises control *of* the exercise of the first of these powers. (Such a living thing's control of the exercise of the first of these powers itself does not require any control by it.)

It does not exercise control of it unless the exercise of it is not caused deterministically *or* indeterministically.

It does not exercise control of it unless it believes that it attends to a particular situation.

It does not exercise control of it unless it believes that an exercise of such a power is enough to bring about the exercise of a (or its) power to will ... to do that this or that. (See (ix).)

It does not exercise control of it unless it believes that any exercise of a (or its) power to will ... to do that this or that is enough to bring about the exercise of a (or its) power to bring about that this or that. (See (x).)

It exercises control *by* the exercise of the first of these powers. Here are some of the ways that it exercises control:

it exercises control of the exercise of the other powers which constitute its power to do that this or that freely (in effect), *viz.* the powers referred to in (v) and (viii), by the exercise of it ;

it exercises control in that it exercises its power to do that this or that rather than its power to not do that this or that by the exercise of it.[18]

It exercises its power to do that this or that. Why? Well, it believes that it attends to a particular situation[19] and it possesses the first of these powers apart from anything else.[20, 21, 22]

*

With (i) - (xii) in mind, let us consider the following two cases.

First case

(i) a living thing is rational in the way identified in the illustration in (iv) *and* it is in a particular situation: it possesses the power to acquire grounds from some other living thing for it to will ... to do this or that *and* it possesses the power to understand that these are grounds for it to will ... to do that this or that and enough for it to will ... to do that this or that in let us say the period t-1 - t-2i. (The exercise of these powers begins at t-1; it continues: t-1 + i + i ... - i is a small fraction of time in the period t-1 - t; it ends at t-2i.) ;

it possesses the power to attend to grounds (including these grounds) for it to will ... to do that this or that and to understand in the period t - t1 that these grounds are enough for it to begin to exercise a (or its) power to will ... to do that this or that.

the exercise of this power is enough to bring about the exercise of a (or its) power to will ... to do that this or that. (It in a (or this) way does not possess the power to will ... to do that this or that freely.) ;

it is not the case that an exercise of this power is caused deterministically *or* indeterministically.

but, an exercise of this power is not by chance ;

it possesses the power to will ... to do that this or that in the period t1 - t2.

the exercise of this power is enough to bring about the exercise of a (or its) power to bring about that this or that - that this or that is at issue in its will ... to do that this or that ;

it possesses the power to bring about that this or that - that this or that is at issue in its will ... to do that this or that - in the period t2 - t3 ;

-

prior to any exercise of its power to attend to grounds for it to will ... to do that this or that and to understand in the period which begins at t that these grounds are enough for it to begin to exercise a (or its) power to will ... to do that this or that, it possesses the power to believe that an exercise of such a power is enough to bring about the exercise of a (or its) power to will ... to do that this or that ;

prior to any exercise of its power to attend to grounds for it to will ... to do that this or that and to understand in the period which begins at t that these grounds are enough for it to begin to exercise a (or its) power to will ... to do that this or that, it possesses the power to (also) believe that an exercise of a (or its) power to will ... to do that this or that is enough to bring about the exercise of a (or its) power to bring about that this or that ;

(ii) its power to acquire grounds from some other living thing for it to will ... to do that this or that is exercised *and* the grounds are that it (*viz.* that other living thing) would bring about a state of affairs which is contrary to what it (very strongly) prefers in case it were not to will ... to do that this or that *and* its power to understand that these are grounds for it to will ... to do that this or that and enough for it to will ... to do that this or that is exercised in the period t-1 - t-2i ;

-

its power to believe that an exercise of a (its) power to attend to grounds for it to will ... to do this or that and to understand that these grounds are enough for it to begin to exercise a (or its) power to will ... to do that this or that is enough to bring about the exercise of a (or its) power to will ... to do that this or that is exercised by let us say t-I ;

its power to (also) believe that an exercise of a (or its) power to will ... to do that this or that is enough to bring about the exercise of a (or its) power to bring about that this or that is exercised by t-i ;

-

its power to attend to, say, the grounds which are referred to in the first paragraph of *(ii)* for it to will ... to do that this or that and to understand in the period t - t1 that they are enough for it to begin to exercise a (or its) power to will ... to do that this or that is exercised[23] ;

its power to will ... to do that this or that in the period t1 - t2 is exercised ;

its power to bring about that this or that - that this or that is at issue in its will ... to do that this or that - in the period t2 - t3 is exercised.

The subject of this case does not possess a power to attend to grounds for it to will ... to not do that this or that and to understand in a period which begins at t that these grounds are enough for it to begin to exercise a (or its) power to will ... to not do that this or that. It, in that case, does not possess the power to not do that this or that freely. So, it does *not* possess the power to do that this or that freely.

Further, it does not possess the power to attend to grounds for it to will ... to do that this or that and to understand freely in the period which begins at t that these grounds are enough for it to begin to exercise a (or its) power to will ... to do that this or that *and* it does *not* possess the power to attend to these grounds for it to will ... to do that this or that ... *independently.* So, it does *not* possess the power to do that this or that in a *morally responsible* way.[24]

Second case

(i) a living thing possesses the power to attend to a particular situation which includes it and some other living thing by let us say t-3.

it possesses the power to attend to grounds for it to will ... to do this or that and to understand that these grounds are enough for it to will ... to do that this or that and the power to attend to grounds for it to will ... to not do this or that and to understand that these grounds are enough for it to will ... to not do that this or that by let us say t-3, too.

(the situation let us say is as follows: it has made a promise to meet that other living thing at a local place and it is at home and it is ill; that other living thing is about to arrive at that place.

the this or that let us say is to meet that other living thing at that place.

there is let us say a single set of grounds which are enough for it to will ... to meet that other living thing at that place, *viz.* a promise which it has made to do so.

there is let us say a single set of grounds which are enough for it to will ... to not meet that other living thing at that place, *viz.* it is ill.) ;

-

it possesses the power to attend to grounds for it to will ... to do that this or that and to understand in the period t - t1 (*or* even the period t + i - t1) that these grounds are enough for it to begin to exercise a (or its) power to will ... to do that this or that.

the exercise of this power is enough to bring about the exercise of a (or its) power to will ... to do that this or that in the period t1 - t2. (It in a (or this) way does not possess the power to will ... to do that this or that freely.) ;

it is not the case that an exercise of this power is caused deterministically *or* indeterministically.

but, an exercise of this power is not by chance ;

it possesses the power to will ... to do that this or that in the period t1 - t2.

the exercise of this power is enough to bring about the exercise of a (or its) power to bring about that this or that - that this or that is at issue in its will ... to do that this or that ;

it possesses the power to bring about that this or that - that this or that is at issue in its will ... to do that this or that - in the period t2 - t3 ;

-

prior to any exercise of its power to attend to grounds for it to will ... to do that this or that and to understand in a period which begins at t that these grounds are enough for it to begin to exercise a (or its) power to will ... to do that this or that, it possesses the power to believe that an exercise of such a power is enough to bring about the exercise of a (or its) power to will ... to do that this or that ;

prior to any exercise of its power to attend to grounds for it to will ... to do that this or that and to understand in a period which begins at t that these grounds are enough for it to begin to exercise a (or its) power to will ... to do that this or that, it possesses the power to (also) believe that an exercise of a (or its) power to will ... to do that this or that is enough to bring about the exercise of a (or its) power to bring about that this or that ;

-

it possesses the power to attend to grounds for it to will ... to not do that this or that and to *begin* to understand in a period which begins at t that these grounds are enough for it to begin to exercise a (or its) power to will ... to not do that this or that.

it is not the case that an exercise of this power is caused deterministically *or* indeterministically.

but, an exercise of this power is not by chance ;

-

prior to any exercise of its power to attend to grounds for it to will ... to not do that this or that and to begin to understand in a period which begins at t that these grounds are enough for it to begin to exercise a (or its) power to will ... to not do that this or that, it possesses the power to believe that a (complete) exercise of such a power is enough to bring about the exercise of a (or its) power to will ... to not do that this or that ;

prior to any exercise of its power to attend to grounds for it to will ... to not do that this or that and to begin to understand in a period which begins at t that these grounds are enough for it to begin to exercise a (or its) power to will ... to not do that this or that, it possesses the power to (also) believe that an exercise of a (or its) power to will ... to not do that this or that is enough to bring about the exercise of a (or its) power to not bring about that this or that ;

-

its power to attend to grounds for it to will ... to not do that this or that and to begin to understand in a period which begins at t that these grounds are enough for it to begin to exercise a (or its) power to will ... to not do that this or that is exercised *in case* its power to attend to ... grounds for it ... to do that this or that ... in the period t - t1 ... is *not* exercised ;

some other living thing begins to bring it about at let us say t + i that its power to attend to grounds for it to will ... to do that this or that and to understand in what remains of the period t - t1 that they are enough for it to begin to exercise a (or its) power to will ... to do that this or that is exercised *just in case* its power to attend to grounds for it to will ... to not do that this or that and to begin to understand in a period which begins at t that these grounds are enough for it to begin to exercise a (or its) power to will ... to not do that this or that is exercised ;

it does not possess the power to be aware (*or* believe) that this is so[25] ;

(ii) its power to attend to the particular situation which includes it and the other living thing is exercised by t-3.

its power to attend to grounds for it to will ... to do this or that in it and to understand that these grounds are enough for it to will ... to do that this or that and its power to attend to grounds for it to will ... to not do this or that in it and to understand that these grounds are enough for it to will ... to not do that this or that is exercised by t-3, too ;

-

its power to believe that an exercise of a (or its) power to attend to grounds for it to will ... to do this or that and to understand that these grounds are enough for it to begin to exercise a (or its) power to will ... to do that this or that is enough to bring about the exercise of a (or its) power to will ... to do that this or that is exercised by t-3 ;

its power to (also) believe that an exercise of a (or its) power to will ... to do that this or that is enough to bring about the exercise of a (or its) power to bring about that this or that is exercised by t-3 ;

-

its power to believe that an exercise of a (its) power to attend to grounds for it to will ... to not do this or that and to understand that these grounds are enough for it to begin to exercise a (or its) power to will ... to not do that this or that is enough to bring about the exercise of a (or its) power to will ... to not do that this or that is exercised by t-3 ;

its power to (also) believe that an exercise of a (or its) power to will ... to not do that this or that is enough to bring about the exercise of a (or its) power to not bring about that this or that is exercised by t-3 ;

-

its power to attend to grounds for it to will ... to do that this or that and to understand in the period t - t1 that these grounds are enough for it to begin to exercise a (or its) power to will ... to do that this or that is exercised[26] ;

its power to will ... to do that this or that in the period t1 - t2 is exercised ;

its power to bring about that this or that - that this or that is at issue in its will ... to do that this or that - in the period t2 - t3 is exercised.

The subject of this case does not possess a power to attend to grounds for it to will ... to not do that this or that and to understand in a period which begins at t that these grounds are enough for it to begin to exercise a (or its) power to will ... to not do that this or that. It, in that case, does not possess the power to not do this or that freely. So, it does *not* possess the power to do that this or that freely.

Still, there is at least nothing which is referred to in the description of this case and which is such that its subject does not possess the power to do that this or that in a *morally responsible* way.[27, 28]

In particular, there is at least nothing which is referred to in the description of this case and which is such that it does not possess the power to do that this or that *independently.*

Notes

1. They refer to a living thing which possesses the power to act *freely.*

2. It can be (as we have seen in the course of the first chapter) that God possesses the power to bring about (in the very first instance) other living things which possess the power to do this or that freely in case it can be that he exists and it can be that a living thing possesses this power.

A living thing which possesses the power to do this or that freely is *a self.*

So, it can be that God possesses the power to bring about (in the very first instance) selves in case it can be that that is so. (The second chapter among other things identifies other powers of these selves.)

3. The exercise of its power to attend to grounds for it to will ... to do that this or that and to understand in the period which begins at t that these grounds are enough for it to begin to exercise a (or its) power to will ... to do that this or that does not occur unless it believes that it attends to a particular situation.

Accordingly, (i'):

(i') a living thing does not possess the power to do this or that freely in it unless it possesses the power to attend to grounds for it to will ... to do that this or that in it and to understand in let us say the period t - t1 that these grounds are enough for it to begin to exercise a (or its) power to will ... to do that this or that in it.

4. The exercise of this power is an event. An event is caused *deterministically* just in case there are natural laws which prevail and physical conditions which prevail and these natural laws and physical conditions cause (or bring about) that event and that event had to occur given these natural laws and physical conditions. (An *event* includes a change in something *or* it is a change in something.)

Here is a brief argument for (ii):

this power of a living thing does not have to be exercised in case it possesses an alternative power ;

this power of a living thing has to be exercised in case the exercise of it is causally determined ;

so, it does not possess an alternative power in case the exercise of it is causally determined.

The conclusion follows from the first premise and the second premise. The first premise is true. The second premise is true. So, the conclusion is true. It does not possess an alternative power in case the exercise of it is causally determined. (It in other words does not possess an alternative power unless the exercise of it is not causally determined. This is the claim in (ii).)

*

A living thing does not possess the power to attend to grounds for it to will ... to do that this or that and to understand in the period t - t1 that these grounds are enough for it to begin to exercise a (or its) power to will ... to do that this or that unless it is *not* the case (that it exists for a period up to t and) that it does not exist at t (and after) is caused deterministically.

A living thing does not possess the power to attend to grounds for it to will ... to do that this or that and to understand in the period t - t1 that these grounds are enough for it to begin to exercise a (or its) power to will ... to do that this or that unless it is *not* the case that it does not possess a power to attend to grounds for it to will ... to do that this or that *or* to grounds for it to will ... to not do that this or that ... is caused deterministically.

5. An event is caused *indeterministically* just in case there are natural laws which prevail and physical conditions which prevail and these natural laws and physical conditions cause (or bring about) that event and that event is just one of a number of events which each had a probability of occurring given these natural laws and physical conditions.

6. Among other things in case it is caused deterministically. See (xi) (and (ii)).

See (iv), too.

7. A living thing does not possess the power to do this or that freely unless it is *not* the case that the (mere) exercise of a (or its) power to attend to (one *or* more) grounds for it to will ... to do that this or that in a period of time just prior to t is enough to bring about the exercise of its power to attend to grounds (including one or other of these grounds) for it to will ... to do that this or that and to understand in the period t - t1 that these grounds are enough for it to begin to exercise a (or its) power to will ... to do that this or that.

8. See the 3rd note.

9. See what follows and the 16th note, too.

10. See what follows and the 18th note, too.

11. In some other accounts, a living thing's *will* is its *effective desire(s).* Here is an illustration: let us suppose that a living thing has a desire to walk and this desire brings it about that it walks; its will is to walk. (It is not its will in the absence of a (or its) power to walk.) See, for example, Gary Watson, "Free Agency", in Gary Watson (ed.), *Free Will* (2nd Edition, Oxford, 2003), pp.337-351. See, in particular, p.338 and p.347 of this article. (This article was originally published in the *Journal of Philosophy*, 72/8 (1975), pp.205-220.)

In the account of this Appendix, a living thing's *will* is any exercise - any exercise which is brought by the exercise of the power referred to in (i) by it itself - of a (or its) power to will ... to do this or that. (It is its will in the absence of a (or its) power to do that this or that.)

12. Moore sets out an analysis of free will in the sixth chapter of his work *Ethics* (Oxford, 1912). It is a conditional analysis of free will.

Here is a statement of Moore's analysis **:**

let us suppose that someone wills or "chooses" to do this or that *and* he does that this or that **;**

he does that this or that because he wills or "chooses" to do that this or that *and* he is able to or "can" do that this or that ;

although the first of these occurrences, *viz.* he wills or "chooses" do that this or that, is caused, he wills or "chooses" to do that this or that *freely* for he is able to or "can" *not* do that this or that - that is to say, he would not have done that this or that in case he had willed or "chosen" to not do it.

Let us observe in passing that he (*viz.* the subject) possesses a power to will or "choose" to do that this or that and he possesses a power to do (or bring about) that this or that - that this or that is at issue in his will or "choice" to do that this or that.

Let us also observe that he does not possess the power to will or "choose" to not do that this or that in case the exercise of his power to will or "choose" to do that this or that is caused deterministically.

Let us also observe that he does not possess the power to not do (or bring about) that this or that in case the exercise of his power to will or "choose" to do that this or that is caused deterministically *and* the exercise of his power to will or "choose" to do that this or that is enough to bring about the exercise of a (or his) power to do (or bring about) that this or that - that this or that is at issue in his will or "choice" to do that this or that.

Finally, let us observe the following: in the analysis of Moore (as we shall see more explicitly in the course of what follows), he does not possess the power to will or "choose" to do that this or that *freely* unless he is able to or "can" (or possesses the power to) not do (or bring about) that this or that; in the analysis of this Appendix, it is *not* the case that someone (*or* he) does not possess the power to will or "choose" to do that this or that *freely* unless he is able to or "can" (or possesses the power to) not do (or bring about) that this or that.

That done, here is a re-statement of Moore's analysis :

let us suppose that someone wills or "chooses" (or completes the exercise of his power to will or "choose") to do this or that at more or less t2 and he does that this or that at t3.

(M1) someone wills or "chooses" (or completes the exercise of his power to will or "choose") to do that this or that at more or less t2 ... he does that this or that at t3 ;

he does that this or that at t3 because he wills or "chooses" (or completes the exercise of his power to will or "choose") to do that this or that at more or less t2 *and* he is able to or "can" (or possesses the power to) do (or bring about) that this or that in the period of time t2 - t3. (He possesses the capacity, *viz.* the appropriate cells, neurones, ... to do or bring about that this or that and the opportunity to exercise this capacity in the period t2 - t3. The exercise of this power begins at t2; it continues: t + i ... ; it ends at t3.)

For Moore:

(M2) he does that this or that at t3 in case he wills or "chooses" to do that this or that at more or less t2

just in case

(M3) he is able to or "can" (or possesses the power to) do (or bring about) that this or that in the period t2 - t3. (He possesses the capacity, *viz.* the appropriate cells, neurones, ... to do or bring about that this or that and the opportunity to exercise this capacity in the period t2 - t3. The exercise of this power begins at t2; it continues: t + i ... ; it ends at t3.) ;

although the first of these occurrences, *viz.* he wills or "chooses" do that this or that, is caused, he wills or "chooses" to do that this or that freely for he is able to or "can" (or possesses the power to) *not* do (or bring about) that this or that in let us say the period t2 - t3 - that is to say, he would not have done that this or that at t3 in case he had willed or "chosen" to not do that this or that at let us say more or less t2.

For Moore:

(M4) he would not have done that this or that at t3 in case he had willed or "chosen" to not do that this or that at more or less t2

just in case

(M5) he is able to or "can" (or possesses the power to) not do (or bring about) that this or that in the period t2 - t3. (He possesses the capacity, *viz.* the appropriate cells, neurones, ... to not do or bring about that this or that and the opportunity to exercise this capacity in the period t2 - t3. The exercise of this power begins at t2; it continues: t + i ... ; it ends at t3.)

For Moore, he wills or "chooses" to do that this or that *freely* at more or less t2 because (M5) *or* (M4). (See the discussion which follows of Chisholm's argument for a claim which is contrary to the claim made by Moore.)

It is a conditional analysis because (M4).

*

Chisholm sets out an argument for the claim that it can be that someone would not have done this or that in case he had willed or "chosen" to not do that this or that *and* he is *not* able to or "cannot" not do that this or that. This is contrary to the claim made by Moore. (See, for example, "Human Freedom and the Self", The Lindley Lecture, Department of Philosophy, University of Kansas, 1964, pp.3-15. This is reprinted in G. Watson (ed.), *op. cit.*, pp.26-37).

Here is a statement of Chisholm's argument. (The page which is referred to in the paragraphs which follow is a page in Gary Watson (ed.), *op. cit.*.) :

it can be that someone wills or "chooses" to do this or that and he does that this or that ;

and he would not have done that this or that in case he had willed or "chosen" to not do that this or that. ("... he happens ... to be a man such that, if he had chosen not to ... he would not have ..." (p.29).) ;

and he would not have done that this or that *unless* he is able or "can" will or "choose" to not do that this or that. ("If the man could not have chosen to do otherwise, then he would not have done otherwise ..." (p.29).) ;

and he is *not* able to or "cannot" will or "choose" to not do that this or that. ("Suppose that [he] ... could not have *chosen* ... otherwise" (p.29).) ;

so, it can be that he would not have done that this or that in case he had willed or "chosen" to not do that this or that *and* he is not able to or "cannot" not do that this or that. ("... our man might be such that, if he had chosen to do otherwise, then he would have done otherwise, and yet *also* such that he could not have done otherwise" (p.29).) (This is contrary to the claim made by Moore.)

Here is a re-statement of Chisholm's argument :

(C1) it can be that someone wills or "chooses" (or completes the exercise of his power to will or "choose") to do this or that at let us say more or less t2 ... he does that this or that at let us say t3 ;

and

(C2) he would not have done that this or that at let us say t3 in case he had willed or "chosen" to not do that this or that at more or less t2 ;

and

(C3) he would not have done that this or that at t3 *unless* he is able to or "can" (or possesses the power to) will or "choose" to not do (or bring about) that this or that in let us say the period t1 - t2 ;

and

(C4) he is *not* able to or "cannot" (or does not possess the power to) will or "choose" to not do (or bring about) that this or that in the period t1 - t2. (It is not the case that he possesses the capacity, *viz.* the appropriate cells, neurones, ... , to will or "choose" to not do or bring about that this or that and the opportunity to exercise this capacity in the period t1 - t2. The exercise of this power begins at t1; it continues: t + i ; it ends at more or less t2.) ;

(C5) so, it can be that he would not have done that this or that at t3 in case he had willed or "chosen" to not do that this or that at more or less t2 *and* he is not able to or "cannot" (or does not possess the power to) not do (or bring about) that this or that in the period t2 - t3. (It is not the case that he possesses the capacity, *viz.* the appropriate cells, neurones, ... to not do or bring about that this or that and the opportunity to exercise this capacity in the period t2 - t3. The exercise of this power begins at t2; it continues: t + i ... ; it ends at t3.) (This is contrary to the claim made by Moore.)

In passing, let us note the following with regard to (C4). (C4) refers to the following power: the power to will or "choose" to not do that this or that in the period t1 - t2.

Moore refers to such a power. Indeed, we are able to add that, for Moore:

(M6) someone completes the exercise of a (or his) power to will or "choose" to not do that this or that at more or less t2 in case he begins to exercise this power at t1

just in case

(M7) he possesses the power to will or "choose" to not do (or bring about) that this or that in the period t1 - t2. (He possesses the capacity, *viz.* the appropriate cells, neurones, ... , to will or "choose" to not do or bring about that this or that and the opportunity to exercise this capacity in the period t1 - t2.)

Here is Moore:

"... many people...will say

...: Granted that we often *should* have acted differently, *if* we had chosen differently, yet it is not true that we have Free Will, unless it is also often true in such cases that we *could* have *chosen* differently

... And since there is some plausibility in this contention

... If by saying that we *could* have done, what we did not do, we ... mean merely that we *should* have done it, *if* we had chosen to do it, then obviously, by saying that we *could* have *chosen* to do it, we ... mean merely that we *should* have so chosen, *if* we had chosen *to make the choice*" (*op.cit.*, p.135).

For Moore, there is "some plausibility" for the claim that someone (*or* he) wills or "chooses" to do that this or that *freely* at more or less t2 because (M5) *or* (M4) *and* (M7) *or* (M6). (Let us observe the following: in the analysis of Moore, there is "some plausibility" for the claim that he does not possess the power to will or "choose" to do that this or that freely unless he possesses the power to will or "choose" to not do (or bring about) that this or that; in the analysis of this Appendix, someone (or he) does not possess the power to will or "choose" to do that this or that freely unless he possesses the power to will or "choose" to not do (or bring about) that this or that.)

It is a conditional analysis because (M4) *and* (M6). (See Moore, *op.cit.*, pp.136-137, too.)

That done, let us return to Chisholm's argument. Does his argument establish that his claim is true?

Well, his argument does not establish that his claim is true for Moore. The following is so after all for Moore :

(C2) (or (M4)) *entails* (6) (or (M5)):

(6) he is able to or "can" (or possesses the power to) not do (or bring about) that this or that in the period t2 - t3. (He possesses the capacity, *viz.* the appropriate cells, neurones, ..., to not do or bring about that this or that and the opportunity to exercise this capacity in the period t2 - t3.) ;

but, (C3) and (C4) *entail* (C7):

(C7) it is *not* the case that he is able to or "can" (or possesses the power to) not do (or bring about) that this or that in the period t2 - t3. (It not the case that he possesses the capacity, *viz.* the appropriate cells, neurones, ..., to not do or bring about that this or that *and* the *opportunity* to exercise this capacity in the period t2 - t3.) (Chisholm writes: "... if he could *not* have chosen *not* to ..., then he could not have done anything other than just what it was that he did do" and "Suppose that [he] ... could not have *chosen* ... otherwise ... " (p.29).) ;

so, (C5) - (C5) claims that it can be that (C2) *and* (C7) - is *untrue.*

His argument in any case does not establish that his claim is true :

(C3) and (C4) entail (C7):

(C7) it is *not* the case that he is able to or "can" (or possesses the power to) not do (or bring about) that this or that in the period t2 - t3. (It not the case that he possesses the capacity, *viz.* the appropriate cells, neurones, ..., to not do or bring about that this or that and the opportunity to exercise this capacity in the period t2 - t3.) ;

(C2) in that case is *untrue* ;

so, (C5) - (C5) claims that it can be that (C2) *and* (C7) - is *untrue.*

*

Keith Lehrer, an analytic philosopher, sets out an argument for the claim that it can be that someone is not able to not do this or that *and* he would not have done that this or that in case he had willed or "chosen" to not do that this or that. This is contrary to the claim made by Moore. (Keith Lehrer, "Cans Without Ifs", *Analysis*, 29 (1968), pp.29-32. Incidentally, there has been considerable discussion about his argument. See, for example, G.E.M. Anscombe, "Soft Determinism", *Collected Philosophical Papers*, vol.2, *Metaphysics and the Philosophy of Mind* (Oxford, 1981), pp.163-172.)

Here is a statement of Lehrer's argument :

it can be that someone wills or "chooses" to do this or that and he does that this or that ;

and he is *not* able to not do that this or that *unless* he wills or "chooses" to not do that this or that ;

and he does *not* will or "choose" to not do that this or that ;

and he would not have done that this or that *in case* he had willed or "chosen" to not do that this or that ;

so, it can be that someone is not able to not do that this or that *and* he would not have done that this or that in case he had willed or "chosen" to not do that this or that. (This is contrary to the claim made by Moore.)

Here is a re-statement of Lehrer's argument :

(L1) it can be that someone wills or "chooses" to do this or that at more or less t2 ... he does that this or that at t3 ;

and

(L2) he is *not* able to or "cannot" (or does not possess the power to) not do (or bring about) that this or that in the period t2 - t3 *unless* he wills or "chooses" to not do that this or that at more or less t2 ;

and

(L3) he does *not* will or "choose" to not do that this or that at more or less t2 ;

and

(L4) he would not have done that this or that at t3 *in case* he had willed or "chosen" to not do that this or that at more or less t2 ;

(L5) so, it can be that someone is not able to or "cannot" (or does not possess the power to) not do (or bring about) that this or that in the period t2 - t3 *and* he would not have done that this or that at t3 in case he had willed or "chosen" to not do that this or that at more or less t2. (This is contrary to the claim made by Moore.)

Incidentally, the first conjunct of (L5) (*viz.* someone is not able ...) is ("rendered") true *because* (L3) for Lehrer. We are able to take it alternatively that the first conjunct of (L5) is true prior to the period t1 - t2. (It is in this period that he, *viz.* the subject, wills or "chooses" to do that this or that *or* he wills or "chooses" to not do that this or that.) He would in that case have been able or "could" have (or would have possessed the power to) to not do (or bring about) that this or that *in case* he had willed or "chosen" to not do that this or that at more or less t2.

Here is *a* response on behalf of Moore. Let us suppose, for the sake of argument, that Lehrer's argument establishes that his claim is true. Still, his (*viz.* the subject's) will is free for (L4) (or (M4)).

And, this is still dependent on the following: he is able or "can" (or possesses the power to) not do (or bring about) that this or that in the period t2 - t3. This is so for the following is so:

(L4) (or (M4)) he would not have done that this or that at t3 in case he had willed or "chosen" to not do that this or that at more or less t2

just in case

(M5′) he would have been able or "could" have (or would have possessed the power to) to not do (or bring about) that this or that in the period t2 - t3 in case he had willed or "chosen" to not do that this or that at more or less t2.

13. An exercise of its power to bring about that this or that in the period t2 - t3 is *not* by chance due to the following among other things: the powers - the powers themselves - which bring it about; the exercise of these powers is enough to bring it about.

14. A living thing does not possess the power to do this or that freely unless it is *not* the case that the (mere) exercise of the powers referred to in (ix) - (x) prior to t is enough to bring about the exercise a (or its) power to attend to grounds for it to will ... to do this or that and to understand in the period which begins at t that these grounds are enough for it to begin to exercise a (or its) power to will ... to do that this or that.

15. A living thing possesses the power to *not* do this or that freely during a period of time just in case it possesses the power to do something other than this or that in it.

16. Let us suppose that the following is so:

(i) it possesses a power to do this or that and a power to not do that this or that at a time.

(It possesses, for example, a power to be considerate of other living things and a power to not be considerate of other living things at t.) ;

(ii) it also possesses a power to diminish {its power to not do that this or that}.

It also possesses a power to diminish {its power to not do that this or that} for it possesses a power to diminish {its power to attend to grounds for it to will ... to not do that this or that and to understand that these grounds are enough for it to begin to exercise a (or its) power to will ... to not do that this or that}.

(With our example in mind, it also possesses a power to diminish {its power to not be considerate of other living things}.

It also possesses a power to diminish {its power to not be considerate of other living things} for it possesses a power to diminish {its power to attend to grounds for it to will ... to not be considerate of other living things and to understand that these grounds are enough for it to begin to exercise a (or its) power to will ... to not be considerate of other living things}) ;

(iii) it exercises this power such that it does *not* possess {its power to attend to grounds for it to will ... to not do that this or that and to understand that these grounds are enough for it to begin to exercise

a (or its) power to will ... to not do that this or that} at a later time. So, it does not possess a power to not do that this or that after that time.

(With our example in mind, it exercises this power such that it does *not* possess {its power to attend to grounds for it to will ... to not be considerate of other living things and to understand that these grounds are enough for it to begin to exercise a (or its) power to will ... to not be considerate of other living things} at say t9. So, it does not possess a power to not be considerate of other living things after t9.)

An exercise of its power to attend to grounds for it to will ... to do that this or that and to understand that these grounds are enough for it to begin to exercise a (or its) power to will ... to do that this or that - an exercise of its power to do that this or that - after that time is not by chance in this way. (An exercise of it after that time is not by chance in this way and in other ways - see (iii).)

(With our example in mind, an exercise of its power to attend to grounds for it to will ... to be considerate of other living things and to understand that these grounds are enough for it to begin to exercise a (or its) power to will ... to be considerate of other living things - an exercise of its power to be considerate of other living things - after t9 is not by chance in this way. An exercise of it after t9 is not by chance in this way and in other ways.)

17. It is untrue (as we have seen in the course of the first chapter) that it can be that God does not exercise a (or his) power to bring about (in the very first instance) some other living things which possess the power to do this or that freely at a time in case it can be that he exists and it can be that a living thing possesses this power.

Let us suppose that it can be that he exists and it can be that a living thing possesses this power and he exercises a (or his) power to bring about (in the very first instance) some other living things which possess the power to do this or that freely at a time and one of these other living things exercises its power to do this or that freely (at some time) and the grounds which it attends to for it to do that this or that ... are (for example) *overly self-interested.*

It cannot be that it does not (at least) possess a power to develop a power to understand that it has exercised this (or such a) power and to develop a power to diminish this (or such a) power.

Otherwise, it can be that these other such living things do not possess these powers in a universe which is brought about by God. That's absurd!

18. Let us suppose that it exercises the first of these powers.

It *itself* exercises *it.*

Is it the case that it does not exercise it freely unless it exercises a (or its) power to attend to grounds for it to exercise it and to understand by let us say t-i that these grounds are enough for it to exercise it (and it does not exercise this power freely unless it exercises a (or its) power to attend to grounds for it to attend to these grounds and to understand by let us say t-2i that these grounds are enough for it to exercise it ...)?

Well, no. (*Cf.* G. Strawson, *Freedom and Belief* (Oxford, 1986), chapter 2.)

*

Let us suppose that it exercises the first of these powers.

It *itself* exercises *it* as opposed to its alternative.

Is it the case that it does not exercise it freely unless it exercises a (or its) power to attend to grounds for it to exercise it as opposed to its alternative and to understand by let us say t-i that these grounds are enough for it to exercise it as opposed to its alternative (and it does not exercise this power freely unless it exercises a (or its) power to attend to grounds for it to attend to these grounds as opposed to its alternative and to understand by let us say t-2i that these grounds are enough for it to exercise it as opposed to its alternative ...)?

Well, no. (*Cf.* G. Strawson, *ibid.*, chapter 2 and T. Nagel, *The View from Nowhere* (Oxford 1986), chapter 7. Chapter 7 of *The View from Nowhere* is re-printed in Gary Watson (ed.), *op.cit.*, pp.229-256. Such a requirement is a misunderstanding of such a living thing.)

It does *not* exercise it *freely* in case the following is so:

(i) it exercises a (or its) power to attend to grounds for it to exercise {a (or its) power to attend to grounds for it to do this or that and to understand in the period which begins at t that these grounds are enough for it to begin to exercise a (or its) power to will ... to do that this or that} as opposed to its alternative and to understand by t-i that these grounds are enough for it to exercise it as opposed to its alternative ;

(ii) it is in a (or this) way rational: to exercise it in that case is in a (or this) way rational; it is such that then it possesses - and exercises - this power and it does not possess its alternative.

It does not possess its alternative. So, it does not exercise it freely.

19. It cannot be (as we have seen in the course of the first chapter) that God does not exercise a (or his) power to bring about (in the very first instance) some other living things which possess the power to do this or that freely in a universe at a time in case it can be that he exists and it can be that a living thing possesses this power.

These other living things (as we have seen in the course of the second chapter) possess (among other powers) the power to know about this or that situation. (Such a living thing - a living thing - does not know about this or that situation unless it believes that it attends to it.)

20. Here is another account of a living thing, *viz.* a human being, which possesses the power to do this or that freely.

It is the account of Carl Ginet, an analytic philosopher. (Carl Ginet, *On Action* (Cambridge, 1990). See also, for example, his article "Freedom, Responsibility and Agency", *The Journal of Ethics,* 1:1 (1997), pp.374-380. This article is in large part re-printed in Robert Kane (ed.), *Free Will* (Blackwell, 2002), pp.207-220.)

Here is a statement of this account. (It, unlike the statement which follows, does not in the main refer to "powers". The pages which are referred to in the paragraphs which follow are pages in Robert Kane (ed.), *op. cit.*. The page which is referred to in particular is p.210. He writes on this page: "... let me state my view more fully ....".)

Someone's "action" is either a "causally simple mental action" or one which begins with a "causally simple mental action". ("Every action ... either is or begins with a causally simple mental action" (p.210).)

A mental event is an "action" just in case it has "a certain intrinsic phenomenal quality", *viz.* it seems to someone that it occurs due to him. ("A ... mental event is an action if and only if it has a certain intrinsic phenomenal quality ... seems to me ... it is ... as if I make it occur" (p.210).)

A "causally simple mental action" is a mental event which is an "action" *and* which is not constituted of this mental event causing some other mental event(s). ("... a causally simple mental action ... does not consist of one mental event causing others" (p.210).) Here is an example of an "action" which is a "causally simple mental action": someone *willing to* .... ("... a [causally] simple mental act of willing...." (p.210).)

Here is an example of "action" which begins with a "causally simple mental action": a door being opened by someone ("... [the] action of opening [a] door ..." (p.210).) It begins with the "[causally] simple mental action" of him willing to open it. (It "... begins with a volition, a [causally] simple mental act of willing to [open it] ..." (p.210).) It causes ultimately it being opened by him. It is an example of a "causally complex action" (p.210).

Someone's "causally simple mental action" occurs (merely) because it is his. ("... I make my own ... [causally] simple acts occur ... simply by being their subject ..." (p.210).)

Someone's "causally simple mental action" does not occur because it is caused by him. ("... I make my own ... [causally] simple acts occur not by causing them..." (p.210).)

Someone is in control of a (or his) "[causally] simple mental action" just in case it is "free". ("... my own simple acts ... are ... controlled by me, provided they are free ... " (p.210).)

A "[causally] simple mental action" which is "free" is not determined. ("... my own simple acts ... are ... controlled by me, provided they are free, that is, not determined by something else, not causally necessitated by antecedent states and events" (p.210).)

An "action" of someone is "free" just in case he possessed the power to not do it up to the time he does it. ("Let us say that an action is free if and only if until the time of the action the agent had it open to her not to perform it ...." (p.207).)

Someone's "action" occurs sometimes for "a certain reason". There is in that case an "intention", too. ("... when an action is ... one an agent did for a certain reason supplied by an antecedent motive ... [there is] an *intention* concurrent with the action (pp.216-217).)

This "intention" is a (or his) mental state that the "action" occurs in order to accommodate the "reason". ("The intention has the following content: it ... says that this action is to satisfy that motive ..." (p.217).)

Someone possesses the power to do this or that (a "causally complex action") freely in case the following is so:

(G1) he possesses the power to will .... to do that this or that in let us say the period t1 - t2.

The exercise of this power is enough to bring about the exercise of a (or his) power to bring about that this or that - that this or that is at issue in his will ... to do that this or that ;

and

(G2) he possesses the power to bring about that this or that - that this or that is at issue in its will ... to do that this or that - in let us say the period t2 - t3 ;

and

(G3) he possesses the power to will .... to not do that this or that in let us say the period t1 - t2.

The exercise of this power is enough to bring about the exercise of a (or his) power to not bring about that this or that - not that this or that is at issue in his will ... to not do that this or that ;

and

(G4) he possesses the power to not bring about that this or that - not that this or that is at issue in its will ... to not do that this or that - in let us say the period t2 - t3.

An exercise say of his power to will .... to do that this or that is an instance of a "causally simple mental action". (He is in control of it just in case it is "free"; it is "free" just in case (or because) he possesses the power to will .... to not do that this or that.)

An exercise say of his power to will .... to do that this or that is enough to bring about the exercise of his power to bring about that this or that and he does that this or that. That he does that this or that is an instance of a "causally complex action". (It is "free" just in case (or because) he possesses the power to will .... to not do that this or that and he possesses the power to not bring about that this or that - not that this or that is at issue in its will ... to not do that this or that.)

This "causally complex action", let us take it in the paragraphs which follow, is for "a certain reason". (There is in that case a (or his) mental state that it occurs in order to accommodate that "reason".)

There are a number of similarities between this account of a living thing's, *viz.* a human being's, power to do this or that (a "causally complex action") freely and the account of a living thing's power to do this or that freely in this Appendix. They include the following **:**

someone's *or* its power to do this or that *freely* during a period includes the power to *not* do that this or that freely during it **;**

the exercise of a part of it, *viz.* its first part, is *not* caused (or brought about) deterministically **;**

the exercise of a part of it, *viz.* its first part, is *not* by chance **;**

he *or* it exercises control by the exercise of a part of it, *viz.* its first part. (Here are two ways that he *or* it exercises control:

(i) he *or* it exercises control of the exercise of all of the other powers which constitute his *or* its power to do that this or that freely (in effect) by the exercise of it ;

(ii) he *or* it exercises control in that he *or* it exercises his *or* its power to do that this or that rather than his *or* its power to not do that this or that by the exercise of it.) **;**

the exercise of someone's *or* its power to do this or that freely is constituted *solely* by events**.**

There are a number of dissimilarities between this account of a living thing's, *viz.* a human being's, power to do this or that (a "causally complex action") freely and the account of a living thing's power to do this or that freely in this Appendix. They include the following:

in this account, it is *not* the case that someone does not exercise his power to do this or that (a "causally complex action") freely unless the power which he exercises to control all of the other powers which constitute his power to do that this or that freely is a (or his) power to attend to grounds for him to will ... to do that this or that and to understand that these grounds are enough for him to begin to exercise a (or his) power to will ... to do that this or that; in the account of this Appendix, a living thing does not exercise its power to do this or that freely unless the power which it exercises to control all of the other powers which constitute its power to do that this or that freely *is* a (or its) power to attend to grounds for it to will ... to do that this or that and to understand that these grounds are enough for to begin to exercise a (or its) power to will ... to do that this or that;

in this account, someone exercises control of the exercise of the first part of his power to do this or that (a "causally complex action") freely (merely) because it is his and it is "free"; in the account of this Appendix, it is *not* the case that a living thing exercises control of the exercise of the first part of its power to do this or that freely (merely) because it is its and it is "free";

in this account, it is *not* the case that someone does not exercise his power to do this or that (a "causally complex action") freely unless his power to will ... to do that this or that is caused (or brought about) by something else; in the account of this Appendix, a living thing does not exercise its power to do this or that freely unless its power to will ... to do that this or that *is* caused (or brought about) by something else, *viz.* the exercise of a (or its) power to attend to grounds for it to will ... to do that this or that and to understand that these grounds are enough for it to begin to exercise a (or its) power to will ... to do that this or that.

*

Here is another account of a living thing, *viz.* a human being, which possesses the power to do this or that freely.

It is the account of Robert Kane, an analytic philosopher. It is the account which is set out in an article entitled "Responsibility, Luck, and Chance: Reflections on Free Will and Indeterminism". (Robert

Kane, "Responsibility, Luck, and Chance: Reflections on Free Will and Indeterminism", *Journal of Philosophy*, 96/5 (1999), pp.217-240. This article is reprinted in Gary Watson, (ed.), *op.cit.*, pp.299-321.)

Here is a statement of this account. (It, unlike the statement which follows, does not in the main refer to "powers". The pages which are referred to in the paragraphs which follow are pages in Gary Watson (ed.), *op. cit.*. Kane is concerned with "free and responsible action" in his article. He considers among other things the following claim: someone's "action" is by chance and it in that case is not a "free and responsible action" in case it is "undetermined". It is his claim that it is untrue. See, for example, p.299.)

Someone's "will" includes at least an exercise of a (or his) power to attend to "motives" or "reasons" (or grounds) for him to do this or that and to "want", "desire", ... to do that this or that and to "make an effort" or "try" to "choose", "decide", ... to do that this or that. ("Perhaps we are torn between doing the moral thing or acting from self-interest,

... In all such cases, we are faced with competing motivations [or "reasons" or grounds; in this case, "moral" *or* "self-interest[ed]"] and have to make an effort to overcome the temptation to do something else we also strongly want [in this case accordingly we "want" to do "the moral thing" and "want" to act "from self-interest" and we "make an effort" to do the "moral thing" and we "make an effort" to act "from self-interest"]

... the uncertainty we feel ... is reflected in the indeterminacy of our neural processes themselves.

... When we do decide [or "choose" (pp.306-307)] ... the outcome is not determined ... - and yet it can be willed (and hence rational and voluntary) either way owing to the fact that ... the agents' prior wills are divided by conflicting motives" (p.306).)

[Here, there is a description of "agents'" wills. In this case, consider the agent's will in relation to "doing the moral thing": "motivations" (or "reasons" or grounds): "moral"; a "want" to do "the moral thing"; an "effort" (or "trying" to "choose", "decide", ...) to do "the moral thing". See also the example of someone who is "trying" to "solve" a "mathematical problem" in what follows; and the example of a "businesswoman" in what follows.]

Someone has "voluntary control" of what he "chooses", "decides", ... just in case he possesses the power to "choose", "decide", ... in "accordance with" his "will" or "realize his purpose". ("... voluntary control over what they chose [, "decided", ...], where voluntary control means being able to bring about something in accordance with one's will ... "; "... voluntary control ... his ability to realize his purpose or what he is trying to do ..." (p.318).)

Someone "chooses", "decides", ... to do this or that (and brings about this or that) "voluntarily" and "intentionally" in case that is what he was trying to do. ("If [people] ... succeed in doing what they are trying to do ... they will do it *voluntarily* (in accordance with their wills) and *intentionally* (knowingly and purposely)" (p.309).)

Someone does *not* "choose", "decide", ... to do this or that (and bring about this or that) by chance in case he does so "voluntarily" and "intentionally". ("To say something was done 'by chance' usually means ... it was done ... 'involuntarily,' or 'as an unintended fluke' " (p.316).)

Someone's "choice" ("decision", ...) [in at least one place] is an "action". ("... suppose a choice occurred as the result of an undetermined event ... in one's brain ... it would appear to be more of a fluke or accident than a free and responsible action" (p.301).)

Someone brings about this or that is an "action". [Someone's "choice", "decision", ... is also distinguished from an "action".] ("Nor would it help to suppose that indeterminism or chance came *between* our choices ... and our actions" (p.302).)

[Let us take it in what follows that both are "actions".]

Someone who attends to and understands a particular situation at let us say t-1 possesses the power to do this or that freely (and responsibly) in case the following is so:

(K1) he possesses the power to attend to grounds for him to do this or that and to "want", "desire", ... to do that this or that and to "make an effort" or "try" to "choose", "decide", ... to do that this or that in let us say the period t-1 - t ;

and

(K2) he possesses the power to "choose", "decide", ... to do that this or that in let us say the period t - t1.

The exercise of this power is *not* "determined" by the exercise of the power referred to in (K1). (The exercise of this power is "undetermined" - it is left "uncertain" - by the exercise of the power referred to in (K1).)

Since he possesses this power, he has (keeping in mind the power referred to in (K1)) "voluntary control" of a (or his) "choice", "decision", ... to do that this or that.

But, his "voluntary control" is "hindered", ... because the exercise of this power is not determined. ("... indeterminism, wherever it occurs, functions as a hindrance or obstacle to our purposes ... " (p.318).)

The exercise of this power is enough to bring about the exercise of a (or his) power to bring about that this or that ;

and

(K3) he possesses the power to bring about that this or that in let us say the period t1 - t2.

Let us suppose that the powers referred to in (K1) - (K3) are exercised. (He "chooses", "decides", ... to do that this or that and brings about this or that "voluntarily" and "intentionally". He does not "choose", "decide", ... to do that this or that and bring about that this or that by chance.)

He "chooses", "decides", ... to do that this or that and brings about this or that "freely" (and "responsibly").

He "chooses", "decides", ... to do that this or that and brings about this or that "freely" (and "responsibly") even though it is "undetermined" that he does so. ("Suppose [for example] that you are trying to think through a difficult (say, mathematical problem) [and you exercise in that case the power referred to in (K1)] and there is some indeterminacy in your neural processes

... Whether you are going to succeed in solving the mathematical problem is uncertain and undetermined.

... Yet if you concentrate [and you exercise in that case the power referred to in (K2)] and solve the problem [and you exercise in that case the power referred to in (K3)] ... I think we can say that you did it [freely] and are responsible for doing it even though it was undetermined whether you would succeed" (p.308).)

Further, let us suppose that the following was so:

(K4) he (*viz.* the subject of our supposition) also possessed the power to attend to grounds for him to do some other this or that and to "want", "desire", ... to do this other this or that and to "make an effort" or "try" to "choose", "decide", ... to do this other this or that in the period t-1 - t ;

and

(K5) he also possessed the power to "choose", "decide", ... to do this other this or that in the period t - t1.

The exercise of this power is *not* "determined" by the exercise of the power referred to in (K4). (The exercise of this power is "undetermined" - it is left "uncertain" - by the exercise of the power referred to in (K4) in this case because of the exercise of the power referred to in (K1).)

Since he possesses this power, he has (keeping in mind the power referred to in (K4)) "voluntary control" of a (or his) "choice", "decision", ... to do this other this or that. (Indeed, he has "plural voluntary control" for he possesses this power *and* the power referred to in (K2). See p.319.)

(Further, he also possessed the power to "identify with", "endorse", ... a "choice", "decision", ... to do that this or that at t1 *and* the power to "identify with", "endorse", ... a "choice", "decision", ... to do this other this or that at t1) ;

Finally, let us suppose that the power referred to in (K4) was exercised. (The exercise of the power referred to in (K2) is "undetermined" - it is left "uncertain" - by the exercise of the power referred to in (K1) in this case because of the exercise of the power referred to in (K4). Further, the second of the powers referred to (in parenthesis) in (K5), *viz.* his power to "identify with", "endorse", ... a "choice", "decision", ... to do that this or that, was exercised at t1.)

He "chooses", "decides", ... to do that this or that and brings about this or that (as we have seen by way of an example) "freely" (and "responsibly").

He "chooses", "decides", ... to do that this or that and brings about this or that "freely" (and "responsibly") even though it is "undetermined" that he does so.

He "chooses", "decides", ... to do that this or that and brings about this or that "freely" (and "responsibly") even though it is "undetermined" that he did so for (as in the example of the person who was trying to solve a mathematical problem) he did what he was "trying" to do. ("Imagine that ... [a] businesswoman is *trying* ... to solve two cognitive problems at once ... to make a moral choice [*viz.* "to help the victim" of "an assault" (p.307)] [and she exercises in that case the power referred to in (K1) and she possesses the power referred to in (K2)] and to make a choice for her ambitions [and she exercises in that case the power referred to in (K4) and she possesses the first power referred to in (K5)]

... With respect to each task, as with the mathematical problem, she is being thwarted in her attempt to do what she is trying to do by indeterminism ... But, in her case the indeterminism ... is coming from her own will ... the two crossing neural networks involved are connected, so that the indeterminism which is making it uncertain that she will do the moral thing is coming from her desire to the opposite, and vice versa.

["Prior to choice, there was some indeterminacy in her neural processes stirred up by the conflict in her will" (p.307).

"She ... will identify with the choice reached by either of them as her choice" (pp.318-319). She possesses in that case the second and third powers referred to (in parenthesis) in (K5)]

... I argue that, if she nevertheless *succeeds* [and makes a choice to do one of these things - she exercises in that case the power referred to in (K2) and she exercises in that case the second power referred to (in parenthesis) in (K5) - and returns "to help the victim" (p.307) - she exercises in that case the power referred to in (K3)], then she [did it, *viz.* makes "her choice", and she "help[s] the victim" "freely" and] can be held responsible because ... she will have succeeded in doing *what she was trying to do* ... this will be true of her, *whichever choice is made*, because she was trying to make both choices and one is going to succeed" (pp.312-313).

Incidentally, the businesswoman's "will" - unlike the will of the person who was "trying" to solve a mathematical problem - is not identifiable until she "chooses". ("... the wills of agents ... like the businesswoman ... are not already settled or 'formed' until they choose ... " (p.312).)

Further, someone's will is not *free* unless he possesses the powers referred in (K1) *and* (K4). ("... agents trying to do two competing things at once ... that capacity, I believe, is essential for the exercise of free will" (p.313).)

There are a number of similarities between this account of a living thing's, *viz.* a human being's, power to do this or that freely and the account of a living thing's power to do this or that freely in this Appendix. They include the following:

it is *not* the case that the exercise of it is not free unless it is caused (or brought about) deterministically;

the exercise of it is *not* by chance;

he *or* it is *in control of* the exercise of his or its power to do that this or that freely;

the exercise of someone's *or* its power to do this or that freely is constituted *solely* by events.

There are a number of dissimilarities between this account of a living thing's, *viz.* a human being's, power to do this or that freely and the account of a living thing's power to do this or that freely in this Appendix. They include the following:

in this account, indeterminism ("wherever it occurs") is a "hindrance" ... in the control of someone's exercise of his power to do this or that freely; in the account of this Appendix, indeterminism ("wherever it occurs") is *not* a "hindrance" ... in the control of a living thing's exercise of its power to do this or that freely;

in this account, someone exercises his power to do this or that freely even in case the exercise of his power to attend to grounds to do that this or that ... is determined; in the account of this Appendix, it is *not* the case that a living thing exercises a (or its) power to do this or that freely even in case the exercise of its power to attend to grounds to do that this or that ... is determined;

in this account, someone exercises his power to do this or that freely even in case he exercises his power to attend to grounds to do that this or that ... *and* his power to attend to grounds to do some other this or that; in the account of this Appendix, it is *not* the case that a living thing exercises a (or its) power to do this or that freely even in case it exercises its power to attend to grounds to do that this or that ... *and* its power to attend to grounds to do some other this or that;

in this account, it is *not* the case that someone does not exercise his power to do this or that freely unless his power to will (or choose ...) to do that this or that is brought about by his power to attend to grounds to do that this or that ... ; in the account of this Appendix, it *is* the case that a living thing does not exercise its power to do this or that freely unless its power to will (or choose ...) to do that this or that is brought about by its power to attend to grounds to do that this or that .... .

Here is a very brief consideration of Kane's account. In passing, let us observe that *a self* is identifiable in, in particular, the powers referred to in parenthesis in (K5). That done, let us ask the following question about this account apart from anything else.

Is it the case that someone possesses the power to do this or that *freely* in case (K1) - (K3)? Well, no. Why? Well, he does not do so unless the exercise of the power which is referred to in (K1) is not caused deterministically *or* indeterministically.

21. Here is another account of a living thing, *viz.* a human being, which possesses the power to do this or that freely.

This account refers to someone or an "agent". The first part of the exercise of this power consists in the following: the "agent" causes (or brings about) an "event" which occurs in the exercise of this power. This is in the main referred to as "agent causation". (Chisholm sets out such an account in "Human Freedom and the Self". Chisholm refers to it as "immanent causation". Thomas Reid sets out such an account in the 18th century. He does so in *Essays on the Active Powers of the Human Mind* (Cambridge Mass.: MIT Press, 1969).)

It is even less similar to the account of this Appendix than the accounts which are referred to in the previous note. Here is a statement of this account. (For an instance of this account along the lines of this statement, see, for example, Timothy O'Connor, "The Agent as Cause" in Peter van Inwagen and Dean W. Zimmerman (eds.), *Metaphysics: The Big Questions* (Blackwell, 1998), pp.374-380. These instances, unlike the statement which follows, do not in the main refer to "powers".)

Someone's (or his) power to do this or that freely *or* responsibly includes the power to will ... (on this or that grounds) to do that this or that and the power to do (or bring about) that this or that.

The exercise of the first of these powers is enough to cause (or bring about) the exercise of the second of these powers.

The exercise of any one of these powers is such that there is a change with it. Any change is an "event". (An "event" is a change *or* a state such as a state of belief in someone.) So, the exercise of any one of these powers is such that there is an "event". These "events" are a part of the exercise of a (or his) power to do that this or that freely *or* responsibly.

He does not possess the power to do that this or that freely *or* responsibly unless he possesses the power to *not* do that this or that freely. So, he possesses the power to *not* do that this or that freely.

He does not possess the power to not do that this or that freely *or* responsibly in case the exercise of his power to will ... (on this or that grounds) to do that this or that is caused (or brought about) deterministically. So, the exercise of his power to will ... (on this or that grounds) to do that this or that is *not* caused (or brought about) deterministically.

He does not possess the power to do that this or that freely *or* responsibly in case the exercise of his power to will ... (on this or that grounds) to do that this or that is caused (or brought about) indeterministically (*or* deterministically) by an "event" *or* it is by chance.

Here is an argument for this claim:

he does not possess the power to do that this or that freely *or* responsibly unless he possesses the power to control the exercise of his power to will ... (on this or that grounds) to do that this or that ;

he does not possess the power to control the exercise of his power to will ... (on this or that grounds) to do that this or that in case the exercise of it is caused (or brought about) indeterministically (*or* deterministically) by an "event" *or* it is by chance ;

so, he does not possess the power to do that this or that freely *or* responsibly in case the exercise of his power to will ... (on this or that grounds) to do that this or that is caused (or brought about) indeterministically (*or* deterministically) by an "event" *or* it is by chance.

So, the exercise of his power to will ... (on this or that grounds) to do that this or that is *not* caused (or brought about) indeterministically (*or* deterministically) by an "event" and it is *not* by chance.

But, he does not possess the power to do that this or that freely *or* responsibly unless he possesses the power to control the exercise of his power to will ... (on this or that grounds) to do that this or that.

How does he possess the power to control the exercise of his power to will ... (on this or that grounds) to do that this or that? Well, he himself, *viz.* the "agent", possesses the power to cause (or bring about) its exercise. He himself, *viz.* the "agent", thereby possesses the power to control its exercise.

Its exercise is not caused (or brought about) by an "event". (It is not caused or brought about by a state *or* a change in the "agent".)

Further, the "agent's" exercise of his power to cause (or bring about) its exercise is *not* itself caused (or brought about).

Further still, it is *not* by chance even though it is not caused (or brought about). He himself, *viz.* the "agent", exercises it having been aware of and attended to grounds which are enough for it to do so.

In passing let us consider an argument for the claim that the event of the exercise of his power to will ... to do this or that is not caused by an "agent". (An "agent" possesses the power to cause or bring about the event of the exercise of his power to will ... on this or that grounds to do this or that according to this account. The "agent" does *not* possess this power in case this claim is correct.)

Here is the argument. (An argument along these lines is set out by C.D. Broad, an analytic philosopher. It is set out by him in *Ethics and the History of Philosophy* (London, 1952), p.215.)

The argument refers to a thing *or* things which are "dateable". A "dateable" thing, x, is such that we are able to refer to it as follows: x-at-t. Here is an example of such a thing: the event of the Tate closing. It is "dateable": the Tate closing-at-noon today.

Its initial premises are as follows. (The initial premises are true according to an advocate of this argument.) **:**

events *alone* are "dateable" **;**

an event is not caused by something *unless* that thing is "dateable"**.**

It is the claim of an advocate of "agent causation" that an "agent" causes (or brings about) the event of the exercise of his power to will ... to do this or that *and* that the event of the exercise of his power to will ... to do this or that is not caused (or brought about) by an event ;

The event of the exercise of his power to will ... to do this or that in that case is not caused (or brought about) by something which is "dateable". (This initial conclusion follows from the first premise and the claim.) ;

So, the event of the exercise of his power to will ... to do this or that is not caused by an "agent". (This ultimate conclusion follows from the second premise, the claim (in particular, its first conjunct), and the initial conclusion.)

Here is a reply for an advocate of "agent causation": an "agent" causes (or brings about) the event of the exercise of his power to will ... to do this or that at say t1; this is so even though the event of the exercise of his power to will ... to do this or that is not caused (or brought about) by an event and it in that case is not caused (or brought about) by something which is "dateable"; the second premise in that case is untrue; so, this argument does not establish that its conclusion is true.

There are a number of similarities between this account of a living thing's, *viz.* someone's or an "agent's", power to do this or that freely as it is stated above and the account of a living thing's power to do this or that freely in this Appendix. They include the following :

someone's *or* its power to do this or that *freely* during a period includes the power to *not* do that this or that freely during it ;

the exercise of a part of it, *viz.* its first part, is *not* caused (or brought about) ;

the exercise of a part of it, *viz.* its first part, is *not* by chance even though it is not caused (or brought about) ;

he *or* it exercises control by the exercise of a part of it, *viz.* its first part *or* at least a part of it. (Here are two ways that he *or* it exercises control:

(i) he *or* it exercises control of the exercise of all of the other powers which constitute his *or* its power to do this or that freely (in effect) by the exercise of it ;

(ii) he *or* it exercises control in that he *or* it exercises his *or* its power to do that this or that rather than his *or* its power to not do that this or that by the exercise of it.)

There are a number of dissimilarities between this account of a living thing's power to do this or that freely as it is stated in this note and the account of a living thing's power to do this or that freely in this Appendix. They include the following **:**

this account refers to "agent causation" (or "immanent causation"); the account of this Appendix does *not* refer to "agent causation" (or "immanent causation") **;**

in this account as it is stated in this note, he himself, *viz.* the "agent", exercises control by the exercise of his power to cause (or bring about) the exercise of his power to will ... (on this or that grounds) to do that this or that; in the account of this Appendix, a living thing exercises control by the exercise of *its* power to attend to grounds for it to will ... to do that this or that and to understand that these grounds are enough for to begin to exercise a (or its) power to will ... to do that this or that **;**

in this account as it is stated in this note, it is *not* the case that there is an "event" *or* there are "events" *alone* with the exercise of a part, *viz.* the first part, of his, *viz.* the "agent's", power to do that this or that freely; in the account of this Appendix, it *is* the case that there is an event, *viz.* a change, *alone* with the exercise of a part, *viz.* the first part, of a living thing's power to do that this or that freely **;**

in this account as it is stated in this note, the exercise of his, *viz.* the "agent's", power to that this or that freely is *not* constituted solely by "events"; in the account of this Appendix, the exercise of a living thing's power to do that this or that freely *is* constituted solely by events**.**

That done, let us observe, apart from anything else, the following about this account as it is stated in this note: it is untrue that someone, *viz.* an "agent", exercises his power to do this or that freely!

Here is an argument for this claim. Its initial premises are as follows:

someone, *viz.* an "agent", possesses a power to cause (or bring about) the exercise of his power to will ... (on this or that grounds) to do that this or that and exercises it in case he exercises his power to do that this or that freely;

the exercise of his power to will ... (on this or that grounds) to do that this or that is not caused (or brought about) by an "event" and it in that case is not caused (or brought about) by a change - a change at that time - in something (*viz.* the "agent");

there is a change in something in case it *begins* to exercise this or that power.

Let us suppose that someone, *viz.* an "agent", exercises his power to do that this or that freely.

He in that case possesses a power to cause (or bring about) the exercise of his power to will ... (on this or that grounds) to do that this or that and exercises it and the exercise of his power to will ... (on this or that grounds) to do that this or that is not caused (or brought about) by a change in something (*viz.* the "agent"). (This initial conclusion follows from the first premise and the second premise and the supposition.)

He in that case possesses a power to cause (or bring about) the exercise of his power to will ... (on this or that grounds) to do that this or that and exercises it and he does *not* begin to exercise it. (This further conclusion follows from the third premise, the supposition, and the initial conclusion.) That's absurd!

So, it is not the case that someone, *viz.* an "agent", exercises his power to do that this or that freely.

The first premise is true according to this account as it is stated in this note. The second premise is true according to this account as it is stated in this note. The third premise is true. The supposition is such that an absurdity follows with its addition. So, the conclusion - the conclusion is the denial of the supposition - is true. It is not the case that someone, *viz.* an agent, exercises his power to do that this or that freely!

22. Here are three other examples of accounts of a living thing, *viz.* a human being, which possesses the power to do this or that freely.

*

The first account is the account of Harry Frankfurt, an analytic philosopher. (It is an account of someone's power to do this or that freely *and* responsibly.) It is the account which is set out in an article entitled "Freedom of the Will and the Concept of a Person". (Harry Frankfurt, "Freedom of the Will and the Concept of a Person", *Journal of Philosophy,* 68/1 (1971), pp.5-20. This article is reprinted in Gary Watson (ed.), *op.cit.*, pp.322-336.)

It is even less similar to the account of this Appendix than the account which is referred to in the previous note. Here is a brief statement of it. (The pages which are referred to in the paragraphs which follow are pages in Gary Watson (ed.), *op. cit.*. Frankfurt's account, unlike the statement which follows, does not refer to "powers". Incidentally, Frankfurt uses the verbs "to desire" and "to want" interchangeably. See note 2, p.324. The statement which follows uses the word "desire" rather than the word "want".)

Someone possesses the power to do this or that freely in case the following is so:

(F1) he possesses the power to *bring about* that this or that - that this or that is at issue in a (or his) desire to do that this or that ;

and

(F2) he possesses the power to have a desire to do that this or that. (This is an instance of a "first-order desire". See, in particular, p.323 and pp.324-325.) ;

and

(F3) he possesses the power to desire that a desire (which he has) to do that this or that is effective (or his "will" (p.325)). (The desire that a desire which he has to do that this or that is effective is an instance of a "second-order volition". It is a particular kind of "second-order desire". See, in particular, p.327. Further, this power entails that the power referred to in (F2) has been exercised. See p.326.) ;

and

(F4) he possesses the power to "identify himself ... *decisively*" (p.332) with a (or his) desire that a desire (which he has) to do that this or that is effective, (*viz.* with the (or his) pertinent "second-order volition") ;

and

(F5) the exercise of the powers referred to in (F3) and (F4) is such that it brings about that a desire (which he has) to do that this or that *is* effective.

For Frankfurt, (F3) entails the following:

(F3.1) he possesses a "rational" power. ("... it is only in virtue of his rational capacities that a person is capable of becoming aware of his own will and of forming volitions of the second order. The structure of a person's will presupposes, accordingly, that he is a rational being" (p.328).)

For Frankfurt, he, "roughly" speaking, has "freedom of action" (p.331) in relation to that this or that in case he possesses the power referred to in (F1).

For Frankfurt, he, "roughly" speaking, has "freedom of the will" in relation to that this or that in case he possesses the power which is referred to in (F3) and the exercise of the power referred to in (F3) is such that it brings it about that a desire (which he has) to do that this or that is effective. ("... freedom of the will means (... roughly) ... that he is free ... to have the will he wants" (p.331). "It is in securing the conformity of his will to his second-order volitions ... that a person exercises freedom of the will" (p.331).)

For Frankfurt, he (*or* anyone) has "all the freedom it is possible to desire or to conceive" in case he has "both freedom of action and freedom of the will" (pp.333-334).

Incidentally, the exercise of the power expressed in (F3) is essential in order that something is a person for Frankfurt. ("... it is having second-order volitions ... that I regard as essential to being a person" (p.327).)

Why does the statement of Frankfurt's account in this Appendix refer to the additional powers expressed in (F4) and (F5)? (According to the statement of Frankfurt's account in this Appendix, he has "freedom of the will" in relation to that this or that in case he possesses the powers referred to in (F3) *and* (F4) *and* (F5).)

Well, it does so in order to avoid the difficulty (for his account) raised by the following question: does he *desire* to desire that a desire (which he has) to do that this or that is effective, ... ? (Frankfurt himself recognises such desires: "... a person may have ... desires ... of a higher order than the second" (p.332). He identifies the power which is referred to in (F4). Incidentally, he writes the following despite his identification of the power referred to in (F4): "The unwilling addict identifies himself ... , through the formation of a second-order volition, with one rather than the other of his conflicting first-order desires" (p.329).)

Here is a brief consideration of Frankfurt's account. In passing, let us observe that *a self* is identifiable in, in particular, the power expressed in (F4). That done, let us ask the following questions about this account apart from anything else.

First of all, is it the case that someone possesses the power to do this or that *freely* in case (F1) - (F5)? Well, no. Why? Well, he does not do so unless the exercise of the powers which are referred to in (F3) and (F4) are not caused deterministically *or* indeterministically.

(In passing, here is a claim of another analytic philosopher, Thomas Nagel, in chapter 7 of his work *The View from Nowhere*: normally, there is an "increase" in "one's freedom" in case one is "prudent" for it is a "higher order" or "higher level" operation and it "increases" the control of one's "first-order motives". ("... in its normal form, prudence increases one's freedom by increasing one's control over the operation of first-order motives ....". Chapter 7 of *The View from Nowhere* recall is re-printed in Gary Watson (ed.), *op. cit.*, pp.229-256. See Gary Watson (ed.), *op.cit.*, p.251).

Is this so? Well, no. Why? Well, there is *no* "freedom" - there is in that case *no* "increase" in "one's freedom" - unless one being "prudent" (or the exercise of one's power to be "prudent") is not caused deterministically *or* indeterministically.)

Secondly, is it the case that someone does not possess the power to do this or that *freely* unless (F1) - (F5)? Well, no. Why? Well, he possesses the power to do that this or that freely (in terms of the kinds of powers which are at issue in Frankfurt's account) in case the following is so:

(F1) he possesses the power to bring about that this or that - that this or that is at issue in a (or his) desire to do that this or that ;

and

(F2) he possesses the power to have a desire to do that this or that ;

and

(F4′) he possesses the power to "identify himself ... *decisively*" with a (or his) desire (which he has) to do that this or that (*viz.* with the (or his) pertinent "first order desire". Further, this power entails that the power referred to in (F2) has been exercised.) ;

and

(F5′) the exercise of the power referred to in (F4′) is such that it brings it about that a desire (which he has) to do that this or that is effective.

He possesses the power to do that this or that freely for he possesses the power to bring about that this or that - that this or that is at issue in a (or his) desire to do that this or that - *viz.* (F1), and he himself possesses the powers to bring it about that a desire (which he has) to do that this or that is effective, *viz.* (F4′) and (F5′). He possesses (as a result of (F4′) and (F5′)) the power to have his *own* will. He possesses the power to have his own will in the absence of the powers referred to in (F3) and (F5). (He does so in the absence of powers to secure "the conformity of his will" to a (or his) second-order volition to desire that a desire which he has to do that this or that is effective.)

*

The second account is the account of Gary Watson, an analytic philosopher. It is the account which is set out in an article entitled "Free Agency". (Gary Watson, "Free Agency", *Journal of Philosophy*, 72/8 (1975), pp.205-220. This article is reprinted in Gary Watson (ed.), *op.cit.*, pp.337-351.)

Again, it is even less similar to the account of this Appendix than the account which is referred to in the previous note. Here is a brief statement of it. (It, unlike the statement which follows, does not refer to "powers". The pages which are referred to in the paragraphs which follow are pages in Gary Watson (ed.), *op. cit.*.)

Someone possesses the power to do this or that freely in a particular situation in case the following is so:

(Wa1) he possesses the power to *bring about* that this or that - that this or that is identified in a (or his) judgement that to do that this or that is for him greater in value than to do anything else in it. ("The free agent has the capacity to translate his values into actions..." (p.347); see (Wa2), too.) ;

and

(Wa2) he possesses the power to judge that to do that this or that is for him greater in value than to do anything else in it.

(He judges that to do that this or that is for him greater in value than to do anything else in it as a result of his "principles and ends" *and* his "factual beliefs" *and* his assessment of the probability of the success of the courses of action which are available to him. He makes an "all things considered" judgement.

His "principles and ends" are the "principles and ends" which he identifies in a "cool and non-self-deceptive moment" as "definitive of the good, fulfilling, and defensible life" (p.346).

They constitute his "evaluational system" or "valuation system". ("... the ends and principles that constitute one's evaluational system ..." (p.347).)

"*The valuation system* of an agent is that set of considerations which, when combined with his factual beliefs (and probability estimates), yields judgements of the form: the thing for me to do in these circumstances, all things considered, is *a*" (p.346).

"To ascribe free agency to a being presupposes it to be a being that makes judgements of this sort" (p.346).) ;

and

(Wa3) the exercise of the power referred to in (Wa2) is such that it brings it about that the power referred to in (Wa1) is exercised. (He is "moved to get" what he "most values". Watson does not state this explicitly; but, it is implicit in what he states. See, in particular, p.341.)

For Watson, the exercise of the power referred to in (Wa2) is such that there is *or* it brings about a "want" to do that this or that. (" ... wants that are (or perhaps arise from) evaluations" (p.340).)

This want is *in a way* stronger than any other which he has for what he wants to do is something which he judges is for him greater in value than anything else which he is able to do in that situation. ((Wa1) refers to his power to bring about that this or that - that this or that is at issue in this want.)

For Watson, his "motivational system" (p.347) consists of the want *or* desire which brings him to do this or that in a particular situation.

For Watson, someone does *not* do this or that freely in a particular situation in case he possesses the power to judge that to do something or other is for him greater in value than do anything else in it and this power is exercised and this judgement is such that it identifies something *other than that this or that* and he is (nonetheless) brought to do that this or that by another want *or* desire. ("... in the case of actions that are unfree, the agent is unable to get what he most wants, or *values*, and this inability is due to his own 'motivational system'. In this case the obstruction to the action that he most wants to do is his own will" (p.338). "The problem of free action arises because what one desires may not be what one values, and what one most values may not be what one is finally moved to get" (p.341).)

This other want *or* desire is *in a way* stronger than a want which is brought about by the subject's "[e]valuation[al] system" for it brings about what he does.

This other want *or* desire is something which he does not value at all *or* he values (merely) to some degree.

He does what he wants *or* desires and he does *not* do it freely. (This explains the case of someone who does what he wants *or* desires and he does not do it freely - *eg,* an addict.)

Here is a brief consideration of Watson's account. In passing, let us observe that *a self* is identifiable in, in particular, the power expressed in (Wa2). That done, let us ask the following questions about this account apart from anything else.

First of all, is it the case that someone does this or that *freely* in a particular situation in case (Wa1) - (Wa3) and the powers which are referred to in (Wa2) and (Wa1) are exercised? Well, no. Why? Well, this is not the case for the following reason among others: his power to judge that to do that this or that is for him greater in value than to do anything else in it is exercised and it is *merely* because this is so that his power to bring about that this or that is exercised (*cf.* the account of this Appendix).

Secondly, is it the case that someone does not do this or that *freely* in a particular situation unless (Wa1) - (Wa3) and the powers which are referred to in (Wa2) and (Wa1) are exercised? Well, no. Why? Well, this is not the case for consider among other things the following. (The following is stated in terms of the kinds of powers which are at issue in Watson's account.):

someone judges that to do this or that in it has for him a certain "value" and this "value" is for him sufficient to do that this or that although he does not judge that to do that this or that is for him greater in value than to do anything else in it *and* this brings it about that a (or his) power to bring about that this or that is exercised.

He does that this or that freely (and responsibly) although he does not judge that to do that this or that is for him greater in value than to do anything else in it.

Here is an illustration. Consider someone whose "principles and ends" include to alleviate the suffering of the poorest in the world by donating to charities and to donate to a charity which is efficient in its activity and his "factual beliefs" include that he is in a situation which is such that there are a number of suitable charities to donate to and his "probability estimates" include that one of these charities – say, Oxfam – has a certain probability of realising this "principle and end".

Let us suppose that he judges that to donate to Oxfam has for him a certain "value" and that this "value" is for him sufficient to do so although he does not judge that to donate to Oxfam is for him greater in value than to donate to any other charity and this brings it about that a (or his) power to donate to Oxfam is exercised.

He does so freely (and responsibly) although he does not judge that to do so is for him greater in value than to than to donate to any other charity.

*

The third account is the account of Susan Wolf, an analytic philosopher. (It is an account of someone's power to do this or that freely *and* responsibly.)

It is the account which is set out in "Sanity and the Metaphysics of Responsibility" in F. Shoeman (ed.), *Responsibility, Character and the Emotions* (Cambridge, 1987), pp.46-62. (It is reprinted in Gary Watson (ed.), *op. cit.*, pp.372-387.)

Again, Wolf's account is even less similar to the account of this Appendix than the account which is referred to in the previous note.

Wolf considers the accounts of some philosophers. They include the accounts of Frankfurt and Watson in the articles which have been referred to. (The pages which are referred to in the paragraphs which follow are pages in Gary Watson (ed.), *op. cit.*. For Wolf, it is, as noted, a matter of both "freedom" and "responsibility". See, for example, p.380.)

She writes: "... all these philosophers seem to be saying that the key to [freedom and] responsibility lies in the fact that [free and] responsible agents are those for whom it is not just the case that their actions are within the control of their wills, but also the case that their wills are within the control of their *selves* in some deeper sense" (p.375).

She writes: "... we may speak of their separate positions as variations of one basic view on [freedom and] responsibility: the *deep-self view*" (p.376).

She writes: "... the conditions of [free and] responsible agency offered by the deep-self view are necessary but not sufficient" (p.382).

She writes: "The conception of [freedom and] responsibility I am proposing ... requiring that a [free and] responsible agent be able to govern her (or his) actions by her desires and to govern her desires by her deep self. In addition, my conception insists that the agent's deep-self be sane, and claims that this is *all* that is needed for [free and] responsible agency ... let us call this new proposal the *sane deep-self view*" (p.382).

She writes: "Sanity involves the ability to know the difference between right and wrong" (p.382).

In that case, someone possesses the power to do this or that freely and responsibly in case, for example, the following is so for Wolf:

(Wo1) he possesses the power to bring about that this or that - that this or that is at issue in a (or his) desire to do that this or that ;

and

(Wo2) he possesses the power to have a desire to do that this or that ;

and

(Wo3) he possesses the power to desire that a desire (which he has) to do that this or that is effective (or his "will"). (This power entails that the power referred to in (Wo2) has been exercised.) ;

and

(Wo4) the exercise of the power referred to in (Wo3) is such that it brings it about that a desire (which he has) to do that this or that is effective ;

and

(Wo5) he (*viz.* his "deep-self") is *sane* (that is to say, his "deep-self" is a "*sane* deep-self").

For Wolf, (Wo5) entails the following:

(Wo5.1) he possesses the power to "have the resources and reasons on which to base 'self-correction' " (p.384).

Wolf believes that (Wo5.1) is such that someone or a "sane deep-self" possesses the power to do this or that freely and responsibly even in case his "sane deep-self" is causally "unavoidable" (pp.383-384).

Wo1 - Wo4 refer to powers which are at issue in Frankfurt's account. One of the powers which is at issue in Frankfurt's article and which is included in the statement of his account in this Appendix is the power to "identify himself ... *decisively*" with a (or his) desire that a desire (which he has) to do that this or that is effective, *viz.* (F4).

But, this power is not referred to in the statement of Wolf's account. Why? Well, it is not referred to in the statement of Wolf's account for Wolf does not refer to it in her account of Frankfurt's account. Here are the key parts of Wolf's brief account of Frankfurt's account:

"In ... "Freedom of the Will and the Concept of a Person,"[1] Harry Frankfurt notes a distinction between freedom of action and freedom of the will. A person has freedom of action ... if she (or he) has the freedom to do whatever she wills to do ... Even a person who has freedom of action may fail to be responsible for her actions ... if the wants or desires she has the freedom to convert into action are themselves not subject to her control ... [if she lacks] freedom of the will ... freedom of the will is the freedom to will whatever one wants to will .... Frankfurt introduces a distinction between first-order and second-order desires. First-order desires are desires to do or to have various things; second-order desires are desires about what desires to have or what desires to make effective in action. In order for an agent to have both freedom of action and freedom of the will, that agent must be capable of governing his or her actions by first-order desires *and* capable of governing his or her first-order desires by second-order desires" (pp.373-374).

Let us recall that a "self" is identifiable in, in particular, (F4). Wolf does not refer to the power expressed in (F4). Still, let us take it that a "self" is identifiable in (Wo3).

Further, let us observe, with regard to Wolf's account of Frankfurt's account, that, for someone to have "freedom of the will" (with just "second-order desires" in mind), he is required to possess the power to "govern" his "first-order desires" by a *particular kind* of "second-order desire", *viz.* a "second-order volition".

Finally, let us observe that a "self" or a "deep-self" is not particularly well-identified by Wolf in her account of Frankfurt's account. (Still, it is correct to say that a "self" is identifiable in Frankfurt's account. It is also identifiable in Watson's account.)

Here is a brief consideration of Wolf's account. Let us ask the following questions about this account apart from anything else.

First of all, is it the case that someone possesses the power to do this or that *freely* in case (Wo1) - (Wo5) or (Wo1) - (Wo5) - (Wo5.1)? Well, no. Why? Well, he does not do so unless the exercise of the power which is referred to in (Wo5.1) is not caused deterministically. (He does not do so unless the exercise of the power which is referred to in (Wo5.1) is not causally "unavoidable" in the terms of Wolf's account.)

Secondly, is it the case that someone does not possess the power to do this or that *freely* unless (Wo1) - (Wo5) or (Wo1) - (Wo5) - (Wo5.1)? Well, no. Why? Well, let us suppose, for example, the following:

(Wo1) he possesses the power to bring about that this or that - that this or that is at issue in a (or his) desire to do that this or that ;

and

(Wo2) he possesses the power to have a desire to do that this or that ;

and

(Wo3) he possesses the power to desire that a desire (which he has) to do that this or that is effective (or his "will"). (This power entails that the power referred to in (Wo2) has been exercised.) ;

and

(Wo4) the exercise of the power referred to in (Wo3) is such that it brings it about that a desire (which he has) to do that this or that is effective ;

but

(5) he does not possess the power to know whether that this or that is right *or* wrong. (So, it is not the case that (Wo5).)

and

(6) he possesses the power to know this is so.

And, he exercises the power referred to in (6). He then exercises the powers which are referred to in (Wo3) and (Wo1). In that case, he (in the terms of the kinds of powers which are at issue in Wolf's account) does that this or that freely (and responsibly) although it is *not* the case that (Wo5).

23. It exercises control of the exercise of all of the other powers which constitute its power to do that this or that (in effect) by the exercise of it.

24. Frankfurt sets out two particular cases of someone who does this or that in an article entitled "Alternate Possibilities and Moral Responsibility" (*Journal of Philosophy*, 66 (1969), pp.829-839. This article is reprinted in G.Watson (ed.), *op. cit.*, pp.167-176.)

He claims that they are cases of someone who does this or that freely and (as a result) morally responsibly although he does not possess the power to not do that this or that or "could not do otherwise".

There is in what follows a statement of the first case which is set out by Frankfurt. (The case which follows is stated in some of the terms of this Appendix. The pages which are referred to in the paragraphs which follow are pages in Gary Watson (ed.), *op. cit.*.)

There is an argument which is addressed tacitly and which is identifiable in this article. It is (in some of the terms of this Appendix) as follows :

someone does not possess the power to do this or that in a morally responsible way unless he possesses the power to do that this or that freely ;

he does not possess the power to do that this or that freely unless he possesses the power to *not* do that this or that ;

so, he does not possess the power to do that this or that in a morally responsible way unless he possesses the power to not do that this or that.

The conclusion follows from the first premise and the second premise. The first premise is true for Frankfurt. The second premise is *untrue* for Frankfurt. So, this argument does not establish that its conclusion is true for Frankfurt.

Here is the first case set out by Frankfurt in order to seek in effect to demonstrate that the second premise of this argument is untrue and that in that case it does not establish that its conclusion is true.

Frankfurt's first case

(i) someone possesses the power to identify grounds for him to do this or that and to understand in let us say the period t-2 - t-1 that these grounds are enough for him to do that this or that and to "decide" in line with that to do that this or that ;

he possesses the power to acquire other grounds from someone else for him to do that this or that and to do nothing other than that this or that and to understand in let us say the period t-1 - t that these grounds are enough for him to do that this or that and to do nothing other than that this or that ;

he possesses the power to attend to what occurs in the exercise of the powers referred to in the preceding two paragraphs in the period t - t2.

and, his power to attend to what occurs in the exercise of the power referred to in the second paragraph of *(i)* in the period t - t2 is exercised *in case* his power to attend to what occurs in the exercise of the power referred to in the first paragraph of *(i)* in the period t - t2 is *not* exercised.

and, what he attends to is enough to bring about the exercise of a (or his) power to bring about that this or that ;

he possesses the power to bring about that this or that in the period t2 - t3 ;

(ii) his power to identify grounds for him to do this or that and to understand in the period t-2 - t-1 that these grounds are enough for him to do that this or that and to "decide" in line with that to do that this or that is exercised. ("... he ... provided himself with a sufficient motive for performing the action in question" (p.170). "[He] decides for reasons of his own to do something ..." (p.169).) ;

his power to acquire other grounds from someone else for him to do that this or that and to do nothing other than that this or that and to understand in the period t-1 - t that these grounds are enough for him to do that this or that and to do nothing other than that this or that (and the grounds are that a state of affairs which is contrary to what he very strongly prefers would obtain in case he were not to do that this or that) is exercised. (" ... then someone threatens him with a very harsh penalty (so harsh that any reasonable person would submit to the threat) unless he does precisely that ..." (p.169). "The threat impressed him, as it would impress any reasonable man ..." (p.170). "... he himself recognized that ... he had to do it ..." (pp.170-171).) ;

but, his power to attend to what occurs in the exercise of the power referred to in the first paragraph of *(i)* in the period t - t2 is exercised ;

his power to bring about that this or that in the period t2 - t3 is exercised. ("... he performed the action ... on the basis of the decision he had made before the threat was issued" (p.170).

"When he acted, he was not actually motivated by the threat but solely by the considerations that had originally commended the action to him. It was not the threat that led him to act, though it would have done so if he had not already provided himself with a sufficient motive ..." (p.170).)

The subject of this case does not possess the power to not do that this or that. He nonetheless possesses the power to do that this or that freely and (as a result) in a morally responsible way according to Frankfurt. (He nonetheless does that this or that freely and as a result in a morally responsible way according to Frankfurt.)

Incidentally, Frankfurt believes that it is "unclear" whether the subject of this case is coerced. ("... it is unclear whether the example [or this case] constitutes a genuine instance of coercion" (p.170).)

Is he coerced? Well, he is *not* coerced for his power to attend to what occurs in the exercise of the power referred to in the second paragraph of *(i)* in the period t - t2 is not exercised. . ("... the threat did not in fact influence his performance of the action" (p.170).)

Is it the case that he possesses the power to do that this or that freely? Well, it is *not* the case that he possesses the power to do that this or that freely for (leaving aside the consideration of other matters) he does not possess the power to not do that this or that.

Still, there is at least nothing which is referred to in the description of this case and which is such that its subject does not possess the power to do that this or that in a morally responsible way.

In particular, there is nothing which is referred to in the description of this case and which is such that he does not possess the power to do that this or that independently.

25. Let us suppose that the following is so:

(i) it possessed the power to attend to grounds for it to not to possess {a (or its) power to attend to grounds for it to will ... to do that this or that and to understand in the period which begins at t that these grounds are enough for it to begin to exercise a (or its) power to will ... to do that this or that} and to understand by let us say t-2 that these grounds are enough for it to begin to will to not to possess it

and

it possessed the power to will ... to not possess it in the period t-2 - t-1

and

it possessed the power to bring it about that it does not possess it in the period t-1 - t ;

(ii) the exercise of the first of these powers would have been enough to bring about the exercise of the second of these powers, and the exercise of the second of these powers would have been enough to bring about the exercise of the third of these powers.

The exercise of the first of these powers in that case would have been enough to bring it about that it does *not* possess a (or its) power to attend to grounds for it to will ... to do that this or that and to understand in the period which begins at t that these grounds are enough for it to begin to exercise a (or its) power to will ... to do that this or that.

It possessed the power in effect to not possess a power to do that this or that freely.

But, its power to not possess a (or its) power to attend to grounds for it to will ... to do that this or that and to understand in the period which begins at t that these grounds are enough for it to begin to exercise a (or its) power to will ... to do that this or that was not exercised for it possesses it.

Given its powers (which are referred to in *(i)*) in the period just before t, this other living thing does *not* possess the power to bring it about at t + i that a (or its) power to attend to grounds for it to will ... to do that this or that and to understand in what remains of the period t - t1 that they are enough for it to begin to exercise a (or its) power to will ... to do it is exercised. Why?

Well, let us further suppose that it possesses this power.

It (*viz.* the subject of the case) in that case possesses a (or its) power to attend to grounds for it to will ... to do that this or that and to understand in what remains of the period t - t1 that they are enough for it to begin to exercise a (or its) power to will ... to do it. (This initial conclusion follows from the further supposition.)

It (*viz.* the subject of the case) in that case does not possess a power to not possess a power to attend to grounds for it to will ... to do that this or that and to understand in the period which begins at t that these grounds are enough for it to begin to exercise a (or its) power to will ... to do that this or that *and* it possesses a power not to possess it. (This further conclusion follows from the initial conclusion and our supposition.) That's absurd!

So, it is untrue that it (*viz.* this other living thing) possesses this power.

Still, let us say that it possesses this power *just in case* it (*viz.* the subject of the case) does not exercise a (or its) power to attend to grounds for it to not to possess {a power to attend to grounds for it to will ... to do that this or that and to understand in the period which begins at t that these grounds are enough for it to begin to exercise a (or its) power to will ... to do that this or that} and to understand by t-2 that these grounds are enough for it to begin to will to not to possess it. (*Cf.* David Widerkar, "Libertarianism and Frankfurt's Attack on the Principle of Alternative Possibilities", *Philosophical Review*, 104 (1995), pp.247-261. See, in particular, Section 3 of this article. This article is reprinted in G. Watson (ed.), *op. cit.*, pp.177-189.)

Or let us say, to begin with, the following: it (*viz.* the subject of the case) possesses a power to attend to grounds for it to will ... to not do that this or that and to understand in the period t - t1 that these grounds are enough for it to begin to exercise a (or its) power to will ... to not do that this or that *instead of* a (or its) power to attend to grounds for it to will... to not do that this or that and to begin to understand in the period t - t + i that these grounds are enough for it to begin to exercise a (or its) power to will ... to not do that this or that.

Further, let us say that a (or its) power to attend to grounds for it to will... to not do that this or that and to understand in the period t - t1 that these grounds are enough for it to begin to exercise a (or its) power to will ... to not do that this or that is exercised *in case* its power to attend to ... grounds for it ... to do that this or that ... in the period t - t1 ... is *not* exercised.

Further still, let us suppose that this other living thing brings it about at t1 that its power to will ... to do that this or that in the period t1 - t2 is exercised *just in case* its power to attend to grounds for it to will... to not do that this or that and to understand in the period t - t1 that these grounds are enough for it to begin to exercise a (or its) power to will ... to not do that this or that is exercised.

Its power to bring about that this or that - that this or that is at issue in its will ... to do that this or that - in the period t2 - t3 in that case is exercised. (It is exercised whether its power to attend to grounds for it to will ... to do that this or that and to understand in the period which begins at t that these grounds are enough for it to begin to exercise a (or its) power to will ... to do that this or that is exercised *or* not.)

It is *not* the case that in that case a (or its) power to do that this or that in the period t - t3 - a (or its) power to undertake that act in the period t - t3 - is exercised. This power after all is not exercised in case a (or its) power to attend to grounds for it to will... to not do that this or that and to understand in the period t - t1 that these grounds are enough for it to begin to exercise a (or its) power to will ... to not do that this or that is exercised.

*

Let us suppose instead that the following is so:

(iii) this other living thing possessed - it *only* possessed - the power to bring it about that it (*viz.* the subject of this case) exercises a (or its) power to attend to grounds for it to will... to not do that this or that and to begin to understand in the period t - t + i that these grounds are enough for it to begin to exercise a (or its) power to will ... to not do that this or that ;

(iv) this other living thing had exercised this power.

It (*viz.* the subject of this case) in that case would not have possessed a power to attend to grounds for it to will ... to do that this or that and to begin to understand in the period t - t + i that these grounds are enough for it to begin to exercise a (or its) power to will ... to do that this or that.

But, it is *not* the case that in that case it would not have possessed a power to attend to grounds for it to will ... to do this or that and to understand in the period t + i - t1 that these grounds are enough for it to begin to exercise a (or its) power to will ... to do that this or that.

*

Finally, let us suppose instead that the following is so:

(v) this other living thing possessed - it *only* possessed - the power to bring it about that it (*viz.* the subject of this case) exercises

a power to attend to grounds for it to will ... to not do that this or that and to begin to understand in the period t - t + 2i that these grounds are enough for it to begin to exercise a (or its) power to will ... to not do that this or that. (*(v)* entails that it possesses a power to attend to grounds for it to will ... to not do that this or that and to begin to understand in the period t - t + 2i that these grounds are enough for it to begin to exercise a (or its) power to will ... to not do that this or that.) ;

(vi) this other living thing had exercised this power.

It (*viz.* the subject of this case) in that case would not have possessed a power to attend to grounds for it to will ... to do that this or that and to begin to understand in the period which begins at t + i that these grounds are enough for it to begin to exercise a (or its) power to will ... to do that this or that.

But, it does not possess a power to attend to grounds for it to will... to do that this or that and to understand in the period which begins at t that these grounds are enough for it to begin to exercise a (or its) power to will ... to do that this or that unless it possesses (at least) this power.

So, it would not have possessed a power to do that this or that freely.

*

It does not possess a power to do that this or that freely in the period t - t3 unless it is *not* the case that something brings it about that it exercises a (or its) power to attend to grounds for it to will ... to not do that this or that and to begin to understand in the period t - t + 2i that these grounds are enough for it to begin to exercise a (or its) power to will ... to not do that this or that.

26. It exercises control of the exercise of all of the other powers which constitute its power to do that this or that (in effect) by the exercise of it.

It exercises control in that it exercises its power to do that this or that rather than its power to attend to the grounds to will ... to not do that this or that ... by the exercise of it, too.

27. In "Alternate Possibilities and Moral Responsibility", Frankfurt sets out two particular cases of someone who does this or that.

He claims that they are cases of someone who does this or that freely and (as a result) morally responsibly although he does not possess the power to not do that this or that or he "could not do otherwise".

There is in what follows a statement of the second case which is set out by Frankfurt. This statement amends the case slightly. (The case which follows is stated in some of the terms of this Appendix. The pages which are referred to in the paragraphs which follow are pages in Gary Watson (ed.), *op. cit.*.)

There is in this second case someone (*viz.* the subject) and someone else who wants him to exercise his power to bring about this or that (or "...wants ... [him] to perform a certain action" (p.172)).

Frankfurt's second case

(i) someone possesses the power to identify grounds for him to do this or that and to understand in let us say the period t-1 - t that these grounds are enough for him to do that this or that **;**

he possesses the power to attend to these grounds *or* to some other grounds for him to do that this or that and to understand or "to decide" (or "to make up his mind") in the period t - t2 (*or* even the period t + i - t2) that they are enough for him to begin do that this or that. [The verb "to decide" is used in a slightly different sense in this case than in the first case set out by Frankfurt: to begin to do that this or that given that he "decides" to do that this or that in this case; to do that this or that (at some time) given that he "decides" to do that this or that in the first case.]

his exercise of this power is enough to bring the exercise of a (or his) power to bring about that this or that **;**

he possesses the power to bring about that this or that in the period t2 - t3 **;**

someone else knows all of this is so ;

-

he (*viz.* the subject) possesses the power to attend to grounds for him to *not* do that this or that and to *begin* to understand or "to decide" in a period which begins at t that they are enough for him to begin to not do that this or that ;

his power to do so is exercised *in case* his power to attend to ... grounds for him to do that this or that ... in the period t - t2 (*or* even the period t + i - t2) ... is *not* exercised ;

that someone else begins to bring it about at t + i that he exercises his power to attend to some or other grounds for him to do that this or that and to understand or "to decide" in what remains of the period t - t2 that they are enough for him to begin to do that this or that *just in case* his power to attend to grounds for him to not do that this or that and to begin to understand or "to decide" in a period which begins at t that they are enough for him to begin to not do that this or that is exercised.

(that someone else accordingly is not required to be an "excellent judge" of what he is "going to decide" in this statement of the case set out by Frankfurt. That someone else is required to be so in the case set out by Frankfurt. ("If it does become clear that ... [he, *viz.* the subject of the case] is going to decide to do something else, ... [he] takes effective steps to ensure that ... [he] decides to do, and he does do, what he wants him to do" (p.172). "... he waits until ... [he] is about to make up his mind what to do, and he does nothing unless it is clear to him ... that ... [he] is going to decide to do something other than what he wants him to do" (p.172). "...[he] is an excellent judge of such things..." (p.172).) This is the principal amendment to the case in this statement.

that someone else begins to bring it about at t + i that he exercises his power to attend to some or other grounds for him to do that this or that ... : these grounds are that otherwise a state of affairs, *viz.*what is referred to in a "terrible threat", would obtain; *or*, this power is exercised due to a "potion" *or* due to "hypnosis"; *or*, this power is exercised due the subject's "brain" being manipulated by that someone else. (See p.173.)) ;

he (*viz.* the subject) is not aware that this is so ;

(ii) his power to identify grounds for him to do this or that and to understand in the period t-1 - t that these grounds are enough for him to do that this or that is exercised ;

his power to attend to these grounds for him to do that this or that and to understand or "to decide" in the period t - t2 that they are enough for him to begin to do that this or that is exercised. ("... [he], for reasons of his own, decides to perform the ... action" (p.173). "... [the] fact [that "he could not have done otherwise"] played no role at all in leading him to act as he did" (p.173). "... everything happened just as it would have happened without ... [his, *viz.* that someone else's] presence in the situation ... " (p.173).) ;

his power to do that this or that in the period t2 - t3 is exercised. ("... [he] does perform the ... action" (p.173).)

The subject of this case does not possess the power to not do that this or that. (He does not possess the power to attend to grounds for him to not do that this or that and to understand or "to decide" in a period which begins at t that they are enough for him to begin to not do that this or that *and* he does not possess the power to not do that this or that.)

He nonetheless possesses the power to do that this or that freely and (as a result) in a morally responsible way according to Frankfurt. (He nonetheless does that this or that freely and as a result in a morally responsible way according to Frankfurt.)

Is it the case that he possesses the power to do that this or that freely? Well, it is *not* the case that he possesses the power to do that this or that freely for (leaving aside the consideration of other matters) he does not possess the power to not do that this or that.

Still, there is at least nothing which is referred to in the description of this case and which is such that its subject does not possess the power to do that this or that in a morally responsible way.

In particular, there is nothing which is referred to in the description of this case and which is such that he does not possess the power to do that this or that independently.

28. Does someone possess the power to do this or that in a morally responsible way in case it is causally determined that he exercises his power to do that this or that?

Well, let us consider the following line of argument for the claim that he does *not* do so in case that is so. This line of argument has two stages.

Stage one:

he does not possess the power to do that this or that in a morally responsible way unless he possesses the power to *not* do that this or that ;

he does not possess the power to not do that this or that in case it is causally determined that he exercises his power to do that this or that ;

so, he does not possess the power to do that this or that in a morally responsible way in case it is causally determined that he exercises his power to do that this or that.

The conclusion follows from the first premise and the second premise. The second premise is true. Is the first premise true? Well, the second stage of this line of argument is an argument for the claim that the first premise is true.

Stage two:

he does not possess the power to do that this or that in a morally responsible way unless he possesses the power to do that this or that *freely* ;

he does not possess the power to do that this or that freely unless he possesses the power to *not* do that this or that ;

so, he does not possess the power to do that this or that in a morally responsible way unless he possesses the power to not do that this or that.

The conclusion follows from the first premise and the second premise. But, the second premise is untrue in case Frankfurt's claim that there are cases of someone who does this or that freely and (as a result) morally responsibly although he does not possess the power to not do that this or that or he "could not do otherwise" is correct. (The 24th note and the 27th note refer to this claim and there is a consideration of this claim in these notes.) So, this line of argument does not establish that the conclusion of the first stage is true in case Frankfurt's claim is correct.

An advocate of Frankfurt's claim would claim that *another line of argument* is required in order to demonstrate that someone does not possess the power to do this or that in a morally responsible way in case it is causally determined that he exercises his power to do that this or that. (See, for example, John Martin Fischer, "Frankfurt-style Examples; Responsibility and Semi-compatibilism", *Ethics,* 110 (1999).)

But, Frankfurt's claim is incorrect. Is this line of argument in that case correct? Well, the first premise of its second stage states that someone (*viz.* the subject) does not possess the power to do that this or that in a morally responsible way unless he possesses the power to do that this or that freely.

Is this true? Well, the subject of the second case of this Appendix does *not* possess the power to do (that) this or that freely. But, there is at least nothing which is referred to in the description of this case and which is such that the subject does not possess the power to do that this or that in a morally responsible way.

Finally, let us consider the original question: does someone possess the power to do this or that in a morally responsible way in case it is causally determined that he exercises his power to do that this or that? Well, he does not do so - he does not do so freely *and* he does not do so independently. (See, in particular, (xi) and (iii).)

Select Bibliography

Alexander, H.G., (ed.), *The Leibniz-Clarke Correspondence* Manchester, 1956

Aquinas, Thomas, *Summa Theologiae* trans. T.McDermott London: Eyre & Spottiswoode, 1964

Augustine, *On the Free Choice of the Will,* trans. A Benjamin Indianapolis, 1964

Boethius, A.M.S., *The Consolation of Philosophy* trans. S. J. Tester Harvard, 1973

Charlesworth, M., *St. Anselm's Proslogion* Oxford, 1965

Cottingham, J., (ed.), *The Philosophical Writings of Descartes* Cambridge, 1994

Hume, D., *Dialogues concerning Natural Religion* N. Kemp-Smith, ed., Edinburgh, 1947

Enquiry concerning Human Understanding, L.A. Selby-Bigge, ed., Oxford, 1975

Kemp Smith, N., *Immanuel Kant's Critique of Pure Reason* London, 1929

Molina, Luis de, *On Divine Foreknowledge: Part IV of "The Concordia"* trans. Alfred J. Freddosso Cornell, 1998

Reid, Thomas, *Essays on the Active Powers of the Human Mind* Cambridge Mass.: MIT Press, 1969

Index

A

Abelard, Peter, 118
abstract things, 17, 47, 55, 57, 125, 277, 278, 279, 282, 284, 285, 286, 287, 288
actualise(s)
  a possible world, 160
  weakly, 161
analysis, 11
analytic philosophy, 10, 11, 17
Anscombe, G.E.M., 396
Anselm, Saint, 173, 174, 175, 176, 177, 178, 179, 181, 182, 185, 257, 258, 259, 273
Aquinas, Saint Thomas, 85, 201
argument(s), 13
āśrava, 267
Augustine of Hippo, Saint, 338, 340, 343, 344, 345, 347

B

Boethius, 75, 76, 78, 119, 120
Brahman, 250, 251, 252, 267
Broad, C.D., 414
Buddha, 9, 25
Buddhism, 9, 25, 250

C

Cantor, Gregor, 153
Chāndogya Upaniṣad, 267
change
  and God, 112, 125
  extrinsic, 24
  in a thing, 24
  in the momentum of a physical thing, on whether it can be brought about by a non-physical thing, 41
  intrinsic, 24
Charlesworth, M., 257
Chisholm, R.M., 152, 392, 412
Christianity, 9, 10
Clarke, Samuel, 201, 212, 263
concrete things, 17, 89, 90, 91, 96, 97, 98, 110, 124, 125
consequentialism, 149
cosmological argument
  which includes a line of argument associated with early Islamic rational theology, 208
  which includes a line of argument of Aquinas, 201
  which is a line of argument associated with Clarke and Leibniz, 212
  which provides *some* grounds for God's existence, 220, 226, 274

D

Descartes, René, 117, 123, 124
design argument(s)

which is an argument by analogy, 185
which use the principle of likelihood (and increase any degree of belief that God can exist), 187, 192, 196, 197
Draper, Paul, 326, 327, 332

E

eternally in time, God exists, 78, 79
event, 387
evil
and God, some discussions of, 295
another response (to the existence of), 166
as grounds for the claim that God does not exist, 155
as grounds for the claim that, very probably, God does not exist, 315, 320, 325, 326
liable to experience due to the conditions which prevail, 133, 134, 135
moral, 160
natural, 160
Plantinga's response to the existence of in *The Nature of Necessity*, 159
state of affairs being overridden, 127, 128, 148, 273, 295, 299, 302
states of affairs, 127
experience, of a thing which is just like something, 228, 264
explanation, of God's existence, 101

F

fact(s)
and (intrinsic) *value*, 21
brute, 102, 213
fact, 20
how a human being knows (a), 46, 47, 48
past, 69, 70, 71
First Cause, 202
Fool, of *Psalms*, 176, 259
Frankfurt, Harry, 418, 429, 437
Frege, Gottlob, 10

G

Gettier, Edmund, 45
Ginet, Carl, 401
Gods, on whether there can be two, 113

H

Hasker, William, 355
Herodotus, 26
Hick, John, 335, 343, 344, 345
Hinduism, 9, 250
Hoffman, Joshua, 119
Homer, 26
Hume, David, 185, 186

I

immutability, and God, 33, 76, 77, 78, 111, 113, 270
Irenaeus, Saint, 335, 343, 344, 345
Īśa Upaniṣad, 267

Islam, 9, 10

J

Judaism, 9, 10

K

Kane, Robert, 401, 405, 406
Kant, Immanuel, 259
knowledge
  human capacity to acquire it, 47, 48
  of God, 53, 54, 55
  tripartite analysis of, 11, 44
  tripartite analysis of amendment(s), 44, 45, 46

L

Lane Craig, William, 261
Lehrer, Keith, 395, 396
Leibniz, Gottfried, 201, 212, 263
Lewis, David, 170
living and non-physical thing, on whether instances of this kind, or it, can exist, 33, 35, 38, 41

M

Mackie, John (Leslie), 295, 300
McCann, Hugh, 293
modal expressions, 15
Molina, Luis de, 120, 121, 122
Moore, George Edward, 10, 389
morally perfect, God being and bringing about a particular kind of universe, 305

N

Nagel, Thomas, 400, 420
nature (or essence)
  of an individual thing, 213
  of things of a particular kind, 263
Nielson, Kai, 25
nirvāṇa, 9, 25, 250, 251, 253, 267

O

O'Connor, Timothy, 412
Ockham, William of, 68
omnipotent (or all-powerful) thing
  definition of, 83
  on whether God can be omnipotent, 32, 99, 107, 108, 109, 269
  on whether there can be an omnipotent thing, 89, 90, 91, 92, 93, 94
omniscient (or all-knowing) thing
  definition of, 43
  on whether God can be omniscient, 32, 62, 269
  on whether there can be an omniscient thing, 48, 49, 50, 51, 52, 53
ontological argument
  in the second chapter of the *Proslogion*, 177, 179
  in the third chapter of the *Proslogion*, 183
Open Theists, 354

P

Pali Canon, 25, 253
philosophy of religion, 10, 11
Plantinga, Alvin, 159, 162, 163, 166, 170, 171
Plato, 120
possible world(s)
  account of, 16, 160, 170
  as a way to understand modal expressions, 16
power
  analysis of, 84
  morally significant, 142, 159
  not morally significant, 142
  of God, 94, 95, 99
  of living things to do this or that freely and God's (fore-) knowledge, 66, 67, 68, 82, 83, 270
  to act [or to do this or that] freely, 129, 130, 336, 338, 341, 348
  to act *independently* of God, 130, 136, 138, 141, 142, 266, 272, 341
  to do this or that [or to act] *freely*, 32, 270, 369, 420, 424, 428
  to do this or that in a *morally responsible* way, 381, 386
  which can be possessed by a thing at some time, 89
  which other free and independent living things are imbued with by God, 131, 136, 137, 141
principle of likelihood, 187, 188, 190, 274
Principle of Sufficient Reason, 213, 264
property
  accidental, 28
  essential, 28
  extrinsic relational, 23
  intrinsic relational, 23
  non-relational, 23, 24
  relational, 23

R

Reid, Thomas, 412
religion, 9
religious experience of God
  an argument from (for the belief that God exists), 226, 227
  as sufficient grounds for the belief that God exists, 235
  nature of, 228, 229
Ṛg Veda, 267
Rosenkrantz, Gary S., 119
Russell, Bertrand, 10

S

sceptic, extreme, 235
self, a, 369, 387, 412, 420, 424
significantly free creature, 159
simplicity, and God, 33, 109, 110, 111, 113, 270, 358, 359, 360
soul, 133
sovereignty, God's, 277
states(s) of affairs
  (a) part of, 19, 27, 152, 343
  and propositions, 27
  examples of, 17

kinds of, 18, 19
not conjunctive *or* conjunctive, 18
relations between, 22
value of, 21
Strawson, G., 400
Stump, Eleonore, 353
Swinburne, Richard, 265, 295, 296, 298

T

teleological argument, 186
The Acts of the Buddha, 25
theist(s), 10, 33, 65, 79, 109, 113, 187, 269, 270
sceptical, 352
theodicy
explanation of, 333
free will, 348, 351, 352
of Augustine, 338, 343, 344, 345
of Irenaeus and Hick, 335, 343, 344, 345
which is identifiable in this work, 340
time
and God, 32, 71, 72, 73, 74, 75, 76, 78, 79, 357
and the Bible, 78, 79
series, 76, 119, 120
traditional account of God, 10, 29, 117, 269

U

universe, 133
Upaniṣad(s), 252, 267

V

Veda, 252, 267

W

Watson, Gary, 389, 421
Widerkar, David, 434
will, 389
Wittgenstein, Ludwig, 10
Wolf, Susan, 425

CPSIA information can be obtained
at www.ICGtesting.com
Printed in the USA
BVHW061931050721
611167BV00015B/1047/J